WHERE AM I IN THE PICTURE?

Researcher Positionality in Rural Studies

Edited by Claudia Mitchell, Katarina Giritli-Nygren, and Relebohile Moletsane

Positionality and researcher reflexivity – how to account for one's subject position – remain as challenges for new researchers. But they also remain as challenges for experienced researchers, who are often involved in multiple research projects simultaneously. *Where Am I in the Picture?* sheds light on the idea of researcher positionality through visual methodologies, particularly in the context of studying rurality in Canada, Sweden, and South Africa.

The book is intended for new and experienced researchers seeking to decolonize their own perspectives in research in the social sciences and humanities. It incorporates photographs, drawings, and memory work to highlight the social constructedness of what counts as rural. Drawing together compelling narratives from researchers about their positionality in studying rurality, the book highlights a need for greater attention to "where we are in the picture" more broadly. It suggests that when it comes to the rural, researchers need to rethink the interplay of dominant images, insider and outsider perspectives, and what this interplay means in relation to interpretation. *Where Am I in the Picture?* presents a new vision of how to take into consideration positionality in research.

CLAUDIA MITCHELL is a distinguished James McGill professor in the Department of Integrated Studies in Education at McGill University and an honorary professor in the School of Education at the University of KwaZulu-Natal.

KATARINA GIRITLI-NYGREN is a professor of sociology at Mid Sweden University.

RELEBOHILE MOLETSANE is the J.L. Dube chair in rural education in the School of Education and the pro vice chancellor of social cohesion at the University of KwaZulu-Natal.

Where Am I in the Picture?

Researcher Positionality in Rural Studies

EDITED BY CLAUDIA MITCHELL, KATARINA GIRITLI-NYGREN, AND RELEBOHILE MOLETSANE

UNIVERSITY OF TORONTO PRESS
Toronto Buffalo London

© University of Toronto Press 2024
Toronto Buffalo London
utorontopress.com

ISBN 978-1-4875-0622-3 (cloth)   ISBN 978-1-4875-3356-4 (EPUB)
ISBN 978-1-4875-4782-0 (paper)   ISBN 978-1-4875-3355-7 (PDF)

Library and Archives Canada Cataloguing in Publication

Title: Where am I in the picture? : researcher positionality in rural studies /
   edited by Claudia Mitchell, Katarina Giritli-Nygren, and Relebohile Moletsane.
Names: Mitchell, Claudia, editor. | Giritli-Nygren, Katarina, 1971– editor. |
   Moletsane, Relebohile, editor.
Description: Includes bibliographical references and index.
Identifiers: Canadiana (print) 20230529682 | Canadiana (ebook) 20230529739 |
   ISBN 9781487547820 (paper) | ISBN 9781487506223 (cloth) |
   ISBN 9781487533557 (PDF) | ISBN 9781487533564 (EPUB)
Subjects: LCSH: Sociology, Rural – Research – Canada. | LCSH: Sociology,
   Rural – Research – Sweden. | LCSH: Sociology, Rural – Research –
   South Africa.
Classification: LCC HT421 .W44 2024 | DDC 307.72 – dc23

Cover design: Val Cooke
Cover image: The Mapula Embroidery Project

We wish to acknowledge the land on which the University of Toronto Press
operates. This land is the traditional territory of the Wendat, the Anishnaabeg,
the Haudenosaunee, the Métis, and the Mississaugas of the Credit First Nation.

University of Toronto Press acknowledges the financial support of the
Government of Canada, the Canada Council for the Arts, and the Ontario Arts
Council, an agency of the Government of Ontario, for its publishing activities.

Printed and bound by CPI Group (UK) Ltd, Croydon, CR0 4YY

Canada Council Conseil des Arts
for the Arts du Canada

ONTARIO ARTS COUNCIL
CONSEIL DES ARTS DE L'ONTARIO
an Ontario government agency
un organisme du gouvernement de l'Ontario

Funded by the   Financé par le
Government   gouvernement
of Canada   du Canada

Canadä

Contents

Figures

Acknowledgments

There are so many people we would like to thank, starting with Ann Smith and her careful attention to editing detail that was so necessary in helping us to bring all the chapters together. We would also like to recognize the assistance of Sahar Fazeli of McGill University in preparing the manuscript.

The internal review process involved input from reviewers from our respective institutions in Canada, Sweden, and South Africa, as well as from contributors willing to read and respond to the work of their colleagues. We thank everyone for their generosity. We are also grateful to the two external reviewers who provided such valuable input.

We, of course, would like to acknowledge our funders. Much of the work presented in this book was supported by the Swedish funder Forma in their support to the TGRAN project: "A Transnational Study of the Intersections of Rurality, Gender and Violence against Girls and Young Women: An Urgent Matter in Both the Global North and the Global South."

We also acknowledge the support of the International Partnerships for Sustainable Societies (IPaSS), jointly funded by the Social Sciences and Humanities Research Council (SSHRC; award number 895-2013-3007) and the International Development Research Centre (IDRC; award number 107777-001), for our project "Networks for Change and Well-being: Girl-Led 'from the Ground Up' Policy Making to Address Sexual Violence in Canada and South Africa." These funders made travel possible and ensured that doctoral and postdoctoral fellows could be involved.

Finally, we thank Jodi Lewchuk of the University of Toronto Press for her ongoing support for this book project.

Claudia Mitchell, Katarina Giritli-Nygren, and Relebohile Moletsane

WHERE AM I IN THE PICTURE?

1 Where Am I in the Picture? An Introduction

CLAUDIA MITCHELL, KATARINA GIRITLI-NYGREN, AND RELEBOHILE MOLETSANE

We are all, in one sense, makers of rurality ... [W]e need to undertake a more critical exploration of the power of preconceived notions of the rural.
– Gillander Gådin, Giritli-Nygren, Mitchell, & Nyhlén (2015, p. 116)

Beginning at the Beginning

The inspiration for this collection came out of a transnational project involving a team of feminist researchers from three countries: Sweden, Canada, and South Africa.[1] The entry point for our work together is an overlapping and intersectional interest in place and gender with a specific concern for deepening an understanding of rurality and the high rates of sexual violence suffered by girls and young women in our respective countries. Like many feminist projects, this collection is grounded in both the personal and the political; we have shared stories about our own girlhoods, discussed what counts as violence and what counts as rural, and, critically, considered the commonalities that we see across the so-called Global North and Global South in relation to sexual violence. It is also grounded in the social and in friendship; a special feature of our work together over almost seven years is that, at various points (working towards conceptualizing the project across our three countries, developing it, implementing it, and reflecting on it), we have pondered and strategized through email, Skype, and webinars, but we have also dined together, laughed together, and rolled up our sleeves to write together in each other's countries at conferences and research retreats. These collaborations have taken place in Sweden facilitated by Mid Sweden University (in Sundsvall and Torpshammar), in South Africa facilitated by the University of KwaZulu-Natal and Nelson Mandela University (in Stellenbosch, Monkey Bay, Durban,

Loskop, and La Lucia), and in Canada facilitated by McGill University (in Montreal, Montebello, and Toronto) and have included doctoral students and postdoctoral fellows. Of particular significance to *Where Am I in the Picture?* is that, together, we have also visited the rural parts of Sweden and South Africa, with the promise that sooner or later we will all meet up in rural Prince Edward Island, Canada.

A special feature of our work together has been its visual turn with everything from the tools and methods we have used in the fieldwork in our respective countries (photovoice, drawing, cellphilming, digital stories, collage-making) through to how we have worked together both face to face and online. Indeed, very early on in the three-country project, we engaged in what we termed "picturing rurality," in which all members of the research team participated in finding pictures of rurality, developed captions for them, and shared them with each other in several webinars and face-to-face meetings (see Gillander Gådin and De Lange, chapter 5, this volume). The process of choosing photos (whether from popular culture or from participants' own photo collections), writing captions, and sharing them with the whole group, a practice that comes out of memory-work and visual approaches to autoethnography (Mitchell et al., 2017; Pithouse et al., 2009; Pithouse-Morgan et al., 2019), led to a critical finding that served as the inspiration for this book. We realized that it is almost impossible to begin to make sense of the pictures, find themes, or develop codes without considering our own autobiographies. Given the focus of our work as feminists, we saw that issues related to gender and girlhoods were ever-present in the images and narratives. It was clear that the narratives we offered made each picture more than just a picture and that, in order to really understand the photograph, it was necessary to understand something of the researcher. But across all the narratives emerged a special outsider stance since, with one exception, not one member of the research team engaged in rural studies currently lives in a rural area. Indeed, as we talked about it, we wondered if we could even be living in a rural area and do research on rurality through universities, given that these institutions are located in cities and often implicated in the production of spatial injustices. We saw this issue as yet another angle on the paradoxical nature of doing fieldwork in rural areas.

Positioning Positionality

These contextually confessional moments, generated in our "picturing rurality" retreats, created a heightened sense of the significance of reflexivity and positionality. Positionality, of course, is the hallmark of feminist research. Following the well-established work on class in feminist studies and later in the work of Mohanty (2003), England (1994), and others, positionality is a feature of contemporary social research in the growing work on settler studies, Indigenous studies, migration studies, whiteness, and so on, where it has come to occupy a central role. Clearly, the critical movements surrounding the Black Lives Matter campaign are highlighting even more the significance of privilege itself within positionality. In the introduction to their recent edited collection *Fieldnotes in Qualitative Education and Social Science Research*, Burkholder and Thompson (2020) make explicit the strategies for incorporating positionality.

We are particularly indebted to British visual theorist/activist Jo Spence (1986) and her groundbreaking book *Putting Myself in the Picture* for providing a frame in which we could locate ourselves as researchers in the picture. In Spence's work, the camera in the hands of the subject (Spence herself) becomes a tool for reframing and repositioning. For example, working with Rosy Martin, Spence used re-enactments and other visual play to contest and reimagine their past as schoolgirls, along with critical features of power and sexuality. Later, and as a way of responding to her breast cancer, Spence again used a camera to position her body at the centre. In a 1986 photo exhibition "The Picture of Health," she questions the politics of traditional medicine in treating breast cancer. In the edited collection *Jo Spence: The Final Project* (Lee, 2013), close friends and colleagues comment on Spence's various art and photography projects that she used to address the diagnosis of leukaemia. The visual images (drawings, family photos, maps, artistic pieces, participant-led photos) and narratives used by the contributors to that book also carry with them the traces of Spence's personal and political agenda, particularly in the context of rurality.

Our two previous collections on rurality – *Visual Encounters in the Study of Rural Childhoods*, co-edited by Mandrona and Mitchell (2018), and *Our Rural Selves: Memory, Place and the Visual in Canadian Childhoods*, co-edited by Mitchell and Mandrona (2019a) – set the stage, in a sense, for drawing together writings across our research team on such areas as memory-work and the visual as tools for looking into gendered childhoods and rurality. Moletsane (2018, p. ix), in her foreword to *Visual Encounters*, reflects on her own childhood, observing: "It is this rural childhood and the many happy and sad memories I have of it that led me to rurality and rural girlhoods as a field of research in my academic career." This foreword prefigured what we are doing in this book. Another chapter in that collection, co-authored by Söderberg, Nyhlén, Gillander Gådin, and Giritli-Nygren (2018), highlights the use of memory-work in relation to rurality in girls' literature. And De Lange's (2018) chapter in the same book considers the ways in which participatory visual methods contribute to the reflexivity of participants. In their introductory chapter, "Rural Beginnings," in *Our Rural Selves*, Mitchell and Mandrona (2019b) offer personal narratives of what they think of as growing up rural as an entry point into considering the significance of memory-work and the visual in studying rural childhoods.

Where Am I in the Picture? also expands the feminist collaborations of our team. As co-editors – Claudia Mitchell from Canada, Katarina Giritli-Nygren from Sweden, and Relebohile Moletsane from South Africa – we worked with other members of the research team from each country, as well as with doctoral students, postdoctoral fellows, and colleagues whose research agenda or artistic practices aligned well with the project. As a result, we have a total of sixteen contributing authors from three countries – four from Sweden, six from South Africa, and six from Canada.

About Girlhoods

As highlighted in the opening paragraph of this chapter, our focus on rural girlhoods has been a unifying feature of our work together. "The 'girl subject' and 'young femininity' are repeatedly and with great effect being made increasingly visible as a particular social, cultural and psychical problematic in late capitalist societies," wrote Renold and Ringrose (2013, p. 247). In particular, given the unequal gender norms that often relegate girls and young women to the margins of society, as well as the violence, particularly sexual violence, that characterize these contexts, girlhood as a subject of enquiry continues to be contested, along with its very visibility. While scholarship on the empowered girl is emerging (Taft, 2010), a dominant and enduring discourse is that of the girl at risk. There exists a notion of girlhood as "permanently vulnerable not only because of dire circumstances but also because of something intransigent and intrinsic to girlhood itself" (Gilmore & Marshall, 2010, p. 667). Yet, feminist scholars have pointed out: "Girls and women – young and old – are not only victims. They have multiple identities and through their [various] roles ... they often demonstrate incredible resiliency, coping and survival skills" (Kirk & Taylor, 2007, pp. 13–14). Researchers need to be consistently alert to the diversity and complexity of girlhood, and to girls' agency and voice, even in contexts of marginalization and violence. One way of ensuring this mindset is by understanding girlhood from the perspectives of girls themselves, which can be accomplished, at least to some extent, through the use of participatory visual methods such as photovoice, drawing, and digital storytelling. From this vantage point, researchers need to reflect on the ways in which their positionality as researchers and, often, as outsiders influences their analyses of girls' visual productions in diverse communities.

Finding the Rural?

Something that has intrigued us as we have been working on this book is the very issue of what counts as rural and how and when it is a geographical concept, a social representation, a way of life, or an imaginary. Clearly, there are numerous official markers, including population density and distance, but this book is about social research and not official markers. When our research team made up of Canadians, South Africans, and Swedes travelled together to different rural areas, we recognized how different our perspectives were, and yet we were all writing about rurality. For example, when we travelled to an area described as rural in Sweden (often small villages that included a collection of houses, a church, and so on), some of us asked if it was really rural. But then in South Africa, when several of us spoke at a national conference about research with rural youth from an area that has a clinic, a school, houses, and a tarred road, some of our colleagues offered the critique: "But this isn't deeply rural. It is not far enough away [from a large town], or the state of the road is too urban-like."

As co-editors, we each returned to our own fact finding. In the Swedish context, Swedish authorities and organizations seem to disagree about what should be counted as rural areas. For example, according to the Swedish Association of Local Authorities and Regions (SKR), there are 20 rural municipalities in the country, out of a total of 290 municipalities. When turning to the Swedish Board of Agriculture, rural municipalities can be of two types: "remote rural" areas, which are more than 45 minutes by car from the nearest urban neighbourhood; and "accessible rural" areas, which are 5 to 45 minutes by car from an urban location with more than 3,000 inhabitants. Using this definition, there are 33 remote rural municipalities and an additional 164 accessible rural municipalities. However, the typical physical environment and low number of inhabitants are features that unite the different official definitions of rural areas in Sweden, which is what we refer to when we use the term "rural context" in this study. This term is probably more or less valid for all countries, but what might differ more widely is the definition of urban areas. In Sweden, municipalities with more than 3,000 inhabitants and reachable in 5 minutes by car are regarded as "urban" areas. In the Canadian context, there is increasing attention to what is termed RRN (rural, remote, and northern), with "rural" referring to a community or location with a population of fewer than 10,000 people; "remote" referring to a location that is not accessible by road year-round; and "northern" referring to the northern parts of provinces and to all the territories.[2] These are also loaded terms concerning who lives there (especially taking into considering Indigenous and settler populations); what resources, including safe water, might be available; and what classifications could mean in relation to issues such as addressing gender-based violence (Nonomura & Baker, 2021).

Defining urban and rural spaces in South Africa has a long history informed by colonial and apartheid laws. For example, using the Land Act of 1913, the apartheid system forced the majority Black population to remote, largely unfertile, poorly resourced rural areas referred to as homelands or Bantustans, while the more fertile land was reserved for large, white-owned commercial farms (Makgetla, 2010). Thus, defined in apartheid categories, rural areas referred to "the Bantustans and, in the rest of the country, areas containing smaller towns and commercial farms as well as most mines. By extension, the definition of rural ... includes a number of small towns and relatively dense settlements" (p. 1). In the post-apartheid dispensation, while the Bantustans have been abolished (in terms of geographic boundaries), their legacy endures, and the majority Black population still resides in these areas, with little improvement in terms of infrastructure development and services. Thus, contemporary definitions of the rural include communities made up of areas that fall under the jurisdiction of the traditional authorities and continue to be characterized by lack of infrastructure and services, as well as commercial farms and mining areas historically owned by white people (Department of Planning, Monitoring, and Evaluation, 2015). While "rural" refers to communities that are historically densely populated (due to the legacy of colonialism and apartheid), some are sparsely populated and situated where there is the use of natural resources for livelihood and economic activity (Statistics South Africa, 2005).

Personal Markers

Then there are personal markers, which are the ones that seemed particularly significant as we note in various rural testimonies. Indeed, as we were working on the book, we kept returning to the question, "What is rural?" or "Where is rural?" At times we emailed each other or other colleagues (somewhere) late at night for inspiration. Sara Nyhlén, from Sweden, commented about the complexity of marking location in rural Sweden when she said:

> Along the road every geographical area has a name, even though there might be no houses there. My "village," for example, is not a village. It is just about five houses along a country-side road. However, we call it "the village." The name of the village is Våle, which is an old word for a fallen tree uprooted by the wind. I lived in Våle number 2209. There were no signs or other markings pointing to where 2209 might be. You just had to know. A very important person in this system was the country mailman. They knew where everyone lived, if people were home, what their health status was, and if they could stop for a cup of coffee at some of the houses along their route. If you were going somewhere and you didn't know where it was, you would consult the mailman first to get directions and instructions about where to turn and which gravel road or forest road to follow. There were often landmarks that we used, such as crossroads, to work out where to go. In my area, we had two roads, called the "upper road" and the "lower road." Churches and big houses were also commonly used as landmarks. To get to my house, one had to follow the country road from the village Söråker (where there were grocery stores, a school, a post office, a library, and a health centre). Then, at the intersection, [one had to] take the lower road and follow it towards the church. Several kilometres after the intersection, one would see a chair on a trash bin on the left-hand side of the road. There one would turn left. My house is the only house on that road. We also lived close to a man whom many people knew (before he passed away). He was a hunter and the (informal) village chief. So, turning left after his house could also be part of the instructions to reach my house. If we knew we were having guests or visitors that were from out of the community, we would put signs by the roadside to mark where they should turn. This was often done by putting a garden chair on top of the trash can by the side of the road. (Personal communication, 10 April 2020)

Not that different from Sara's account of how to get there, one of our colleagues in Ethiopia, Solomon Demeke, described it this way in an email:

> It starts from Region (kilil) and goes to Zone (zone), Woreda (district), Kebele (peasant association), and Village (mender) respectively. Each of these has its own known name. In the village, something natural and visible

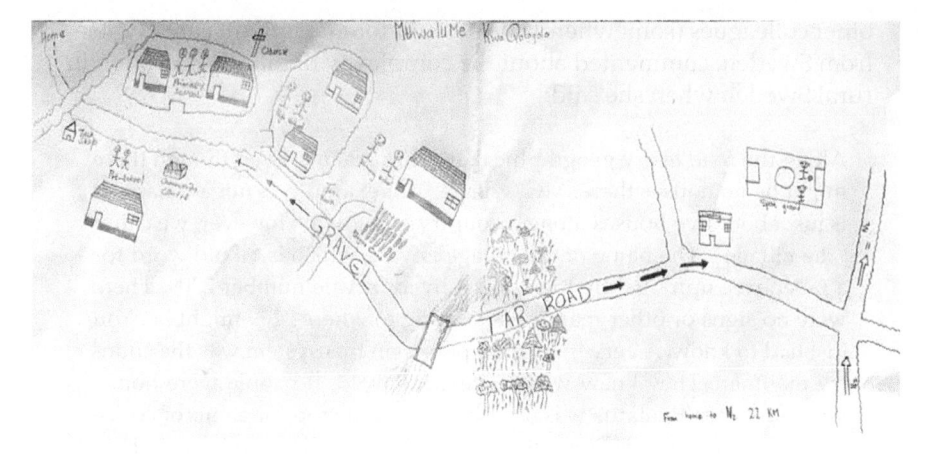

Figure 1.1. A map to your dwelling from the main road. Courtesy of
Nokwanda Myende and Lindelwa Myende, UKZN undergraduate students.

such as uplands, small hills, a foot road, a big tree, a bunch of cactus, a
mosque or church, or a big rock could be used to locate the household.
Once you reach the village, you are advised to ask for the name of the head
of the household. They usually advise you to offer details (appearance of
the hair and face colour, height, body condition, etc. of the person you
are looking for) once you are in the village. We all know each other at the
village level. (Personal communication, 9 April 2020)

For Claudia Mitchell, growing up on the Canadian Prairies, where
the colonizing Dominion Land Survey of the late nineteenth and early
twentieth century mapped the territory, rural is very mathematical.
As highlighted by Sheppard (chapter 3, this volume), the non-urban
spaces of Saskatchewan and Manitoba are divided into numbered sec-
tion-township-range so that a typical rural address is something like
28-10-26. Claudia recalls that, even as a little girl in the first or second
grade in school, she would need to be able to state this address for the
teacher on the first day of the new school year.

At the same time, as Relebohile Moletsane notes, the official forms
for the University of KwaZulu-Natal (UKZN) in South Africa asking
students to give their location indicate that they could include "a map
to your dwelling from a main road" (see Figure 1.1).

These examples serve to illustrate why we also found the question,
"How do you know you know where you are?" a revealing one.

Overview of the Book

We have organized the book into three main sections. When we first started assembling all the chapters, we somehow imagined that they would end up fitting very neatly into sections such as theory and method, or on different methodological frameworks such as memory-work, autoethnography, and visual and arts-based approaches. At one point we even thought that the chapters might break down into insiders and outsiders. But everything was more interrelated, and so we offer a structure that touches on all of the above but is configured in such a way that rurality itself stays front and centre.

Part One: Rural Travelscapes

We start with a section that recognizes the theoretical and methodological positioning of "here" as a research scape that is rural, an idea about rurality advanced in Tony Kelly's (2008) work in educational research in rural Nova Scotia, Canada. His "here" refers to the question that he was so often asked by outsiders when they learned that he was living and doing research in a rural area: "What are you doing *here*?" The "here" suggests a "there," and therefore travel from somewhere, and also suggests shifting positions influenced by landscape and time. The book begins, then, with a chapter by Lisa Starr and Claudia Mitchell about travel. In giving their chapter the title "Travelling in Circles along Roads Less Travelled in Awe of Open Spaces," they make explicit the connections between their shared experience of growing up as prairie girls in white settler families in rural Canada and ending up working together in rural areas in sub-Saharan Africa. Their focus in this chapter is on fieldwork in rural Ethiopia. The notions of driving along with the realities and metaphors associated with being "on the road" and "getting there," which are dominant features of work in rural Ethiopia, provoked the authors into considering why reflexivity and positionality is so critical to this work.

The second chapter in this section is Lou Sheppard's "*Saskatchewan Song Cycle*: A Trans-Reading of Land Survey in the Canadian West." In this chapter, visual artist Sheppard questions their position as a white settler occupying both urban and rural space in Canada and the significance of becoming more accountable to the histories and violences that have privileged the presence of their body in the Canadian landscape. *Saskatchewan Song Cycle* looks at two seminal colonial texts in Canadian geographic and literary history, the Dominion Land Survey produced in 1905 and the early settler Susannah Moodie's (1871) *Roughing It in the Bush*, to see how they have shaped and continue to shape settler relationships to landscape in Canada. The project became a three-part body of work consisting of three interrelated scores, which were then performed in the gallery space in Saskatoon. For Sheppard, "language structures how we experience, interpret, and engage with our identities and the world." Sheppard asks: "Do dominant languages, texts, and structuring principles reflect value systems that have led to oppression and dominance?" This chapter is a narrative reflection on process, situating the artwork itself as both theory and methodology.

To end this section, April Mandrona, in "Picturing Transrurality: Connecting the Rural across Borders," highlights the common experiences of marginalization (in relation to the urban) in rural settings in different geographic spaces. Borrowing from the field of feminist geography, Mandrona, a Canadian scholar who worked with young people in rural South Africa, reflects on the ways in which she is different in terms of her race and class from her participants while at the same time connected to them given her origins in a rural setting, albeit in a different national context; she is in solidarity with them. Using her visual production interactions with the participants, she reflects on the ways in which connections among rural people in different geographic spaces might be fostered and communicated.

Part Two: Girlhoods and Rurality as Context

Context, as we know, matters. But what does rurality as context look like, particularly in relation to rural girlhoods? This was the driving question that brought the team of researchers together in the first place, and so it is fitting that the first chapter in this section brings together the voices and images that frame the project. This section begins with a co-authored chapter by Katja Gillander Gådin of Sweden and Naydene de Lange of South Africa. We locate their chapter at the beginning of this section because it so explicitly, and in so much detail, frames the foundational research project that led to studying the contextual features of rurality through the visual. In "Picturing Rurality: Towards a Shared Understanding of What It Means to Study Rurality in Two Country Contexts," Gillander Gådin and De Lange draw on the results of webinars and seminars involving a group of twelve feminist researchers, working across several disciplinary areas, responding to the prompt "picturing rurality." The webinars and seminars were made in the transnational project aiming at addressing sexualized violence against girls and young women in relation to space and place. Involving researchers from South Africa, Canada, and Sweden, this research marked the beginning of this book. The authors describe a reflexive activity in which the various team members from the three countries share photographs of the rural. As the authors highlight, the photos and descriptions of these images enabled us to discuss our understandings of what rurality is and can be, and perhaps (for some) what it is not.

Samukelisiwe Khumalo's chapter "Drawing Myself into the Picture: What Does It Mean to Be a Rural-Origin Student in an Urban University?" highlights the significance of her positionality in her work in higher education in South Africa. Looking back at her own experiences as a working-class rural-origin student finding herself in an urban university, Khumalo reflects on the ways in which students from similar backgrounds entering higher education continue to face comparable challenges. She reflects on how, as an academic support practitioner in an urban university, she has continued to draw on her past experience, not only to understand her students' struggles but also to use the lessons learned in her own journey to support them as they navigate life in their urban institution.

Next, Emelie Larsson's chapter "'Beyond Getting Something': Reflections on Researching the Closure of a Rural Municipality's Maternity Unit" draws on individual memory-work to explore her position as a (new) researcher from a big city studying the closure of a maternity unit in Sweden's northern inland. Focusing on her positionality as an outsider, she returns to two centre-periphery relationships: urbanity-rurality and south-north – the latter to account for the geographic power imbalance in Sweden. Larsson grew up in Stockholm, the capital of Sweden, and she starts by locating Stockholm as a city where the rural is always geographically close yet can be distant in terms of identification and access. She then returns to some specific memories of her childhood, including the fights between her Polish/urban grandfather and her Finnish/rural grandmother (in which rurality was used as one of several "weapons of othering"). In the second part of the chapter, she relates these memories – and the meanings and feelings with which they are loaded – to her positionality in relation to rurality today and how it affects the way she thinks, writes, and does research. In so doing, she illustrates how her positionality and her research are mutually affected by each other.

The final chapter in this section is Sara Nyhlén's "A Button Thief or an Urban Researcher? Entangled Selves, Positionality, and Knowledge Production," in which she examines researcher positionality and reflexivity through a combination of memory-work, reading a particular novel, and analysing photos she took while doing her fieldwork.

Writing from Sweden, she explores her own memories of growing up in a rural area and how this experience is linked to the research she does. She shows how an understanding of her dual selves as the rural girl "who got away" and the urban adult feminist researcher is crucial to her understanding of what research on the rural is or can be. She argues that the autoethnographic method gives her the opportunity to explore researcher positionality and to question how her understanding of rurality and her twin selves gets entangled in her research.

Part Three: Positionality and the Rural

While all the earlier chapters are linked to positionality, the chapters in this section draw attention to the different ways in which feminist researchers take up this work. The section begins with a chapter by Lisa Wiebesiek and Astrid Treffry-Goatley, "'Hey, Mlungu!': Positionality in Participatory Visual Research in Post-Apartheid South Africa." As a collaborative writing project between the two authors, the chapter draws attention to the comings and goings to the research site itself but also to the comings and goings of researcher identity. The two authors reflect on their work on sexual violence with girls and young women in rural South Africa. In particular, they consider the ways in which their identities as white English-speaking middle-class women grant them (however unwanted) power and privilege over their participants who are Black African rural girls and young women. As outsiders to the community, the authors consider the implications of their power and privilege for their research and for the members of their research community. They discuss the ethics of their work, consider when they thought it best to speak and when to be silent, and explore the extent to which their positionality renders their work with the participants and the community legitimate.

Then Katie MacEntee's chapter, "Acting Like a Skank: Reflections on a Researcher's Involvement in the Production of Participatory Visual Research Texts in a Rural Area," highlights a moment in her research with young people in a South African rural school in which she was literally "in the picture" after a participant asked her to pose for a picture that was to be used in a photovoice exercise. MacEntee interrogates how her intersecting differences – age, race, class, and nationality (Canadian) – from those of the participants – young, Black South Africans from poor rural backgrounds – are necessarily involved in the ethics and implications of this (much regretted) decision.

The chapter draws attention to the value and some of the pitfalls of using photovoice in working with young people on HIV and AIDS, an area of study and public discourse that often renders girls and young women's sexuality problematic. McEntee considers the implications of showing an image that portrays her, the researcher, in a sexually provocative pose.

The next chapter in this section is Ntomboxolo Yamile's "Positioning Girls in Rural Contexts: Then and Now." Also drawing on memory-work in a South African context, Yamile's autobiographical writing takes the reader back to what being a young girl in apartheid South Africa was like. Using this experience as a springboard, she reflects on how the lives of the girls with whom she has been working today are dramatically different from how hers was at their age twenty years earlier, not only because of the passage of time but also because of their response to the violence, including sexual violence, that currently characterizes many communities in this country. She uses memory-work to look back at her childhood and early girlhood, and talks about her current work as a researcher "documenting and analysing ... girls' experiences of sexual violence in their rural community" and how she works with them "to develop strategies to address it."

The chapter by Catherine Vanner, "Positionality at the Centre: An Epistemological and Methodological Approach for Conducting Research in the Postcolonial," is a revised version of an article published in the *International Journal of Qualitative Methods*. In the chapter, she reflects on her doctoral fieldwork in rural schools in Kenya. Her contribution perfectly maps out some critical dilemmas in positionality studies, particularly in the context of studies across the Global North and the Global South. She writes:

> In light of postcolonial critiques of Western researchers and international development, I have often wondered: "Am I doing more harm than good?" The privilege that accompanies my social location as a white, upper class Canadian academic woman means that, despite good intentions, my efforts to support education in postcolonial contexts risk being patronizing, insulting, threatening, imperialist, and recolonizing.
>
> ...
>
> Yet, neglecting and ignoring postcolonial contexts because I am not a member of a community that is directly and negatively affected by colonialism and neocolonialism similarly reflects and reproduces my privileged position without drawing attention to or challenging unequal and oppressive structures.

It seemed particularly appropriate to include this chapter in *Where Am I in the Picture?*, both because it served as a key reading for many of the contributors in preparing their submissions but also in recognition of the author's postdoctoral work at McGill on a related project between Canada and South Africa on gender-based violence and her work with many of the other contributors to this book. Fittingly, there is a full circle back to the travelscapes of part one.

Looking across Chapters

Themes of girlhoods, sexuality, and rurality at the core of the original project that brought together researchers from South Africa, Sweden, and Canada cut across the various chapters. But there is a variety of other unifying features across them. All of the chapters in one way or another draw on critical autoethnography, with many of them (though not all) using this approach as a way of exploring the possibility of taking on a decolonial researcher position. "Decolonizing" here can refer to undoing, disrupting, and delinking knowledge rooted in colonial thinking that ignores or devalues the local knowledges, experiences, and expertise of people occupying rural sites. Decolonizing seeks to disrupt the colonial and apartheid scripts such as those that constitute Black South Africans as the other in their own land (Wiebesiek & Treffry-Goatley, chapter 9) and settler colonialism (MacEntee, chapter 10; Starr & Mitchell, chapter 2; Mandrona, chapter 4). It also seeks to disrupt the values that produce relationships of dominance over nature as well as the colonial supremacy in the construction of the Canadian prairie landscape (Sheppard, chapter 3). All the chapters in one way or another draw on memory. Authors use a range of methods of looking through mapping and installations (Sheppard, chapter 3), looking back including individual memory-work writing (Larsson, chapter 7), working with a literary text (Nyhlén, chapter 8), photographs (Starr & Mitchell, chapter 2; Gillander Gådin & De Lange, chapter 5), drawing (Khumalo, chapter 6), and working through autobiographical writing across two sites of girlhood, then and now (Yamile, chapter 11).

Finally, although not all contributors to this book use visual images, all have set out to evoke a picture that interrogates where they fit into their study of rurality and why it matters. The idea is that, as researchers, we need to locate ourselves and interrogate what that location might mean in a range of social contexts including rurality. Critically, as co-editors writing the last chapter during the time of COVID-19, we recognize the fluidity of the meanings of rurality and our work as researchers in rural contexts. Where are we in the picture? It all depends.

NOTES

1 A Transnational Study of the Intersections of Rurality, Gender, and Violence against Girls and Young Women: An Urgent Matter in Both the Global North and the Global South (TGRAN).
2 See Government of Newfoundland and Labrador (2019); Statistics Canada (2001).

REFERENCES

Burkholder, C., & Thompson, J. (2020). What about fieldnotes: An introduction. In C. Burkholder & J. Thompson (Eds.), *Fieldnotes in qualitative education and social science research* (pp. 1–15). Routledge.

De Lange, N. (2018). Growing up rural in South Africa: On using cellphones to engage children's ideas of social spaces. In C. Mitchell & A. Mandrona (Eds.), *Visual encounters in the study of rural childhoods* (pp. 176–89). Rutgers.

Department of Planning, Monitoring, and Evaluation. (2015). *Twenty year review, South Africa 1994–2014: Background paper: Rural transformation*. https://www.dpme.gov.za/publications/20%20Years%20Review/20%20 Year%20Review%20Documents/20YR%20Rural%20Transformation.pdf

England, K.V.L. (1994). Getting personal: Reflexivity, positionality, and feminist research. *Professional Geographer, 46*(1), 80–9. https://doi.org /10.1111/j.0033-0124.1994.00080.x

Gillander Gådin, K., Giritli-Nygren, K., Mitchell, C., & Nyhlén, S. (2015). Studying the intersections of rurality, gender and violence against girls and young women: An urgent matter in both the Global North and the Global South. In K. Gillander-Gådin & C. Mitchell (Eds.), *Being young in neoliberal time: Transnational perspectives on challenges and possibilities for resistance and social change* (pp. 109–20). Mid Sweden University.

Gilmore, L., & Marshall, E. (2010). Girls in crisis: Rescue and transnational feminist autobiographical resistance. *Feminist Studies, 36*(3), 667–90. https:// www.jstor.org/stable/27919128

Government of Newfoundland and Labrador. (2019). *Rural lens: Assessing regional policy implications: A guide for public bodies*. Public Engagement and Planning Division. https://www.gov.nl.ca/pep/files/Rural-Lens.pdf

Kelly, T. (2008). *Readings from life: Rural educators read our rural selves* [Unpublished doctoral dissertation]. McGill University.

Kirk, J., & Taylor, S. (2007). UN Security Council Resolution 1325. *Forced Migration Review, 27* (January), 13–14. https://www.fmreview.org/sites /fmr/files/FMRdownloads/en/sexualviolence/kirk-taylor.pdf

Lee, L. (Ed). (2013). *Jo Spence: The final project*. Ridinghouse.

Makgetla, N. (2010, 14–16 April). *Overview of rural development in South Africa* [Paper presentation]. International Conference on Dynamics of Rural Transformation in Emerging Economies, New Delhi, India. https://www.researchgate.net/publication/272744192_Overview_of_Rural_Development_In_South_Africa

Mandrona, A., & Mitchell, C. (Eds.). (2018). *Visual encounters in the study of rural childhoods*. Rutgers University Press.

Mitchell, C., de Lange, N., & Moletsane, R. (2017). *Participatory visual methodologies: Social change through community and policy dialogue*. Sage.

Mitchell, C., & Mandrona, A. (2019a). *Our rural selves: Memory, place and the visual in Canadian childhoods*. McGill-Queen's University Press.

Mitchell, C., & Mandrona, A. (2019b). Rural beginnings. In C. Mitchell & A. Mandrona (Eds.), *Our rural selves: Memory and the visual in Canadian childhoods* (pp. 3–19). McGill-Queen's University Press.

Mohanty, C.T. (2003). *Feminism without borders: Decolonizing theory, practicing solidarity*. Duke University Press.

Moletsane, R. (2018). Foreword. In C. Mitchell & A. Mandrona (Eds.), *Visual encounters in the study of rural childhoods* (pp. ix–xi). Rutgers.

Moodie, S. (1871). *Roughing it in the bush; or Forest life in Canada* (3rd ed.). https://www.gutenberg.ca/ebooks/moodie-roughingit1871/moodie-roughingit1871-00-h-dir/moodie-roughingit1871-00-h.html

Nonomura, R., & Baker, L. (2021, May). Gender-based violence in rural, remote & northern communities. *Learning Network Issue 35*. Centre for Research & Education on Violence against Women & Children (London, ON). https://www.vawlearningnetwork.ca/our-work/issuebased_newsletters/issue-35/index.html

Pithouse, K., Mitchell, C., & Weber, S. (2009). Self-study in teaching and teacher development: A call to action. *Educational Action Research, 17*(1), 43–62. https://doi.org/10.1080/09650790802667444

Pithouse-Morgan, K., Pillay, D., & Mitchell, C. (2019). Memory mosaics: New voices, insights, possibilities for working with the arts and memory in researching teacher professional learning. In K. Pithouse-Morgan, D. Pillay, & C. Mitchell (Eds.), *Memory mosaics: Researching teacher professional learning through artful memory-work* (pp. 1–13). Springer.

Renold, E., & Ringrose, J. (2013). Feminisms re-figuring "sexualisation," sexuality and "the girl." *Feminist Theory, 14*(3), 247–54. https://doi.org/10.1177/1464700113499531

Söderberg, E., Nyhlén, S., Gillander Gådin, K., & Giritli Nygren, K. (2018). The place of girls? Collective memory work in the study of portrayals of rural girlhood in Swedish child and youth literature. In C. Mitchell & A. Mandrona (Eds.), *Visual encounters in the study of rural childhoods* (pp. 109–22). Rutgers.

Spence, J. (1986). *Putting myself in the picture: A political, personal and photographic autobiography*. Camden Press.

Statistics Canada. (2001, November). Definitions of rural. *Rural and Small Town Canada Analysis Bulletin*, 3(3). Catalogue no. 21-006-XIE. https://www150.statcan.gc.ca/n1/pub/21-006-x/21-006-x2001003-eng.pdf

Statistics South Africa. (2005). General Household Survey 2005. https://www.datafirst.uct.ac.za/dataportal/index.php/catalog/88

Taft, J.K. (2010). *Rebel girls: Youth activism and social change across the Americas*. New York University Press.

PART ONE

Rural Travelscapes

2 Travelling in Circles along Roads Less Travelled in Awe of Open Spaces

LISA STARR AND CLAUDIA MITCHELL

Introduction

"Where are you from?" We dwell on this question as one that matters a lot when you grow up on the rural prairies of Canada. It is typically one of the first questions you ask when you meet someone. The answer, of course, will vary. It might be "west of town and just east of Manitoba Highway 83." Or it could be about a particular district: "Oh I am from over Lenore way." If you live in town, it could be "across the tracks," "over town," or "out towards the golf course." People want to locate you. The question, of course, has become far more complex over time in recognition of our non-Indigenous settler identities. The question "Where are you from?" now includes "Whose land have you been occupying?" (see also Sheppard, chapter 3, this volume; Mitchell & Mandrona, 2019).

We both spent our childhood in rural farming communities in the Canadian Prairies, but the location of those communities is too simple a response to what we see as an important and complex set of questions about identity. The identity we assume now has been negotiated through our interactions with each other, those with whom we have connected in our work, and the institutions of which we have been, and continue to be, part. What we present here is more of a snapshot of a place and time, a window into our thinking about the hows and whys of who we are and what we do (Harré & Van Langenhove, 1999; Pinnegar, 2005). Although we come from different prairie times separated by a number of years, different prairie places (Saskatchewan and Manitoba are, after all, two very different provinces), and different experiences of prairie life ("in town" and "on the farm"), we find our scholarly selves immersed in rural Ethiopia, Mozambique, and South Africa, researching the impact of gender inequity and gender-based violence on girls and young women as well as on their communities. The coincidence that two "prairie girls," as both our mothers might have described us, would end up in Montreal and travel great distances to do such work may simply be the luck of the draw, but, as we explore here, we believe there is mutual intentionality that traces back to our prairie roots. All the specificity about prairie spaces that characterized our girlhoods has been replaced by an international development context that serves as the site of much of our academic lives. Being "just east of Highway 83" no longer situates us. Or does it? That question is at the heart of what we explore in this chapter.

As researchers working across disciplines, genres, and locations, we discuss here the influence of our sense of rurality on the ontological and epistemological choices we make when we are situating research as well as ourselves within that research. Using visual and narrative prompts, we discuss our sense of rural identity as a threshold concept akin to a "portal, opening up a new and previously inaccessible way of thinking about something. It represents a transformed way of understanding, or interpreting, or viewing something without which the learner cannot progress" (Meyer & Land, 2003, p. 1). We tread lightly in that our sense of transformation is very much continual, in progress, and fluid, since our past and present experiences continue to intertwine themselves in our understandings and perspectives. As we weave our way through our narrative recollections of prairie life, we circle back to several reflective questions. What does engaging in the narrative teach us about ourselves? What does it teach us about others? How have we approached our work and the worlds in which we dwell as a result of our past and evolving understandings? How might we be transformed by process and product?

We frame our exploration of rurality within an autoethnographic approach. Autoethnographic investigation addresses some of the tensions and complexities of identity and the intersections of thinking, feeling, and acting. Ellis and Bochner (2000) have broken down the root words of autoethnography in terms of the self (auto), the culture (ethnos), and the research process (graphy); autoethnography is at the intersection of these three spheres. Morawski and Palulis (2009) put slashes between the auto, the ethno, and the graphy to emphasize the doublings – the need for researchers and educators to dwell in the spaces in-between. The self is situated in culture, and the cultural is in the self; the researcher writes about culture and also re/produces culture through language. With auto/ethno/graphy "the writing writes the writer as a complex (im)possible subject in a world where (self) knowledge can only ever be tentative, contingent, and situated" (Gannon, 2006, p. 474).

The self is conceived of as a text, "a project to be built ... a project for bricoleurs" (Morawski & Palulis, 2009, p. 6). As Trinh (1999, p. 18) suggested, "to write is to become."

Giorgio (2013) described the relationship between memory and autoethnography this way:

> When I write from memory, I re-live and re-imagine, shaping my memories into autoethnography, a suturing of lived experience with theory, memory with the forgotten, the critique of self with those of others and of culture. When we write autoethnography, we retell stories, our own as well as others. (pp. 406–7)

In moving beyond the individual, such autoethnographic exploration requires us to look at a bigger picture to determine how our discoveries can or even should make a difference. Jun (1994) believed that the critical questions of past actions and future possibilities are what build self-conscious ethical action based on two key questions: (1) "Who am I and what kind of person do I want to be?" and (2) "How do I relate to others and to the world around me?" What does engaging in the narrative teach us about ourselves and about others? How have we approached our work and the worlds in which we dwell because of our past evolving understandings? How might we be transformed through both the process and the product? We have embraced Mills's (1959) assertion that "for public theory to influence educational practice it must be translated through the personal" (cited in Bullough & Pinnegar, 2001, p. 15). MacIntyre (1997) claimed that our sense of self comes from our ability to create a coherent narrative that, for Pinnegar (2005), makes sense of the complex and sometimes contradictory obligations and responsibilities that are attached to our fluid identity. Therefore, of importance in this chapter is an examination of the personal meaning created by and for two researchers and its potential impact for those readers who consider its meaning.

Touchstone Stories in Autoethnography

In this section, we each offer "touchstone stories" of the personal. Strong-Wilson (2006) described a touchstone as an experience or text to which individuals return. The touchstone stories here serve as autoethnographic snapshots of our prairie lives. Tanaka et al. (2014, p. 68) characterized touchstone stories as those recollections, memories, or stories that "emerge as a crucial place to find emotional, spiritual and intuitive resonance." Although we have framed ourselves as researchers in this chapter, that role is inextricably linked to our identities as teachers, mothers, children, and sisters. Our method was quite simple, and we had started working on the ideas for this chapter long before we even knew we were going to write it. Almost from our first trip together to Ethiopia several years ago, we were deep into what we think of as "where are you from prairie talk." A year or so later, we participated on a panel at a feminist workshop as part of the Canadian Association of the Study of Women in Education annual meeting in 2017, where our questions of prairie spaces became deepened through the inclusion of photographs along with short narratives. When we decided that we wanted to embark upon writing a chapter related to rurality for this book, we had already landed into collaborative memory-work, the visual, and thinking about what Beckman and Weissberg (2013, p. vii) refer to as "writ[ing] with photography." As part of our process, we agreed on a prompt: to find photo images in our personal albums that captured what we each regarded as touchstone memories of our experience of the prairies where, as we have mentioned above, we both grew up but no longer live. As we discovered in our work together, our selection of photos with which to work was strategic rather than systematic. Following the idea of working with individual photos (see Moletsane & Mitchell, 2007), we then used these images as the basis for short pieces of writing. For Lisa, the images strategically selected were of wind, sky, and people. For Claudia, the images are all about roads and mobility. We consider two sets of stories: Lisa's "If You Aren't from the Prairies" and Claudia's "Pedagogy of the Rearview Mirror."

If You Aren't from the Prairies (Lisa)

David Bouchard (1998) wrote the children's book *If You're Not from the Prairie*, in which he uses verses and illustrations to share an insider's view of living on the Canadian Prairies. I find two verses to be particularly profound in relation to our discussion in this chapter. In the first, Bouchard talks about the sheer power of the wind across a prairie landscape; in the second, he focuses on the limitless prairie sky. Bouchard's focus on these two features of prairie life are catalysts for my discussion.

The Wind as Place

Prairie people have a unique and deep relationship with weather (Figure 2.1). As early settlers moved into the prairies, the harsh prairie winter was a test of both physical and mental survival. The freezing winter

Figure 2.1. The winds at work outside Moose Jaw, Saskatchewan, July 2016. Courtesy of Lisa Starr.

temperatures meant that homesteaders had to hunker down and, in some cases, face the challenge of freezing or starving. Since people were dependent on the land for their survival, the summers posed a different challenge to their livelihood. Storms could bring crop-destroying hail. In other years, rain could all but disappear. Both situations damaged the crops on which people so desperately depended. The sense of the power that weather had over the lives of its new settler inhabitants has become ingrained in the prairie psyche. As a child, when I was speaking to my grandmother on the phone, the conversation would turn inevitably to what the weather was like in Magrath, Alberta, compared to Moose Jaw, Saskatchewan. I did not grow up on a farm, but my grandmother, like countless others, did. Inevitably and almost involuntarily, these prairie people talk about the weather. My sister and I still send each other screen shots from the Weather Network app of extreme weather reports between Saskatoon and Montreal. While the destructive power of prairie weather has been thwarted somewhat by technology and urbanization, I find that the wind remains a daunting force.

Having grown up on the prairies, for me wind is a constant. Rarely will anyone step outside without feeling its presence. The wind is so innately synonymous with the prairies that many people comment more on its absence than on its presence; we think that a day without wind is humid. On hot summer nights, often in the early evening, the wind will intensify, letting everyone know a fantastic thunderstorm is on its way. The sky darkens quickly as thunderheads form. Trees start to bend back and forth unnaturally, garbage cans get blown over, and summer toys left in the yard can be seen sailing down the street.

Even now in Montreal, where I live – far from the prairie flatlands – when I know a storm is coming, my anticipation of the wind makes me uneasy. The wind brings change without consent or agreement. On Montreal nights when I hear the wind whistle, I have trouble sleeping. I can hear the windows rattle; the trees bend just a little further than what I am comfortable with. To me, the wind brings a wave of subtle chaos, just enough to make me feel uncertain but not enough to require significant action – I am just waiting. Most often, these winds bring no change at all, but with them comes a wave of emotional instability that starts in my chest as though my heart rate is trying to challenge the unpredictable rhythm of the gusts that assault the house. I imagine myself standing rock still, head bowed, eyes closed as the force of the wind surges against me. The granules of blowing dirt assault the skin on my face, making me squeeze my eyes till they are tightly closed to protect what little moisture is left behind my eyelids. I wrap my arms around myself more tightly to protect myself from the buffeting wind and also from the uneasiness the blowing wind creates deep inside me.

The Wind and the People

As much as the wind at times brings with it a deep sense of uneasiness, it also has a way of clearing the clutter of daily life to connect me to my childhood, particularly to my dad. I left the prairies in my early twenties ready to forge my way in British Columbia. My father's death when I was twenty-seven had a profound and lingering impact on my adult life. As I fast approach the age when he died, I find myself much more contemplative of my life growing up in the prairies.

I started playing softball in the summers when I was seven; I was supposed to be eight, but my dad talked our way into the league (in fairness I was only a few months too young and turned eight before the season finished). I was excited because I got to play what my dad played. We had to go to the co-op store downtown to sign up, which was kind of a big deal because we never shopped at the co-op. There was an entrance at the side where I and my dad went down some stairs. Two people were sitting at one of those old wooden tables, thin plywood, rounded corners, with the fixed metal legs that, if you sat on them, you were pretty sure they would collapse. My dad filled out a form, and with that simple action, I became a cub.

I loved being a cub. I loved getting my yellow uniform on, the way it hung off me; it had a zipper up the front, so I had to wear a T-shirt underneath because the zipper was cold on the skin. It had some faded black piping down the front of the shirt and the sides of the pants. The uniforms were made of an old material, leftovers from another team, and they were heavy. I didn't have anything like it; there were only two teams, the cubs (we were yellow) and the bears (who were green.) With every game, there was wind: some nights more of a breeze, others a force that whipped the red shale into my eyes and hair. I would get pelted by the dirt in the infield being whipped up into tiny granular daggers. I welcomed the change of innings so I could seek a brief reprieve in the dugout. I would come home from games covered in a layer of dust painted on my skin by the artistry of the wind. Leaning over the sink, I would shake my hair and see the dirt fall from my scalp to cover the white porcelain.

I was the catcher, overwhelmed in the oversized chest protector, mask, and shin guards designed for someone much larger than myself. My dad often volunteered to be the umpire at our games. I could feel him leaning over me as I waited for the next pitch, the smell of his Juicy Fruit gum wafting forward. I don't know that I ever understood how much I wanted him right there with me, leaning in, another layer of protection from the uncertainty. Even at seven, I was preoccupied by uncertainty, constantly wondering, What next? What if? Eventually he stopped volunteering. As I got older and better, we needed real officials, not dads. He still came to all the games, but then we were separated by a large fence. I had the equipment to protect me but not him.

As much as I dwell in place, I cannot separate those memories from people. I did not play softball because of the physical space; I played it because of the connection it created to people (Figure 2.2).

What Is the Sky?

How can anyone who has not been to the prairies do justice to describing its openness, its vastness, as if you could fill the endless sky with possibility? When I go back to visit, I love the breadth of its space. The simple topography of the prairies likely represents the practicality of its inhabitants. You adapted to the harshness of the weather or you perished – it was a simple either/or. I welcome the simplicity of it. In Montreal, I feel the cultural and linguistic tensions of English/French everywhere with little reprieve. Added to that is the chaos of endless

Figure 2.2. Being a cub, Moose Jaw, Saskatchewan, June 1978. Courtesy of Lisa Starr.

construction disrupting even the simplest travel, and I find myself longing for wide-open space – one road, going to one place, unfettered and with clear options to turn left or right as the route requires.

When I visit the prairies, I take many pictures from the car window as we drive from Saskatoon to Moose Jaw. My sister, who has always lived in Saskatchewan (see Figure 2.3, right), laughs at me because to her there is nothing interesting about the flat, mostly beige land stretched out in front of us. I do the same thing when we work in Ethiopia (see Figure 2.3, left). Despite its seeming endlessness, I see two worlds co-existing, born of the line where sky meets earth across the horizon. The two meet and function in harmony, creating a landscape that suggests balance, as if they long ago reached consensus not to interfere with one another unnecessarily. I am fascinated that this earth/sky binary exists so cleanly. My own thinking about the world and about the work I do is much less defined. I enjoy its twists and turns because it takes me to spaces that I may otherwise never experience. I wonder how living in a prairie space has impacted my thinking. Has the openness created space for greater depth of understanding or, perhaps, greater breadth to match the unending skyline? Does the time I spend in either open space

Figure 2.3. Open spaces: Amhara, Ethiopia, March 2016 (left) and Regina, Saskatchewan (right). Courtesy of Lisa Starr.

help me to see the world the way it really is, or am I a privileged tourist who sees only what she wants to see?

The wind and sky go hand in hand, both in their awesomeness and their capacity to intimidate. The wind can rip through the sky without impunity because there is nothing but open space for it to rage through. Once that same wind hits the ground, the story can change quickly. The ground, while firm, must work hard to hold its earthly belongings in place. The multifaceted challenges of working in international development and addressing complex issues like gender-based violence are a bit like standing against the wind. The eventual calm that follows represents the moments when change, however incremental, may happen. Sometimes I think my mind lives within those tumultuous winds, struggling to see clearly the neat boundaries of land and sky.

Pedagogy of the Rearview Mirror (Claudia)

My compulsion to think and write about rural roads in the context of studying rurality is framed within the here and now as much as it is located in memory and the past – hence, the rearview mirror. The point is that, if you live in a rural area, the road is your ticket out, but roads also determine what and who comes in and what stays. Roads are also central to the idea of "getting there from here" when it comes to doing research in a rural area, something my colleagues and I have had to explain and rationalize in so many research grant applications. You

Figure 2.4. The laneway of Devon Farm: spring (left) and winter (right).
Courtesy of Claudia Mitchell.

cannot do research in a deeply rural area of Ethiopia sitting in an office
in the city of Addis Ababa.

It's Always the Same Road

There are dozens of snapshots in our boxes of pictures of this same
scene: looking up the lane from the main road to picture the farm itself –
the barns, the house, and the bluff of trees in which the house and barn
are located (Figure 2.4). The family considers this scene photogenic, it
seems, for there are dozens of versions of this picture. Seasonal pictures
of deep snow, or of early spring and the beginnings of green, or of the
lushness of summer when it is harder to see the house. Looking up the
lane is consoling somehow. There is a sense of destination, boundaries –
you are getting somewhere. You drive up the lane, though the "up"
I think refers to the tiniest of inclines as you get to the barn.

Hopefulness and Suspense

Country roads are part of my childhood.

> I remember hearing the far-off sound of the tires of a car on the gravel of
> the long, straight, open road – what my family always referred to as the
> "main road." This main road is some distance from our farmyard, con-
> nected by another long and very straight and open laneway. No trees or
> bushes or anything to block the view of the prairie expanse. For several

minutes there is suspense. The tires offer a hopeful sound, breaking the silence, and breaking the monotony of the long summer day of a little girl who longs for something, anything, to happen. First, the car is quite a way off. Then it sounds like it is slowing down, and I see that it is turning into our laneway. It stops there, and at that moment I am lost in anticipation. I don't recognize the car. Is it going to come up the lane, or is the driver just turning around? Will there be the sound of the wheels speeding up, kicking up a little dust as it heads back down the main road towards town, or will the vehicle slowly make its way up the narrow passage of the laneway towards the barn and house? (Mitchell, 2015a, p. 7)

If you get down the lane you will be clear; you will get out. Getting out could refer to getting "through," which is what will be a challenge in deep snow or in mud season – will you get through? Getting out is something else. It means getting right to the end of the lane, but there isn't really anything there. It is just open sky, some bush to the right and flat prairie to the left. No, the only way you are going to get anywhere is to follow that road; predictably, every mile there will be another road and then another and then another. You can literally go around in circles always staying on the square.

Field Road

In addition to the laneway for getting to the farm, there is another road, the "field road," which passes right across the fields of our farm starting at the government road allowance on the edge of Virden and leading right through to the farmyard. The main part of the field road is well maintained, with deep trenches like ditches on either side, and is regularly gravelled, having been built by an oil company so the wells could be serviced. The last little section past the second well is more of a dirt track really, but a road anyway. The field road feels like an escape – you could drive out that way and never encounter another vehicle. When I was a child and played softball in the summer in town, I would ride home on the field road after dark since it was safer. It was just me, an eleven-year-old, with my bike and its solid headlamp rumbling through the field road. It horrifies me now, but it seemed the smarter thing to do then.

Car People 1

We are (or were then) what you could call "car people." When I was a child, I think you could have called us "big car people": my father had Oldsmobiles, Chevs, Pontiacs, Chryslers, and Fords – the big five. If you go through photos, you can trace the family history of cars. A high percentage of snapshots have a car in the background. A group can be posed at the front of the car or at the side. I had a student years ago who grew up in East Montreal and talked about doing a family history through an analysis of all the family photos that included a car. His project made me realize that is exactly what we could do too. It is partly, of course, about pre-flash photos, which made it easier to take pictures outside. But then, in these wide-open spaces, where do you take a picture? The car is the focal point.

It is always the same. In the good weather (April to October), we finish Sunday dinner and by 1:00 or 1:30 p.m., my dad has decided that we should go for a drive, take a spin. What else is there to do anyway? No one really works on Sunday, so we might as well. We get down the lane, and then that's when the excitement begins. Will we go left, which could mean driving around town up one street and down the other? How's the renovation going on the Fontana place? Is Mildred's son visiting from Calgary? We will know if there is a car in the driveway. Left could also mean going to the cemetery. A good idea to check the graves. Maybe do a little watering or see where they have buried Jack Frame. Such a sudden death. Or we could go to what we refer to as "the valley" – always my favourite. There is not a single photograph that captures anything of driving down into the Assiniboine Valley, crossing the million dollar bridge to get back out of the valley. If we go right though, we could head up to the old Scallion place, a fascinating stone farmhouse, and even as it is falling down, it is exactly like the Austin Mini in Figure 2.5. Exotic, it could be fixed up. I vow that, when I grow up, I will return to it, fix it up, and live in it.

No one who is in the picture knows where this Austin Mini came from and how it came to be just next to one of the barns. And yet it fits there. The farmyard has always been full of mystery.

Typically, old farm machinery becomes part of the landscape. A small single slope-roofed "shed roof" building smelling of grease and oil, and full of cans of odd nails and perhaps an old hammer, is called "the workshop," but my brothers and I don't really know what that means. We think that someone must have lived there once, but it is so tiny. Who could have lived there and why? The workshop, though, is not nearly as interesting as the Austin Mini. That day in August, when the picture was taken, the four of us pounce through the grass. Sarah, one of my daughters, is the photographer, and my mother and my other daughters, Rebecca and Dorian, come around the corner of the implement shed and into the bright sun.

Figure 2.5. Exotic Austin Mini at the Scallion farmyard. Courtesy of Claudia Mitchell.

I am not sure where I was when this picture was taken. I am not the photographer, but I was definitely there. This car intrigues us, and we are quick to imagine getting it back on the road. There is a sense of wonder and possibility. We are very clearly tourists. The trio seem so clearly to be visiting and not from there. For one thing, no one ever goes for a walk just around the farmyard. People would be working (and therefore not taking pictures) or, if going for a walk, it would be to a park in town or at least on the open road. The image of the trio is slightly blurry, especially in contrast to the sharpness of the Mini. I think that's where I see it as a "memory picture"; the human subjects are not very clear – just a bit fuzzy like the memories.

Resisting Colonizing Eyes: From the Canadian Prairies to Fieldwork in Ethiopia

As prairie folk, we have grown up in a region of Canada that has never been considered an economic or cultural centre, and we are used to hearing people from all other parts of the country commenting on dreading the days of apparent monotony while driving across the flat landscape of Manitoba and Saskatchewan. No mountains, no forests, no oceans. We are used to being vaguely apologetic, even though, as our touchstone accounts above highlight, we love the wide-open space. Perhaps it is about home spaces and the draw of the land in rural settings. Whatever it is for us is perhaps not that different for the instructors and students with whom we work in four rural regions of Ethiopia, and the gaze of outsiders is perhaps not that different from how outsiders from the Global North assess, size up, or conduct a situational analysis of those from the Global South, seeing what is not there rather than what is and with no appreciation for wind or sky. For the last six years, we have worked together on a project in Ethiopia funded by Global Affairs Canada, focusing specifically on capacity building in four agricultural colleges. The work of Agricultural Transformation through Stronger Vocational Education (ATTSVE) concerns agriculture and rural development, and, of course, it takes place in rural settings and represents the fact that agriculture accounts for 80 per cent of productivity in the country. Our work as social scientists on the project, unlike that of most of the team members, is not about the technical aspects of crops, income generation, or post-harvest management, but rather, and in keeping with Canada's Feminist International Agency Policy (FIAP), is about gender equality and related issues that address women, leadership, and gender-based violence (see Starr & Mitchell, 2018).

At one level, and the level that aligns well with the geographic spaces described above, there is something fundamentally prairie-like about the experience of driving in rural Ethiopia. For example, in so much of the work in Ethiopia, it is the long drives from Addis to Jimma or Nedjo, or from Mekele to Maichew, that are so memory inducing.

Sometimes when I am out on one of these roads – being driven – I think I could be anywhere, and then I realize that it is because of the "scape" of it – typically flat, wide-open fields, so that I am driving through the very same landscape as I would have been driving through on a Sunday afternoon as a child when we went for a drive. Even when there is a snaked road that winds down into a valley, as there is on the road to Jimma, I think of heading into the Assiniboine Valley. The main difference now on the drive is that we are going *somewhere*, and we will reach a destination in two or three or seven hours. Once, on the way to Nedjo, we came upon a road that is not unlike the field road. There is no built-up part of the road, no culverts, no cement edging, no ditches or trenches. We drive through tall grasses that are almost as high as the vehicle. As we make our way on the twelve-hour or longer drive to Nedjo, I am transported back in time to the field road. (Claudia)

At another level, and here we run the risk of perhaps sounding overly deterministic, there is a part of our engagement in Ethiopia through the ATTSVE project that somehow hearkens back to being on the prairie.

> As we rumble down smoothly paved roads built and funded by foreign investors, I am easily lost in the open landscape and sky. To say that gender-based violence is a challenging subject is a gross understatement. It is the lived experience of many we have met and with whom we have worked. I have little to offer that will improve the cultural, economic, and social conditions from which many women and children suffer. Conditions, like exchanging sex for food or school supplies or missing a week of class each month because they do not have sanitary pads, are endured by many female students just to get access to basic education. Many of the local female instructors care deeply, even donating money from their own meagre wages to help, but the colleges are dominated by men whose awareness, while growing, lacks understanding of the depth of the struggle women endure. It is the complexity of these challenges that draws me into those open prairie-like spaces because I need space to deconstruct, understand, and respond. Perhaps that is the gift the prairies have given me – a wide-open space to understand the complex intricate tangles of the world. (Lisa)

What is it? Does our "prairie-ness" give us a particular lens through which we view the world? We believe that it does but are less certain how it has happened. In the course of our research, do we ask different questions that are somehow connected to our sense of prairie? We think that we might do because we learned to see the world through wide-open landscapes of superficial similarity yet hidden depth. Those long car rides created opportunities for contemplation, reflection, and thoughtfulness. Our deep prairie roots perhaps fostered a resilience that informs how we view and participate in colonial spaces. We are unsure of whether we are best positioned to say definitely that we have resisted or contested colonizing eyes or adopted Mary Louise Pratt's (2007) idea of imperial eyes in transcultural travel. Instead, we offer that we have intentionally engaged in mindfulness in an attempt to create what Langer (1997, p. 4) described as "new categories; openness to new information; and an implicit awareness of more than one perspective." By doing so, we act with intention to resist the ignorance that leads to "entrapment in old categories; automatic behaviour that precludes attending to new signals; and actions that operate from a single perspective" (Langer, 1997, p. 4).

We speculate here about how our autoethnographic accounts in the previous section also help to situate a certain advocacy in our work in Ethiopia. Well-known Canadian journalist Bruce Hutchison (1956) wrote an article for *McLean's Magazine* about travelling across Manitoba. His description of the "oil capital" of Manitoba, Virden, Claudia's hometown, says it all in terms of how outsiders might regard the space.

The shabby little town of Virden (it would do for a set in a western movie) was filled that Saturday night with men obviously not farmers or tourists, men in jumpers, greasy overalls and the high buckled boots and raffish slouch hats of their craft – the migratory race of drillers, moving from one oil strike to another. One didn't need these men to announce a new oil field. It announced itself by the noise, some stink of crude oil in the middle of some farmer's field, by the steel skeletons of the oil drills, the miles of pipe and the odd little pumps, their arms moving up and down like hammers. The beer parlour was filled with thirsty noisy nomads, the "roughnecks" of the latest prairie migration. They had brought a great industry to the prairies, had moved from southern Alberta to the north, then eastward across Saskatchewan until they finally reached Manitoba. But they were no part of prairie civilization. They were birds of brief passage. To them, Virden was not a town; it was an overnight stop on an endless march wherever the continental oil pool lay hidden beneath the surface of the plains. Among them in the beer parlour, a stranger in his own land, sat an old gentleman who seemed to have been transported, intact and unruffled, from some superior London club. He wore a tweed hat and jacket in large English checks and his face was the face of an English colonel out of a cartoon. Though he had been farming outside Virden for fifty years, he didn't know, so help him God, what had happened to the town. It was ruined by oil and prosperity until a man couldn't drink a glass of beer in peace. Well, the oil drillers would pass on, once they got their beastly wells operating, and then things would get back to normal. "Right now," he protested, "this town's like something out of Hollywood – a gold rush, only it's oil. Why, a four-room house, with no plumbing, rents for ninety or a hundred dollars a month. Good for the country, I dare say, but the people around here seem to think the boom is going on forever. When these fellows get out of town, it'll be just a farm town again with a few oil wells around."

He sipped his beer alone, careless of the clamour around him, as if he were looking out on Pall Mall instead of Virden's threadbare street. (Hutchison, 1956, pp. 41–4)

Hutchison's description drew hostile reactions from the people of Virden. Their reactions in a Canadian context are not that different from the reactions to a photo exhibition of images (*Our Photos, Our Learning, Our Well-being*) taken by a group of students attending the four agricultural colleges in Ethiopia. The students had participated in a photovoice event during which they took pictures in response to the prompt "Being a male/female student in my ATVET."[1] The exhibition travelled to Canada as part of the launch event for the project and then later travelled to the four colleges in Ethiopia. Four faculty members from each of the agricultural colleges were in attendance at the exhibition in Truro, Nova Scotia. The situation of having the faculty members view the exhibition ahead of time was both a good thing and a bit problematic.

> Because the faculty members were otherwise going to be seeing the images for the first time at the launch event, it was important for them to see for themselves how their students regarded their learning. This was particularly important because some of the images were very critical (concerned with the food insecurity in relation to living in residence, sexual violence, absentee instructors) of a specific ATVET (even though no names were used). In fact, even before we unveiled the exhibition to the faculty members, my colleagues and I decided to leave out a set of posters that dealt entirely with images of dirty and inadequate toilets and lack of water. My colleague commented that perhaps these images would simply reinforce the images of Ethiopia, the "othering" of "over there," and that perhaps for this Canadian audience they were not appropriate. Together, we also wondered how the ATVET faculty themselves would feel about having these particular photos exhibited.
>
> My first thought is "but the students took these photos. Is it fair to now not show them?" But then I think that they were taking the photos for a needs assessment. They had been asked to be honest and take pictures of their concerns. My colleague is right: are these images really appropriate for this audience outside of Ethiopia? Is this some type of *National Geographic* portrayal? Why didn't I notice the cumulative effect of fifteen images of dirty toilets when we put that set of posters together? Maybe the fifteen images spread out would be different, but all together on two large posters they seem larger than life.
>
> When the various faculty members viewed the images, they expressed a sense of being pleasantly surprised about the photography skills of the students but also about how much their students knew about topics such as climate change and environmental issues. At the same time, and just as my colleague had predicted, they were concerned about some of the

pictures, although not necessarily the ones we had identified. One photo in particular shows a chair with a half-empty plate on it and the rest of the dining hall in the background. The student who took the pictures offered a caption about the lack of available food.

Three of the faculty members are clustered around the image. One is adamant that it should be taken down. For one thing, he says, the student who took the picture should not be showing a picture of a plate on a chair. Why doesn't the student clean it up instead? A colleague assures him that "actually this is how things are and we should all be open to looking at the truth." It is a back and forth dispute and as an outsider I stay out of it, but in my heart, I am hoping that they will agree to leave the image. It is only the next day at the launch that I learn the outcome. The person who is most adamant about removing the picture asks if he can say something to the assembled group of dignitaries and makes a comment that, although many of the images of the colleges are very negative in that they show problems with sanitation, and it is too bad the students had to take them, but that perhaps at the end of the six years of the project they will be taking different pictures. I heave a sigh of relief, but I find myself compelled to also say something to the group: "These are the pictures a group of ATVET students took on 'being a male or female student.' We have had in the last month a great deal of media coverage about sexual violence on Canadian campuses. What would happen if we gave cameras to our students attending Canadian institutions?" (Claudia's fieldnotes; excerpt from Mitchell, 2015b, p. 54)

We do not mean to conflate the sensitivities related to the two events separated by six decades, several continents, and thousands of kilometres. However, and in keeping with our touchstone accounts in the previous section, we want to suggest that perhaps we both have a strong sense of advocacy for the local and the rural.

Reflecting Forward

As scholars, we typically encourage graduate students to engage in reflexivity intended to help them identify who they are as scholars and to better ground themselves in the research work they will do. But not everyone practices what they preach. In the process of writing this chapter, we have discovered that perhaps those prairie spaces and their windstorms, open skies, and long roads created the conditions for a deeper sense of reflexivity, which has lent itself to the work we do. Reflexivity requires the individual to not just look back and ponder but, more importantly, to consider their contribution to the construction of meanings and the reinterpretation of their actions in light of newly constructed meaning, as Willig (2001) has reminded us. Danielewicz (2001) articulated reflexivity as

> an act of self-conscious consideration that can lead people to a deepened understanding of themselves and others, not in the abstract, but in relation to specific social environments … [and] foster a more profound awareness … of how social contexts influence who people are and how they behave … It involves a person's active analysis of past situations, events, and products, with the inherent goals of critique and revision for the explicit purpose of achieving an understanding that can lead to change in thought or behaviour. (pp. 155–6)

Engaging in reflexivity, we have offered insight into "the ways in which our own values, experiences, interests, beliefs, political commitments, wider aims in life and social identities have shaped the research" (Willig, 2001, p. 10). In this chapter, both as a model and a genuine exploration of understanding generated through deep "reflexion,"[2] we have delved into our understandings of rurality from personal memories of place and space, and have offered some suggestions for what these autoethnographic accounts might mean or how they could be used in relation to our academic fieldwork in rural settings in Ethiopia. We find that it is a perpetual state of meaning-making that remains open, unfixed, and meandering, much like travelling down those prairie roads.

When we think back about the touchstones we shared, the idea of the prairie becomes vivid in our minds as much as in the picture prompts. Drawing on Gadamer (2004), Clark (2008) discussed the concept of horizon as an analogy for understanding

> the superior breadth of vision that the person who is trying to understand must have. To acquire a horizon means that one learns to look beyond what is close at hand, not in order to look away from it but to see it better. Understanding happens when our present understanding or horizon is moved to a new understanding or horizon by an encounter. Thus the process of understanding is a "fusion of horizons," the old and the new horizon combining into something of living value. (para. 5–6)

In our academic work, gender is often a highly contested space with emotionally and culturally charged tangles that are difficult to unravel if they can be at all. We have learned that, in order to understand, we must be able to view the lived experiences of those with whom we work from multiple angles and perspectives like the breadth of vision to which Clark (2008) referred. Each prairie touchstone is part of a fusion of horizons that have contributed to our views of the world. Interestingly, the

Figure 2.6. Prairie skyline, Craik, Saskatchewan, August 2016. Courtesy of Lisa Starr.

horizon skyline of Figure 2.6 is not that different from the horizon skyline on the road between Addis and Jimma. What we appreciate about the horizon metaphor is that the layers of horizon continue to live and breathe. Past is not erased or forgotten but, rather, interwoven.

Perhaps being from just east of Highway 83 matters much more than we had thought.

NOTES

1 Agricultural Technical and Vocational Education and Training (ATVET) programs.
2 We use this spelling intentionally to emphasize that "reflexion" is more than simply looking back or seeing one's self in a mirror. The use of "reflexion" is more in line with how we have taken up reflexivity.

REFERENCES

Beckman, K., & Weissberg, L. (2013). Introduction. In K. Beckman & L. Weissberg (Eds.), *On writing with photography* (pp. ix–xvii). University of Minnesota Press.

Bouchard, D. (1998). *If you're not from the prairie*. Aladdin Picture Books.

Bullough, R.V., & Pinnegar, S. (2001). Guidelines for quality in autobiographical forms of self-study research. *Educational Researcher, 30*(3), 13–21. https://journals.sagepub.com/doi/10.3102/0013189X030003013

Clark, J. (2008). Philosophy, understanding and the consultation: A fusion of horizons. *British Journal of General Practice, 58*(546), 58–60. https://doi.org/10.3399/bjgp08X263929

Danielewicz, J. (2001). *Teaching selves: Identity, pedagogy, and teacher education*. SUNY Press.

Ellis, C., & Bochner, A. (2000). Autoethnography, personal narrative, reflexivity: Researcher as subject. In N. Denzin & Y. Lincoln (Eds.), *Handbook of qualitative research* (2nd ed.). SAGE.

Gadamer, H.-G. (2004). *Truth and method* (2nd revised ed.). Continuum International Publishing Group.

Gannon, S. (2006). The (im)possibilities of writing the self-writing: French poststructural theory and autoethnography. *Cultural Studies ↔ Critical Methodologies, 6*(4), 474–95. https://doi.org/10.1177/1532708605285734

Giorgio, G. (2013). Reflections on writing through memory in autoethnography. In S. Homan Jones, T.E. Adams, & C. Ellis (Eds.), *Handbook of autoethnography* (pp. 406–24). Routledge.

Harré, R., & Van Langenhove, L. (Eds.). (1999). *Positioning theory: Moral contexts of intentional action*. Blackwell Publishers.

Hutchison, B. (1956, 17 March). Bruce Hutchison rediscovers the unknown country. *Maclean's Magazine*.

Jun, J.S. (1994). *Philosophy of administration*. Daeyoung Moonhwa International.

Langer, E.J. (1997). *The power of mindful learning*. Addison Wesley Longman.

MacIntyre, A. (1997). The virtues, the unity of a human life, and the concept of a tradition. In L.P. Hinchman & S.K. Hinchman (Eds.), *Memory, identity, community: The idea of narrative in the human sciences* (pp. 241–63). SUNY Press.

Meyer, J.H.F., & Land, R. (2003). Threshold concepts and troublesome knowledge: Linkages to ways of thinking and practising within the disciplines. In C. Rust (Ed.), *Improving student learning: Theory and practice – ten years on*. Oxford Centre for Staff and Learning Development.

Mills, C.W. (1959). *The sociological imagination*. Oxford University Press.

Mitchell, C. (2015a). Hopefulness and suspense in the autoethnographic encounters of teaching in higher education. *Journal of Education, 62*, 7–12. https://doi.org/10.17159/i62a01

Mitchell, C. (2015b). Looking at showing: On the politics and pedagogy of exhibiting in community based research and work with policy makers. *Educational Research for Social Change*, 4(2), 48–60. http://ersc.nmmu.ac.za /articles/Vol_4_No_2_Mitchell_pp_48-60_October_2015.pdf

Mitchell, C., & Mandrona, A. (2019). Rural beginnings. In C. Mitchell & A. Mandrona (Eds.), *Our rural selves: Memory and the visual in Canadian childhoods* (pp. 3–19). McGill-Queen's University Press.

Moletsane, R., & Mitchell, C. (2007). On working with a single photograph. In N. De Lange, C. Mitchell, & J. Stuart (Eds.), *Putting people in the picture: Visual methodologies for social change* (pp. 131–40). Sense.

Morawski, C.M., & Palulis, P. (2009). Auto/ethno/graphies as teaching lives: An aesthetics of difference. *Journal of Curriculum Theorizing*, 25(2), 6–24. https://journal.jctonline.org/index.php/jct/article/view/MOPAA/37

Pinnegar, S. (2005). Identity development, moral authority and the teacher educator. In G. Hoban (Ed.), *The missing links in teacher education design* (pp. 259–79). Springer Netherlands.

Pratt, M.L. (2007). *Imperial eyes: Travel writing and transculturation* (2nd ed.). Routledge.

Starr, L.J., & Mitchell, C. (2018). How can Canada's feminist international assistance policy support a feminist agenda? Challenges in addressing sexual violence in four agricultural colleges in Ethiopia. *Agenda: Empowering Women for Gender Equity*, 32(1), 107–18. https://doi.org/10.1080/10130950 .2018.1427692

Strong-Wilson, T. (2006). Re-visioning one's narratives: Exploring the relationship between researcher self-study and teacher research. *Studying Teacher Education: A Journal of Self-Study of Teacher Education Practices*, 2(1), 59–76. https://doi.org/10.1080/17425960600557470

Tanaka, M.T.D, Farish, M., Nicholson, D., Tse, V., Doll, J., & Archer, E. (2014). Transformative inquiry while learning–teaching: Entry points through mentor–mentee vulnerability. *Journal of Transformative Education*, 12(3), 206–25. https://doi.org/10.1177/1541344614545129

Trinh, M.T. (1999). *Cinema interval*. Routledge.

Willig, C. (2001). *Introducing qualitative research in psychology: Adventures in theory and method*. Open University Press.

3 *Saskatchewan Song Cycle*: A Trans-Reading of Land Survey in the Canadian West

LOU SHEPPARD

I Am Here

In 2019, I was invited to participate in a project called *Lines of Flight: From Above*, curated by David LaRiviere, artistic director of PAVED Arts in Saskatoon, Saskatchewan.[1] LaRiviere brought three artists, Andrew Maize, Shaheer Tarar, and me, together for an exhibition in Saskatoon to consider the political and aesthetic implications of aerial perspectives in landscape. Each of us approached this question in a different way. Shaheer created a three-channel video installation titled *Falling Archive* that animated images from Landsat observation satellites[2] to show, by pairing the animation with user-uploaded content from the ground in Syria, the impact that the ongoing conflict in that country has had on the physical landscape. Andrew Maize created a kind of do-it-yourself (DIY) drone system by attaching GoPro cameras to kites, which he then flew above the city to capture imagery that mirrored Google satellite images of the city, experimenting with the potentials for glitch and loss in this space. I created *Saskatchewan Song Cycle*, a three-part body of work that considered the Dominion Land Survey,[3] one of Canada's foundational acts of colonial organization. LaRiviere situated our practices in conversation with one another around themes of survey and surveillance, and its political and aesthetic implications.

As a white settler occupying both urban and rural space in Canada, how can I become more accountable to the histories and violences[4] that have privileged the presence of my body in the Canadian landscape? *Saskatchewan Song Cycle* looked to two seminal colonial texts in Canadian geographic and literary history – the Dominion Land Survey (DLS) and early settler Susannah Moodie's *Roughing It in the Bush*[5] – to see how they have shaped and continue to shape settler relationships to landscape in Canada. The project became a three-part body of work consisting of three interrelated scores, which were then performed in the gallery space in Saskatoon.

I am primarily a visual artist, although most of my work begins with language. Language structures how we experience, interpret, and engage with our identities and the world. The languages, data sets, taxonomies, and structuring principles that we use to interpret the world, in turn, construct and conscript the ontologies that shape our world views. Do dominant languages, texts, and structuring principles reflect value systems that have led to oppression and dominance? My practice centres on interrogating structures of power and dominance in language and data. Using metaphor, semiotic shifts, and translation, I find ways to disrupt, translate, and notate the performative powers of a text, re-performing these disrupted performative actions as music, gesture, and installation. These interrogations of language have led me to work with a wide variety of source texts, including diagnostic criteria from the *Diagnostic and Statistical Manual of Mental Disorders* (5th ed.; DSM-5)[6] for assessing gender dysphoria, field recordings of birdsong, sea ice tracking data, executive management principles, and government policy, among others.

Saskatchewan Song Cycle came about after a year of thinking about how my body relates to land and about the reflexive relationship between ways that my body moves in landscape and the landscape that surrounds me. The very language I have with which to comprehend land is rooted in a colonial ontology, a way of understanding the world based on a system of colonial dominance and value. Pointing to this ontological structure from within, and pointing to the places that this ontological structure glitches, has provided some space for me in which to reflect on the values that continue to drive relationships to land based on dominance, ownership, and resource extraction, as well as to consider colonial supremacy in the construction of the Canadian landscape. I continue to unpack this work and recognize the privilege of white settlership that allows me to critique these power structures.

This chapter is a narrative reflection on an artistic process – a series of orienting actions, of wayfinding. It is difficult to retrace these steps. At certain points, I've sought direction from others, read, talked, listened, and followed their pointed fingers. At other times, I've had to follow my own fallible sense of direction, hoping that I'll find my way. Writing about this process has been like following a map: remembering a landmark and then remembering what came before and after. I've tried to recreate my movements as best I can, but there are gaps and leaps of faith. I hope there is enough here that someone else might be able to trace some kind of a path. None of this discussion of process is meant to excuse a lack of rigour or citation in my process. Art-making is rigorous, and artists do (or at least they should) cite their sources, though these citations are not often explicit. It is, however, meant to mark this chapter as coming from outside of a standardized practice of research and writing. Read it like a journal entry, like an artist talk. Read it as a working document that I continue to edit and rewrite as I go on in my own practice.

In this work, I am drawing on an extended period of listening, reading, and making, informed in part by generations of Indigenous thinkers and artists[7] in Canada, whose work has made visible colonial power structures and other ways of thinking and being in this place and has led me to interrogate my own presence and position in so-called Canada.

An Index of Names and Places

Growing up in Nova Scotia, I saw confirmation of my Scottish heritage everywhere I looked, not only from the positioning of Scottish culture in the forefront of Nova Scotia's tourist industry – the consistent drone of bagpipes on the Halifax waterfront and prevalence of tartan in formal dress – but also in the similarities of landscape and weather: rugged coastline, misty valleys, and persistent drizzle. It seemed clear to me that, when my ancestors arrived on this small almost-island that stuck out well into the Atlantic Ocean, they looked around them and recognized themselves as being at home in a new but familiar Scotland, which had been waiting for them across the Atlantic.

Despite its lack of inhabitants, most acres of Nova Scotia bear a name. Some places are named as an approximation of Mi'kmaq place names: Chebucto, Shubanacadie, Antigonish; some are an approximation of Gaelic or French names: Ben Eoin, Inverness, La Have (from La Havre); some are for the families that settled there: Clark's Harbour; and some describe a feature prevalent in the landscape: Bridgewater, Bear River. Many places, however, are named as a memory of another place: Halifax, Amherst, Yarmouth, Dartmouth, Caledonia, Lunenburg, New Germany, Cambridge – the list goes on and on. These names write a history of longing and otherness onto the landscape and point to a slippage between a place constructed in the colonial imagination as home and a place that reminds one of that home.

This list is only one set of names for the place in which I grew up. When I came to understand that there were other names – Mi'kma'ki, K'jipuktuk – I realized that the connection that I felt to this land was mediated through the language I had in which to name it. Colonial names carry not only a colonial history but also a colonial ontology that centres white settlers in the landscape. In Nova Scotia, my Scottish body was of the Scottish land. In Mi'kma'ki, I came to understand my presence as a settler and the colonial legacies that had led to my presence here.

An Index of Signs and Symbols

Land survey and mapping, likewise, are colonial languages. Maps bind territory to a language of systems and symbolism, and land survey makes it possible for land to be measured and thus owned and traded. Maps have a performative relationship with the land that they are meant to represent; in other words, we come to see land through maps rather than seeing maps as representations of land. It is not uncommon to ask, "Where am I on the map?" or to see maps that tell us, "You are here." To understand our place in land, maps insist that we assume an omnipresent view of land: to see where we are, we must see everything at once if we are to understand our place within it.

Recognizing mapping as a language led me to consider the rhetorical properties of that language, namely its potential to make metaphor. Metaphor allows for a momentary slippage in the relationship between the signifier and signified in language, allowing signifiers to resonate with other signifieds. A map, for example, might be a musical score; a coastline might be notated on a musical staff, and playing this music might allow us to apprehend something about the land the map signifies that is not made present in the sign of the map.

Uncharted Territory

I followed this process in my project *Requiem for the Antarctic Coast* (Sheppard, 2017), mapping a 550 kilometre section of the Antarctic Peninsula onto a music staff (see Figure 3.1). I was lucky enough to travel to Antarctica in 2017 as an artist participant in the Antarctic Biennale. I notated the 550 kilometres we travelled along the Antarctic Peninsula while on board the *Akademik Ioffe*, reflecting on the dissonance between seeing those kilometres represented by Google satellite and seeing them first hand. Playing the notation on shore pointed to the slippage between the symbol and the place experience of being there. Antarctica is very much constructed in colonial language, but it is constructed as a wilderness, another space, a space in which the languages of mapping break down. In the work, I was asking what was being lost through the loss of ice off the Antarctic ice sheet. And perhaps this loss happened in the work. But, perhaps more interesting for me, the work pointed

Figure 3.1. Two sections of the Antarctic Peninsula notated as a musical score. Courtesy of Lou Sheppard.

back to the languages we have to comprehend experience and place, the notation finding and figuring the coastline within another colonial language, that of Western musical notation.

My work in Antarctica was the catalyst for a deeper exploration into themes of wilderness closer to home in Canada: how wilderness appeared in Canadian literature and how it was pushed against in Canadian policy and law. Canadian poet Don McKay's (2001, p. 21) figuring of wilderness as a space "beyond the mind's appropriations" was key to my thinking about how wilderness forms a boundary in colonial language and settler identity. The mythology of wilderness in Canada claims it as a space in which you lose yourself, both for better and for worse. In a space like Antarctica, a space that exists in some ways outside of the language of mapping and survey, the mythology is made even more apparent. The relational and symbolic language of mapping, which serves to delineate and situate the individual within the landscape, does not function or, at least, functions poorly. The "you are here" is without its corresponding "here you are not." Without the delineations of mapping, the boundaries between the body and landscape break down. One is lost in wilderness and also lost in language.

Correction Lines / Blend in Distance

In 1871, the DLS gridded and divided the vast territory of the present-day Canadian provinces of Manitoba, Saskatchewan, and Alberta, over 1,100 kilometres across a flat, fertile landscape known as the Canadian Prairies, into one square mile sections to be granted to homesteaders for the settlement of the Canadian West. The DLS covered more than 800,000 square kilometres of land, the world's largest survey laid out in a single grid system. The imposition of a grid on this territory shaped colonial understanding of the land as both property to be owned and traded, and as a productive resource for Canada's economic growth.

The survey led to mass displacement of Indigenous people and the establishment of colonial rule in Canada's new West. The survey was, in fact, not only the justification for the expropriation of lands farmed and settled by Métis people and a precursor to the Red River Rebellion but also the catalyst in the establishment of Treaties 4 to 7 and a land reservation system made with Indigenous communities[8] in what is now commonly called the Canadian Prairies (Yarhi & Regehr, 2006).

Following the purchase of Rupert's Land, as this area was known, from the Hudson's Bay Company, the Canadian government recognized that, to maintain colonial rule (as well as benefit from the agricultural economy), the land would need to be populated by willing colonists. The DLS established a mile by mile square grid across the prairies and then recruited European settlers to occupy each square mile – one homestead per grant. The DLS was the establishment of rural space in the west, constructing the land by township and range. While wilderness is uncharted and unregulated territory, rural space – the country just past the boundaries of the towns – is orderly and defined. Settlers, or homesteaders, were brought in to enforce the boundaries of established rural space against the wilderness and to maintain the boundaries between body and land as owner and owned. You can lose yourself to wilderness, but in rural space, through farming, maintenance of roads, and titles to land, you bring order to what was once wild. Rural space becomes a boundary between wilderness and the self.

The DLS, shown in Figure 3.2, was proposed by John Stoughton Dennis, as Yarhi and Regehr (2006) have reminded us. The task, though massive in scale, seems simple enough: just a question of dividing the 800,000 square kilometres of flat grassland into meridians and baselines; then into thirty-six square mile townships, numbered by range; and finally into one-mile square sections. Road allowances occurred at different points between the sections, meaning that roads

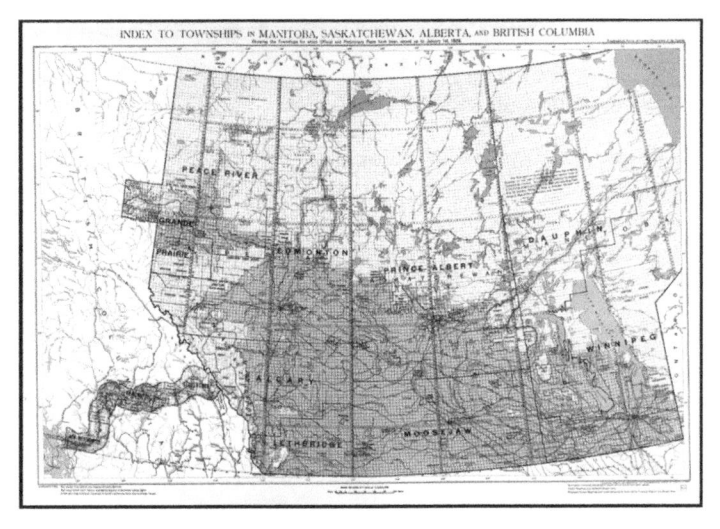

Figure 3.2. Index to townships in Manitoba, Saskatchewan, Alberta, and British Columbia. Source: Canadian Encyclopedia (n.d.).

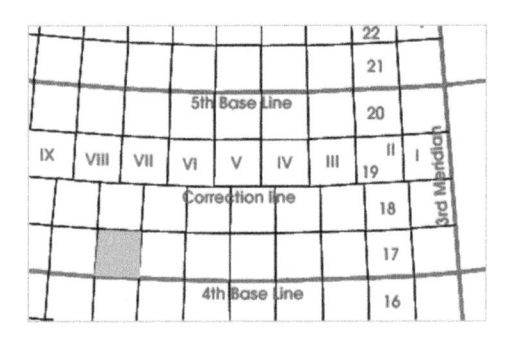

Figure 3.3. Correction line between the fourth and fifth baselines. Modified from Wikimedia Commons (2003).

in the prairies often follow a uniform grid. When applying the planar grid to the flat land of the prairies, however, the DLS official, Dennis, encountered a problem.[9] The rigidity of the planar grid did not allow for the curvature of the earth, and each mile-wide section ended up being slightly wider at its base, narrowing at its top, as the meridians narrowed towards the North Pole, disrupting the integrity of the grid. Rather than question the logic of imposing a flat grid on a curved surface, Dennis devised a series of mathematical corrections so that the grid shifts slightly halfway between each baseline. Figure 3.3 shows a correction line in the DLS between the fourth and fifth baselines.

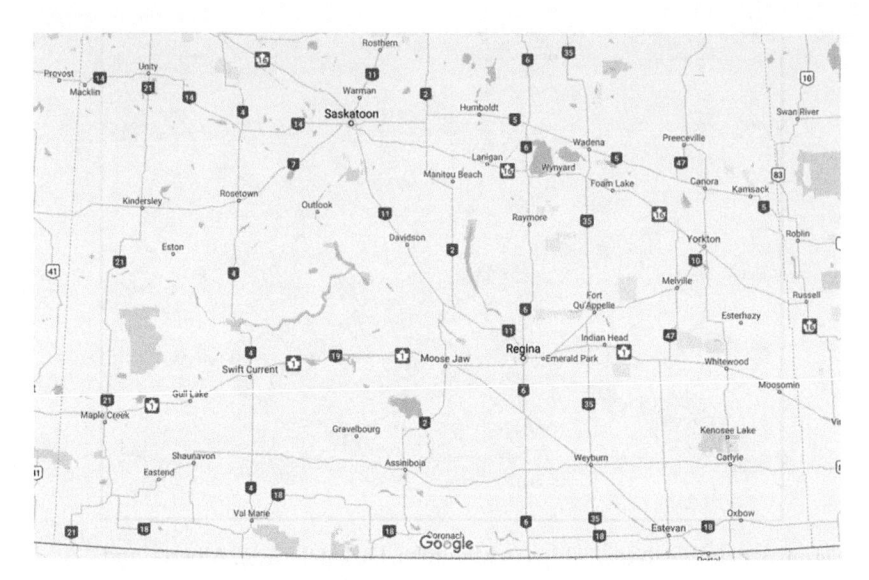

Figure 3.4. Major north/south highways in Saskatchewan. Adapted from Google Maps.

Figure 3.5. Correction line on Highway 60, southwest of Saskatoon, Saskatchewan. Adapted from Google Maps.

North/south roads, following the lines of the sections, were built to accommodate these corrections. Roads jog sharply to the west or east, following the lines of the corrected sections. Roads in the prairies are straight and flat, but every so often they come to a sharp turn and then straighten back out, resuming their north/south orientation. These sharp turns account for the geographic discrepancies of the survey. Figure 3.4 shows the major north/south highways with their corrections in Saskatchewan, and Figure 3.5 shows a correction on Highway 60, just southwest of Saskatoon.

Orienteering the Glitch

I began thinking about correction roads, and the strange task of turning east or west to drive north or south, as a kind of glitch in the colonial language of land survey. These roads make the construction of the land survey apparent, showing that it is an imposed structure and not an inherent truth about the land. I figured the glitched space between the planar grid and the curved earth to be another widening between signifier and signified: land as it was constructed by the DLS and land as it is experienced at a human scale.

I wanted to find a way to make this glitch apparent, to point to the construction of this language and the way in which it had been imposed on the prairie landscape. Since I could see the glitch as a literal gap, a space where language did not lie snugly against the landscape, I began to think about the resonant potential of this space. What would it sound like to sing from either side of these gaps? Could the negative space be sounded by voices singing into that void? Working with a map of present-day Saskatchewan, I found the major corrections on significant north/south highways in the province. Each correction was noted by the point where it entered and the point where it left the correction, so that the corrected space was isolated as a horizontal (or diagonal) line. Figures 3.6 and 3.7 show each correction line taken from a highway map of Saskatchewan and painted onto the gallery wall as a score. I took readings of longitude at both ends of the line so that I could see, by number, the latitudinal distance each correction accounted for. To sound the space of each correction, I translated each pair of longitudes into their corresponding audio frequencies. For example, the latitudinal discrepancy 51.952 and 51.978 (found on Highway 60 just southwest of Saskatoon) became 952 hertz and 978 hertz, respectively, or a very sharp A# and a slightly flat B. The pairs of notes were then sung together to hear the dissonance between them. I imagined this interval as a way of sounding the resonance of this gap.

Figure 3.6. *Correction Lines* (score). Courtesy of Lou Sheppard and PAVED Arts, Saskatchewan.

Figure 3.7. *Correction Lines* (detail of score). Courtesy of Lou Sheppard and PAVED Arts, Saskatchewan.

Desire Lines / These Solitudes

Susannah Moodie's (1852/1871) memoir of settlement in the Canadian wilderness, *Roughing It in the Bush*, was first published in London in 1852 and subsequently published in Toronto in 1871, the same year that the DLS was begun. Although Moodie's experiences took place far east of the prairies, near present-day Peterborough, Ontario, the book became a handbook of sorts for the waves of settlers moving to the Canadian West, providing practical and poetic information about the land and how to live on it.

Moodie arrived in Canada as a homesteader, intending to settle in a cleared acreage near what is known today as Lakefield, Ontario. A professional writer before she arrived in Canada, Moodie wrote about her experiences settling in the Canadian wilderness. As she sailed down the St. Lawrence River in 1830, looking out into her adopted landscape, she wrote the following poem, reflecting on what she saw on the shore:

> Land of vast hills and mighty streams,
> The lofty sun that o'er thee beams
> On fairer clime sheds not his ray,
> When basking in the noon of day.
> Thy waters dance in silver light,
> And o'er them frowning, dark as night,
> Thy shadowy forests, soaring high,
> Stretch forth beyond the aching eye,
> And blend in distance with the sky.
> And silence – awful silence broods
> Profoundly o'er these solitudes;
> Nought but the lapsing of the floods
> Breaks the deep stillness of the woods;
> A sense of desolation reigns
> O'er these unpeopled forest plains.
> Where sounds of life ne'er wake a tone
> Of cheerful praise round Nature's throne,
> Man finds himself with God – alone. (Moodie, 1852/1871)

For Moodie, the Canadian forests are full of beauty, potential danger, and even God. Beyond the boundaries of established rural space, in this case the clearings and homesteads along the St. Lawrence, are the boundless shadowy forests stretching forth beyond their edges and blending with the sky. Her poem, and much literature and art before and after, has established the Canadian forest as unpopulated and silent, the sublime beyond the rural frontier, a place for colonial imaginations to continue their dream of conquest. The wilderness, after all, unmediated by language or by maps, unsurveyed, occupies a territory of jouissance. It is what the settler continues to long for, as well as what they (we, I) define the boundaries of themselves (ourselves, myself) against.

Of course, this wilderness was not silent, but actually full of life, including human life and subsequent sociopolitical structures, place names, territories, and ontologies. What is the impact of the concept of wilderness as a territory of the sublime, and how has this notion contributed to the ideologies that justify the impacts of colonialism on Indigenous communities? Is there a belief that life outside of colonial boundaries is potentially romantic but ultimately invaluable, since its worth cannot be accounted for in colonial language?

Much of *Roughing It in the Bush* is written in prose, which made Moodie's decision to mark her description of the forest in verse stand out. Each line is quite short, most with a punctuation mark at its end. Moodie was following poetic conventions of her time, but their effect on describing the wilderness she sees feels deliberate, a result of her own colonial ontology. Almost every line describes a view and is then punctuated, taking a reader to the edge of the described view and, with the silent pause of the punctuation mark, allowing them to look off into the distance. The poem operates as a kind of poetic land survey, similar to the DLS in that it assumes a surveillance or raised perspective looking out over the landscape.

I began to read Moodie's punctuation marks as a series of survey markers, like the ones that Dennis would have used to survey the prairies. Moodie's punctuation marks marked the edge of what she could see and imagine that day looking out into the landscape from the deck of her ship travelling down the St. Lawrence. At the horizon of her vision, the edge of what she could survey, Moodie tacked these commas, periods, and semicolons onto the landscape, thus claiming it through her description. I wanted to study the action of this survey, the gesture that her poem had established. By removing the words of Moodie's poem, I was left with a surveyor's map, a series of marks that could be used to bind and contain a space. Tracing these marks onto the wall of the gallery (Figure 3.8), I reperformed Moodie's survey, this time onto the floor of the gallery (Figure 3.9). I ran surveyor's tape at 75 degree angles from each punctuation mark, triangulating the place where my tape landed on the floor of the gallery. I then placed survey markers on each of these points. Tracing Moodie's punctuation into a map, and then using these punctuation marks to survey onto the gallery space,

Figure 3.8. *Desire Lines / These Solitudes.* Courtesy of Lou Sheppard and PAVED Arts, Saskatchewan.

Figure 3.9. *Desire Lines / These Solitudes* (wider view). Courtesy of Lou Sheppard and PAVED Arts, Saskatchewan.

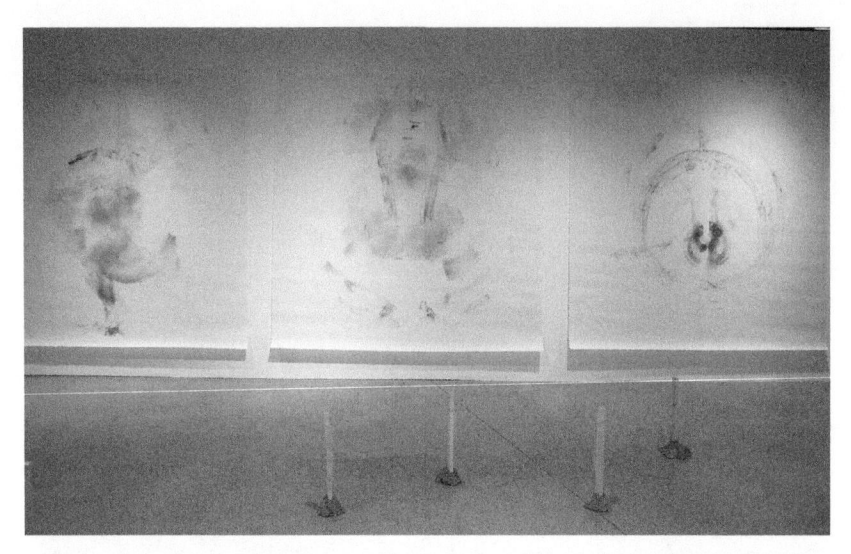

Figure 3.10. Three large kinespheric drawings. Courtesy of Lou Sheppard and PAVED Arts, Saskatchewan.

allowed me to consider how her poetry might have been understood by the Canadian settler, clearing a space from which the wilderness could be viewed. Moodie's poem became a series of obstacles: visitors to the gallery had to navigate these survey markers, which choreographed a pattern of movement into the space.

Survey Lines / Stretch Forth

Chorography is the art of mapping. I came across this word in my research and was struck by its logical similarity to choreography, the writing of a dance. Chorography comes from Greek *khōros*, meaning place, while choreography comes from Greek *khoreia*, meaning dance. *Graphia*, or graphy, indicates the action of writing these ideas down. Chorography tells us what a place is, and choreography tells us how to move in that place. Both terms speak to the act of directing bodies in space, one a sequence of movements that can be followed and the other a map directing motion over the landscape. Can we read maps as choreographies? To what extent do these colonial strategies of mapping and surveying space direct and sequence our own movements over landscape?

Figure 3.11. *Standing*. Courtesy of Lou Sheppard and PAVED Arts, Saskatchewan.

Previous research in dance had brought me to Laban's (1966) concept of the kinesphere – the space surrounding the body that can be reached from any fixed position. The kinesphere can be thought of as a way of establishing personal space. Dancers are keenly aware of their kinespheres, for example, while interacting on stage and dealing with the ways in which other dancers come in and out of the space. Now, standing at the intersection of choreography and chorography, I became interested in the kinesphere as a tool for spatial survey. Like the DLS and Moodie's poem, which reach into the landscape, the kinesphere provides a process for surveying space around the body. And if these bodies are directed by the choreographies of the maps they are given, how do they continue to survey and create new maps of the space around them?

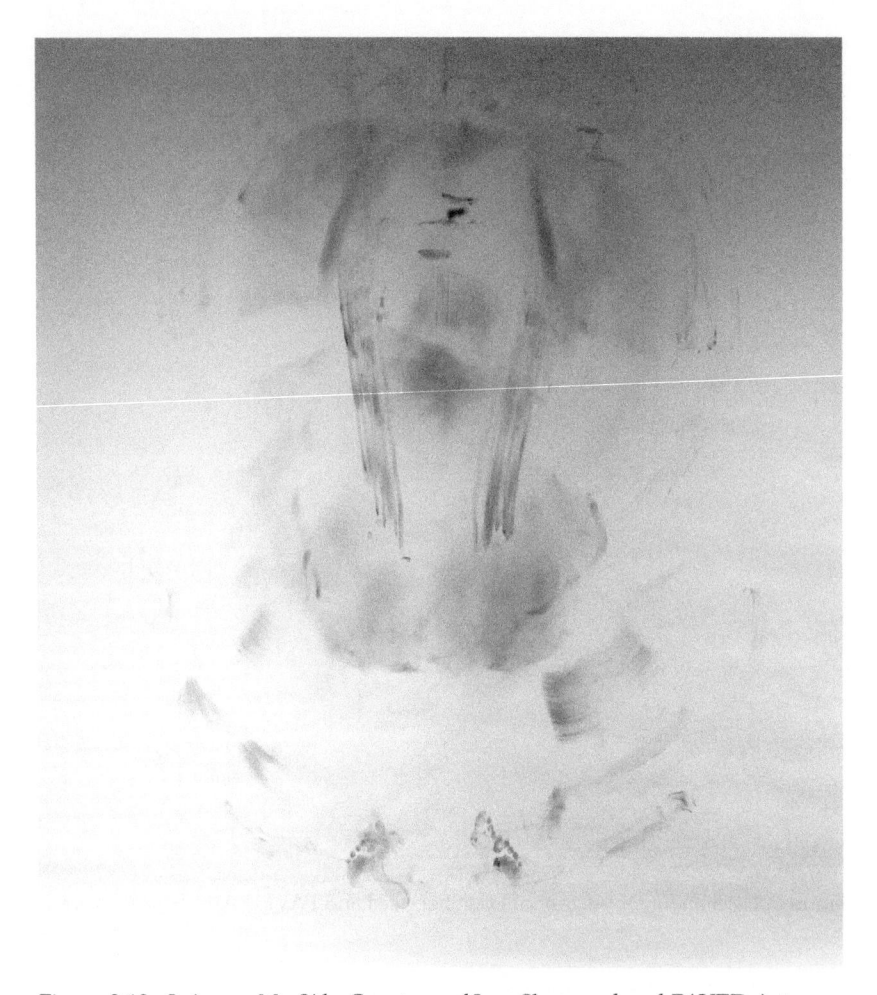

Figure 3.12. *Lying on My Side*. Courtesy of Lou Sheppard and PAVED Arts, Saskatchewan.

The exploration of kinesphere as a process of survey led to the final work in *Saskatchewan Song Cycle* – three large kinespheric drawings (shown in Figure 3.10), traces of my body reaching from three different fixed positions: standing, lying on my side, and lying on my front (Figures 3.11, 3.12, 3.13). These drawings, 2 by 2 metre squares, were hung in a line like sections or homesteads of the DLS, each one a record of a series of movements made in a defined space. Like the language of

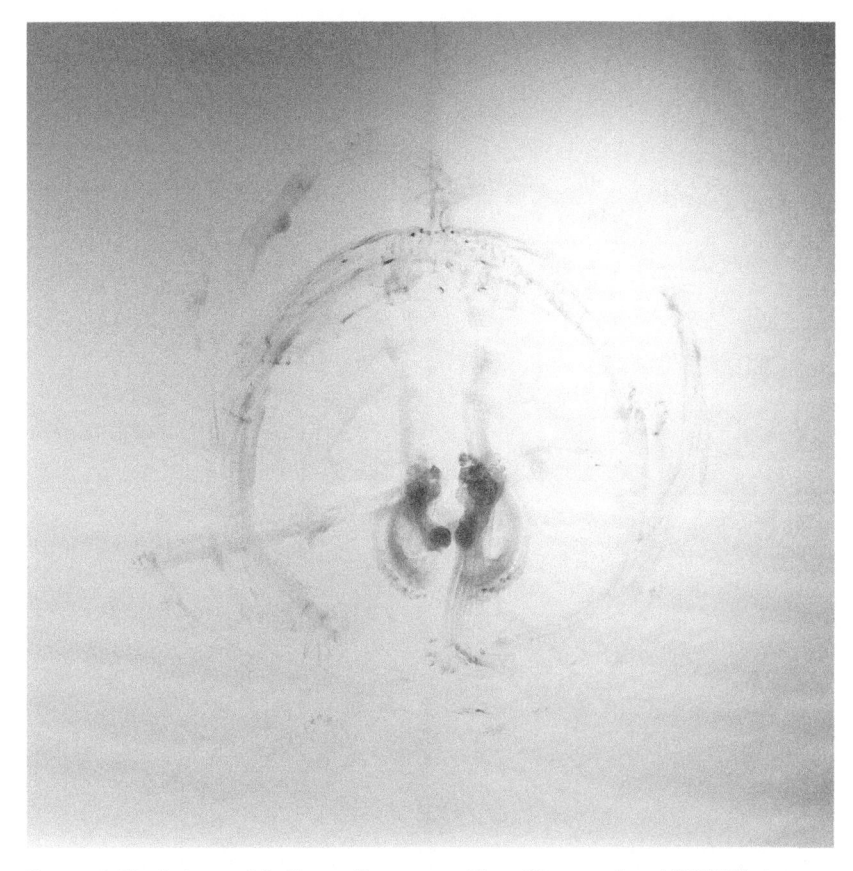

Figure 3.13. *Lying on My Front*. Courtesy of Lou Sheppard and PAVED Arts, Saskatchewan.

Moodie's poem, the kinesphere provided a method for seeing and comprehending space. As my body moved through the extensions of my kinesphere, I was mapping space by what it, like language, could reach. Seeing these kinespheric drawings as a record of movement, in fact, a choreographic score, I imagined future movements in the landscape.

Texts like the DLS and Moodie's poem have likewise scored movement in the landscape, both literally and figuratively. The DLS forced thousands of Indigenous people out of their traditional territories and onto reservations, drove Métis farmers off their land, and resettled thousands of homesteaders from Europe into the Canadian West. Moodie's poem gave homesteaders a metaphoric boundary to

Figure 3.14. Stills from *Correction Road Edinburg Rd – SK 784 – Edinburg Rd N.*
Courtesy of Lou Sheppard and Andrew Maize.

push against, a fight to establish rural space against the wilderness. It also provided (and goes on doing so) a way of looking out into the landscape from an elevated surveyor's perspective, which can see the land as an entire entity rather than understanding it from a human perspective. These texts continue to act as choreographic scores in the landscape and to influence how we move in rural and wilderness space.

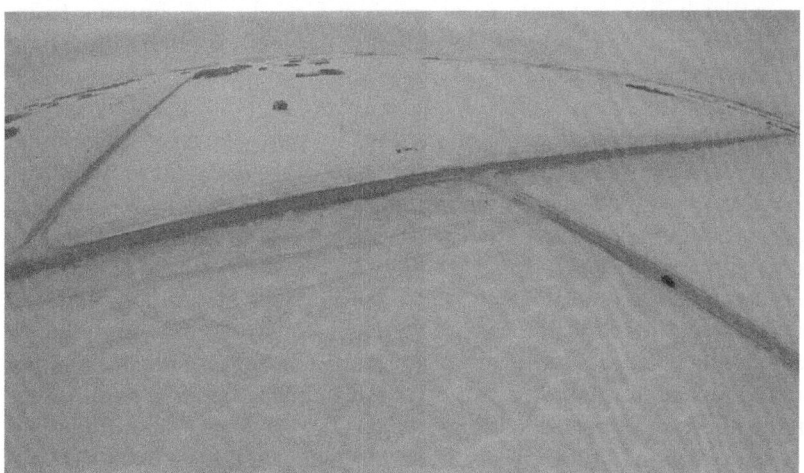

During the residency in Saskatoon, Shaheer, Andrew, and I, wanting to experience the flatness of the prairies, drove out of Saskatoon into the surrounding rural space. I wanted to find a correction road, which I had seen only via Google satellite imagery. With the help of Google Maps, we located one close to the city in the middle of a series of checkerboard fields. Andrew and I had an idea about collaborating on a project using his kite photography method and my thoughts on the DLS as an agent of choreography in the landscape. Together we created *Correction Road*, a minute-long looped video that depicts me walking on the space of correction between two points on a road and spanning this space with flagging tape. We filmed the performance using the GoPro attached to a kite, starting with the kite quite close to me at the beginning of the video and allowing it to unfurl to a distance of almost 300 metres by the end of the video[10] (Figure 3.14). *Correction Road Edinburg Rd – SK 784 – Edinburg Rd N* performs the choreography of the DLS, traversing the glitch between the physical experience of being on the ground and navigating the imposition of the surveyor's perspective (Sheppard & Maize, 2019). The video also makes apparent the near invisible presence of the surveillance perspective of satellite imagery by activating a perspectival shift from near eye level to 300 metres above.

Landing Point

As settler bodies navigate rural space in Canada, we continue to inscribe colonial languages of surveillance, ownership, and control onto the landscape. The tools of our inscription are the corrections roads our bodies follow to adhere to the grid of the DLS, the way we are taught to read and comprehend land via its symbolic representation as a map, and the way many of the place names we use refer to the places that they reminded our settler ancestors of in other lands. My work in general attempts to show the construction and embedded value systems and structures of power in language. In projects like *Requiem for the Antarctic Coast* and *Saskatchewan Song Cycle*, I look at languages of land survey to show that these languages construct and choreograph a particular settler relationship with land, one that is steeped in colonial values of surveillance and ownership, particularly in rural space, at the boundaries between the urban and the wilderness. Finding ways to make colonial ontology visible in familiar languages, texts, and approaches to land use is a way of holding my settler body to account in how I occupy land in Canada.

NOTES

1   LaRiviere used Deleuze and Guattari's (1977) concept of lines of flight as a way of considering how artistic practice might rigorously oppose majoritarian colonial systems of consumption, in particular in relation to military and colonial survey and surveillance. PAVED (Photography, Audio, Video, Electronic, and Digital) Arts is a not-for-profit artist-run centre in

Saskatoon, Saskatchewan, which supports both the production and exhibition of art works that engage with new media and technology.

2 The Landsat observation satellites are a series of low-orbit Earth observation satellites launched in collaboration between the US National Aeronautics and Space Administration (NASA) and the United States Geological Survey. The satellites provide a moderate resolution image of every point on Earth every sixteen days.

3 The Dominion Land Survey, based on the Public Land Survey System in the United States, was the method used to divide most of Western Canada for settlement and agriculture.

4 As an entry point into learning about the violence of colonization in Canada, see the work of the Truth and Reconciliation Commission, which details the experiences of survivors of the residential school system. These schools were "created for the purpose of separating Aboriginal children from their families, in order to minimize and weaken family ties and cultural linkages, and to indoctrinate children into a new culture – the culture of the legally dominant Euro-Christian Canadian society, led by Canada's first prime minister, Sir John A. Macdonald" (Truth and Reconciliation Commission of Canada, 2015, p. v).

5 *Roughing It in the Bush; or, Forest Life in Canada* by Susannah Moodie is an account of settlement in Canada, written in the 1830s and published in 1852 in London and 1871 in Toronto.

6 *The Diagnostic and Statistical Manual of Mental Disorders*, published by the American Psychiatric Association, outlines standard criteria for the classification of mental disorders. Previous versions classified gender identity disorder as a mental disorder. The fifth edition dropped gender identity disorder and introduced, instead, gender dysphoria as an "acute stressor."

7 Of particular relevance to this work was the book *The True Spirit and Original Intent of Treaty 7* by Treaty 7 Elders and Tribal Council (1996); and Jean Telliet's prosecution of Canada's founding father Sir John A. Macdonald on the Canadian Broadcasting Corporation's radio program *Ideas* in a radio drama titled "The Trial of Sir John A. Macdonald," which questioned whether Macdonald could be found guilty of war crimes today.

8 In the area now known as Western Canada, a series of numbered treaties (1 through 11) between Indigenous people and the reigning monarch of Canada was signed between 1871 and 1921. The specifics of each treaty differ because of local negotiations, but all of them concern the interactions between Indigenous people and the Canadian monarch, and the transference of large tracts of land to the crown. Treaties continue in effect today, although there are differing perspectives on the meaning of the

treaties between some Indigenous communities and the government (Canadian Encyclopedia, 2011).

9   At least I call this issue a problem; it is what the *Atlas of Alberta Railways* calls one of several "disadvantages" of the DLS method, the others being adjusted road allowances to account for topography (since the prairies are not actually flat) and isolation and loneliness resulting from a scattered population (Atlas of Alberta Railways, 2005).

10   See Sheppard & Maize (2019) for the URL to watch the video. The password is "linesofflight."

REFERENCES

Atlas of Alberta Railways. (2005). Settlement of Western Canada: Land grant system. In G. Lester (Ed.), *Atlas of Alberta Railways*. University of Alberta Press. https://railways.library.ualberta.ca/Chapters-2-2/

Canadian Encyclopedia. (n.d.). Townships in Manitoba, Saskatchewan, Alberta, and British Columbia. In E. Yarhi (Ed.), *The Canadian Encyclopedia*. Historica Canada. https://www.thecanadianencyclopedia.ca/en/primarysources/townships-in-manitoba-saskatchewan-alberta-and-british-columbia

Canadian Encyclopedia. (2011). Treaties with Indigenous peoples in Canada. In E. Yarhi (Ed.), *The Canadian Encyclopedia*. Historica Canada. https://www.thecanadianencyclopedia.ca/en/article/aboriginal-treaties

Deleuze, G., & Guattari, F. (1977). *Capitalism and schizophrenia* (Vol. 1). Viking Press.

Laban, R. (1966). *Choreutics*. Dance Books.

McKay, D. (2001). *Vis-à-vis: Fieldnotes on poetry & wilderness*. Gaspereau Press.

Moodie, S. (1871). *Roughing it in the bush; or, Forest life in Canada* (3rd ed.). Maclear & Co. (Original work published 1852). https://www.gutenberg.ca/ebooks/moodie-roughingit1871/moodie-roughingit1871-00-h-dir/moodie-roughingit1871-00-h.html

Sheppard, L. (2017). *Requiem for the Antarctic coast* [A composition for piano and strings]. Commissioned by the Antarctic Biennial, curated by Nadim Saaman. https://www.lousheppard.com/work/antarcticcoast

Sheppard, L., & Maize, A. (2019). *Correction Road Edinburg Rd – SK 784 – Edinburg Rd N* [Kite Aerial Video documentation of a performance]. *Vimeo*. https://vimeo.com/329361717

Treaty 7 Elders and Tribal Council, Hildebrandt, W., Rider, D.F., & Carter, S. (1996). *The True Spirit and Original Intent of Treaty 7*. McGill-Queen's University Press.

Truth and Reconciliation Commission of Canada. (2015). *Honouring the truth, reconciling the future: Summary of the final report of the Truth and Reconciliation*

Commission of Canada. https://publications.gc.ca/collections/collection
_2015/trc/IR4-7-2015-eng.pdf

Wikimedia Commons. (2003). Overview of Dominion Land Survey (Canada)
showing township numbering system. https://commons.wikimedia.org
/wiki/File:Dominion-land-system-overview.png

Yarhi, E., & Regehr, T.D. (2006). Dominion Lands Act. In E. Yarhi (Ed.),
The Canadian Encyclopedia. Historica Canada. https://www
.thecanadianencyclopedia.ca/en/article/dominion-lands-policy

4 Picturing Transrurality: Connecting the Rural across Borders

APRIL MANDRONA

Much of my work has been inspired by hearing Ron Tremblay, grand chief of the Wolastoq Grand Council, say, at the National Indigenous Education and Reconciliation Network Gathering in 2019: "It's always been about the land."

Introduction

In this chapter, I present a theorization of the concept of transrurality practices of spatial solidarity across borders by linking explorations of the visual with conceptualizations of feminist researcher reflexivity and the interconnectivity of rural places under globalization. Transrurality was first described briefly by Mandrona and Mitchell (2018) in an edited collection to connect their experiences of growing up as rural girls (on the Canadian East Coast and Prairies, respectively) but also to think through how we negotiate our implication in the lives of rural research participants with whom we work. I draw on conceptualizations of rurality spanning human geography and rural studies that destabilize spatial biases and present rural places in both the Global North and the Global South as related, complex, and shifting. Rural areas are connected by the provision of resources that support collective survival but also by shared experiences of marginalization as auxiliary to the centrality of the urban. Such articulations of rural connectivity help to make visible the ways in which rural experiences and knowledges can create collective processes to address persistent inequity as well as to imagine possible futures. An expansion into aspects of transnational solidarity also harnesses the uniqueness of rural experience and knowledge by imagining methods for social and spatial transformation. By revisiting the text of my doctoral dissertation and reflecting on my fieldwork with young people in rural South Africa, a distant location from my own rural beginnings in New Brunswick, I use the relational encounter of visual production as a point from which to examine how connections across rural people and places can be established. Through this visual narration, transrurality is characterized by three central aspects: (1) a commitment to transnational enactments of decolonization that reveal how rural locations around the world are part of a present history of imperial domination; (2) attention to the intricate ways in which rural places both shape and are shaped by forces of globalization; and (3) an immersion in the distinctive creativity of the rural.

In the following sections, I begin by providing a brief overview of some of the pervasive conceptualizations of the rural and corresponding responses that provide more nuanced understandings by destabilizing deficit and homogeneous interpretations. This discussion provides an entry point from which to begin to build a theorization of transrurality and think through solidarity, particularly between rural researchers and participants, and the interrelatedness of rural places. I use these approaches to thinking about rurality and connections across geographical locations to formulate a politicized allegiance between and among people (and non-human actors) across locations exemplified by creative production in the rural.

Approaching the Rural

Globally, rural landscapes and ways of life are repeatedly represented and understood through oppositional identities of the idyllic and that which lacks (see also Bindewald, 2021; Massey, 2017; Walker-Gibbs, 2019). In the context of the United States, Howley et al. (2016) traced how representations of rural life in textbooks, literature, and popular media have influenced the cultural imagination and the treatment of rural interests by governments. The authors noted that popular media, for example, "treat rural life as at once idyllic (bucolic and pure) and chaotic (lawless, impoverished, and stupid)" (p. 94). Epp and Whitson (2001) have stated that "the countryside is coming to serve two new and very different purposes – playground and dumping ground – as the traditional rural economy declines" (p. 15). The rural idyll or playground conjures up notions of pastoral landscapes that provide spiritual nourishment and respite from the intensity and alienation of the city. Ideas of renewal and escape are rooted in nostalgia for a pre-industrial past, one marked by simpler ways of life far removed from the dirtiness and immorality of the city. The term "dumping ground," employed by Epp and Whitson, highlights the ways in which rural places are also sites of exploitative practices associated with resource extraction – forestry, mining, fishing, farming – as well as repositories for industrial and household waste. Consumption-oriented economies, particularly tourism, have also been positioned as the antedate to rural decline. Rofe (2013) outlined how the powerful discourses of the rural ideal are "deeply entrenched in the modern psyche and hold significant sway over the perception and construction of rural places" (p. 263). The rural idyll exists alongside the rural dystopia, implying "inbreeding, struggle, and sense of callous indifference borne of hardship … [D]arker versions of the rural exist in which sinister, threatening, and insular landscape is evident" (p. 263).

The forces of globalization have, for some time, produced a fear that the survival of rural areas hinges on global centres. South African scholar Gillian Patricia Hart (2002), writing shortly after the dismantling of the apartheid regime, outlined the relationship between globalization, capitalism, and "Bantustans," which were territories consisting most often of rural and undesirable land, set aside for Black inhabitants. She describes these areas as embodying the "key features of the geographies of racial capitalism: historical and contemporary processes of dispossession; industrial decentralization; and direct connections with East Asia" (p. 2). As Hart went on to say, in the 1960s the apartheid state forcibly removed millions of Black South Africans from their land in designated white rural places and packed them into relocation townships in other rural areas (see Yamile, chapter 11, this volume). Twenty years later, the government created some of the most generous subsidies in the world at that time to entice both South African and foreign industrialists, notably from counties like Taiwan, to set up operations in these so-called out of the way places.

Both these narratives of extremes position rural places as something available for the taking, and they seek to control rural places and people in particular ways. This normative interpretation tends to erase the complex ways in which rural places provide food, energy, raw materials, labour, and innovation to support (urban) existence. Similarly, drivers of rural change tend to be identified as exogenous. In both popular and scholarly discourses, the agency of rural inhabitants and lands are largely unacknowledged. Rather, they are seen as being acted upon by other forces such as government and environmentalists (see, for example, Shucksmith, 2018). Cheshire and Woods (2009), in their discussion of a rural leadership course in Australia, note that it "seeks to create economically productive but politically docile rural leaders through its efforts to enhance their entrepreneurial disposition while simultaneously directing their efforts towards embracing, rather than resisting, the changes they face" (p. 117). As argued by Gorlach and Foryś (2003), drawing hard distinctions between rural and urban areas as "worse developed" and "better developed" (p. 296), respectively, destabilizes the functioning of democratic institutions in the long term and impedes holistic and egalitarian prosperity.

This reductionist rhetoric is embedded in various aspects of bureaucracy and instilled in both urban and rural citizens alike. For example, institutionalized schooling in rural and coastal communities has generally educated rural dwellers for city life. Canadian educational sociologist Michael Corbett (2007) referred to this systematized deficiency model as "learning to leave." He signalled that "rather than support placed-based ways of knowing, economic and cultural networks in rural and coastal communities, the school has typically stood in opposition to local lifeworlds" (p. 10). Conventional approaches to education equate urban lifestyles and knowledge with the norm, while the particular experiences that are rural living are often overlooked. In the wake of ongoing issues related to education, economic development, and social mobility, state structures continue to pathologize or position rural peoples as failed citizens (Swanson, 2013). There is a tendency to treat the various forces at play (social class, poverty, student background, poor school performance, and so on) as isolated, rather than as interrelated components of a complex system (see Vally & Spreen, 2014) in which rural inhabitants are blamed for their own disenfranchisement.

There is, however, a growing body of scholarship and practice that foregrounds the uniquely vital character of rural places and inhabitants in both majority and minority worlds (see, for example, the edited collections by Mandrona & Mitchell, 2018; Mitchell & Mandrona, 2019). Balfour et al. (2008) and Balfour et al. (2012) argue for a generative theory of rurality that is embedded in the South African context. Although identifying exactly where the urban ends and the rural begins is difficult, their theory identifies rural environs as transformative, accounts for the dynamic and intricate relationships between humans and rural genotypes, and positions the environment as an active force in the formation of self and community identities. Recently, Guy Robinson (2019) interrogated the notion of resilient ruralities. Through an interaction between human social structures and the local ecological environment, rural communities can adapt and reorganize to minimize the impact of a destabilizing shock. The well-being of community members is directly connected to the resilience of the group. The collective social memory of the community – rites, traditions, social learning processes – helps to form pathways to resilience.

The rural exists both marginally and peripherally to the urban locus. The material and social perimeter space of rural locales and lives results from both the exercising of agency and the deliberate exclusion by those in power. Marginality suggests a form of exclusion whereby those in rural areas are actively prevented from participating fully in sociopolitical and economic life compared to urban dwellers. However, periphery, or existing on the fringes as a way of exerting sovereignty and self-sufficiency, is a powerful form of non-participation in normative systems and structures that is enacted by many rural peoples and is key to Indigenous resurgence. The latter is potentially enabling and presents the possibility of resistance to city-centric policy, governance, and wealth distribution. Despite the positioning of rural areas as recipients of modernization, scholars like Bruno Latour (1993) have argued that "if we have never been modern ... the tortuous relations that we have maintained with the other nature-cultures would also be transformed" (p. 11). Corbett (2013) goes on to note that resilient rural communities have resisted the unrelenting scientific and bureaucratic pressures to standardize analytic and administrative procedures. Therefore, from this perspective, rural development and thrivability does not have to mean being made increasingly more urban.

Articulating Transrurality

Given the specific entanglement of the rural with conflicting and contested perceptions, how then can ethical relations be developed between researchers, participants, and the land that hosts rural research projects? And how can it be done in a way that simultaneously recognizes how rural places and experiences around the world are intimately connected but also highly contextualized and specific? What practices of solidarity, recognition, and resistance might be possible across the rural? The notion of transrurality was put forward by Mandrona and Mitchell (2018) in the edited volume *Visual Encounters in the Study of Rural Childhoods* as a framework for thinking about the ways in which rural places and peoples are connected through global forces that move beyond geographical distance and borders. The notion of transrurality was sparked by my and Mitchell's grappling with our personal history in rural environments and commonalities between our research agendas that address contemporary rurality and what it means for issues such as gender equity, sex-based violence, health and well-being, and social participation. The visual is a primary way through which we approach the rural, whether as a lens through which to represent and understand rural lives, a mechanism of community engagement, or a form of creative skills building (see also the edited collection of Mitchell & Mandrona, 2019).

Around the world, rural lands (at some point, all lands were rural) are sites of struggle where identity and geography intersect. I describe engaging transrurality as a reflexive process. For many researchers and artists like myself who work with the rural, thinking through ways of addressing spatial inequity is essential. Place is fundamentally political, although not always explicitly described as such. Politics shape home and countryside, and determine not just where people live but how they live. The "world is deeply marked and territorialized around lived experiences of gender, race, sexuality, class, age, citizenship, and other social differences, privileges, and oppressions" (Rentschler & Mitchell, 2016, p. 1). I argue that radical possibilities lie in creative alliances across geographic, economic, and cultural divisions. Creative approaches that engage the rural landscape can reconfigure space physically, reframe an experience in relation to place, and help rethink the taken-for-granted. It is also possible to expand understandings of the links between the material environment and the production of new locational meanings. Various social actors take part and interact in these creative activities to produce new meanings and forms of relating to each other and to environments and social structures.

It is important to recognize how the academic research enterprise itself is part of the broader project of globalization and has been for some time, whether or not it involves fieldwork or travel between different locations. Additionally, the effects of globalization like ease of travel and dissemination of knowledge are uneven across the Global North and the Global South. It remains the case that academics from the Global North are empowered both economically and socially (for example, having access to research funds and travel visas, and the ethnographic tradition of Western researchers doing fieldwork in far-away places) to make those in other countries the subject of their enquiry, while the reverse is seldom encouraged or even possible (McEwan, 2001). Scholars who believe that the intellectual and political value of conducting research across borders outweighs the potential philosophical and contextual pitfalls must be responsible for the development of "critical analyses of our multidimensional struggles with such crossings" (Nagar & Geiger, 2007, p. 272). There is a need to connect the situations of the disenfranchised to the lifestyles and associated political and economic practices of those in the Global South. Without such an express linkage, "affected non-citizens are wrongly excluded from consideration – as, for example, when the claims of the poor are shunted into the domestic political arenas of weak or failed states and diverted from the offshore causes of their dispossession" (Fraser, 2013, p. 1). There is a direct relationship between the wealth, natural resources, and commodities accessible to

Global North people and the disenfranchisement of those living in the Global South, particularly in rural areas.

Any theorization of solidarity between researchers and participants must take up the various effects of power and positionality, but in research practices where histories of land and research intersect, it is also essential to take seriously aspects of Indigeneity and approaches to decolonization. Although not all rural lands are sites of the colonization of first people (for example, some locations in England), many are. For researchers who work in rural places, such scholarly pursuits are nonetheless part of a legacy of imperial enterprise and the corresponding exploitation of peoples and lands. Corbett (2013) has noted that a crucial missing piece in the ways in which rurality is currently approached both in the academic and popular spheres is the relationship between Indigenous peoples, settlers, and the land: "The term rural has been used to distance settler populations from both urban and rural aboriginal peoples ... [T]he historical encounters between us have been, and continue to be, significantly located in spaces we understand as rural" (p. 3).

Strong transnational networks that are based in land rights and struggles for sovereignty exist between Indigenous groups (in the so-called Fourth World). However, there is relatively little rural scholarship or activism that directly addresses how those complicit in these legacies of domination that weaponized rurality as an isolating force, specifically people of white settler heritage, might also work to dismantle systemic oppression. What does it mean to be together in this way and to be received by the land itself? Reflexivity and meaningful connections are conceptualized as integral to practices of solidarity between human actors, but what might considering deeply the rural in this dialogical exchange look like? Rural places are not simply locational backdrops against which sociopolitical relations unfold. Nor are they limited to markers of particular identities and experiences. The rural is an entity that actively shapes and reshapes what is possible between people.

In the sections that follow, I use excerpts from my doctoral dissertation, based on my research in rural South Africa, and from my fieldnotes to explore the emergent concept of transrurality. I explore each of the three initial characteristics of transrurality through to interpersonal interactions between the participants and me that are more broadly contextualized by applicable scholarship. This theorization is just one exploration of transrurality, but it could be applied to numerous other research relationships that deal with issues of rurality.

Transrurality in Place: A Canada-South Africa Connection

The fieldwork for my doctoral dissertation took place over approximately four months between 2011 and 2012 in a sub-district of rural KwaZulu-Natal, South Africa, called Vulindlela, which lies within the Midlands region about 150 kilometres northwest of the eastern coastal city of Durban. The sub-district is considered rural and what is known as "underdeveloped." Working mostly with primary and secondary students in after-school and community settings, I explored the possibilities and limitations of community art education. I used an asset-based approach to build relevant and meaningful art practices by identifying and using resources (materials, tools, techniques, knowledges) that were accessible to participants in their surrounding rural environments. Our explorations of sewing, ceramics, beading, woodworking, and found art involved recycled/repurposed materials, naturally occurring substances such as clay, and locally donated goods such as fabric. Community art education (see Barndt, 2011) guided the in-field research and centred on the question, "What can we make with this?" This praxis was grounded in the pedagogy of everyday knowledge and experiences of ordinary young people and included artistic/visual methods to develop hands-on skills and foster imagination (including both the capacity to imagine new futures for oneself or for the community along with artistic innovations), contextual specificity, and the creation of ongoing collaborative partnerships (within and between groups).

The young people all identify as Black and speak isiZulu as a first language. They lived in the rural area and went to school there. At the time of the fieldwork, the young people were between eight and sixteen years of age (in grades 4 to 10). Although all the participants were Indigenous South Africans, their individual relationship to the land was nuanced and negotiated. On the first day that I met this group of students, they were very direct in relaying what art forms they wanted to engage with as well as the ways in which they were actively creating their own identities in regard to race, Indigeneity, and the land.

One of the girls is particularly talkative and asks if they can go around and introduce themselves to me. Of course, I oblige. They tell me their names, their likes and dislikes, and what type of art they have done and would like to do such as jewellery, painting, and fashion design. Then Mondx announces emphatically: "I hate speaking [isi]Zulu." Ntwenhle adds: "Just because we are Black, people think we have strong ties to all aspects of our culture." But, in fact, they have actively chosen to reject various identifiers. (Fieldnotes, 31 August 2011)

This exchange suggests that the young people pushed back against historically rooted stereotypes of rural Zulu people and that a romanticized affinity between these young people and the land belies the true nature of these relationships as negotiated and in flux. Their statements also indicate that the processes of assimilation still exert a powerful influence in their lives.

The schools themselves were typical of the area and were designated as under-resourced. It meant that poverty levels among the students were high, access to learning materials like textbooks and pencils was limited, and the built environment was very basic (pit toilets for students, one central water spout, and only some buildings with electricity). About 10 per cent of students had been formally identified as "vulnerable" by the schools, indicating that they were AIDS orphans, heads of households, or might otherwise have had difficulty accessing basic necessities such as food and clothing. The racist apartheid legislation that included the confinement of Black South Africans to rural areas and the deliberate underfunding of Black schools had effectively maintained cycles of poverty and poor quality of schooling for many young people then living in rural areas.

Marked differences between the young people and me made for divergent experiences of growing up rural. I am a white researcher of settler heritage who, as a child of back-to-the-landers, grew up in rural New Brunswick on a large plot of land that was purchased by my expat American parents in the early 1970s. My parents met in New Brunswick after arriving separately for reasons associated with the Vietnam War draft. For most of my childhood, by national standards, we were land-poor, with an abundance of acreage but little monetary wealth to speak of since we lived below the poverty line. When my parents first got together, they lived in a 120 square foot shack made from old tea box shingles and windows from a demolished church. However, I could then be described as "upwardly mobilizing" or a "class hybrid" (Cousin, 2010, p. 13), because family trusts set up for me and several scholarships allowed me to attend university debt free and become an academic.

1. Transnational Solidarity

Researcher-participant relationships tend to be marked by power differentials that stem in part from categories such as race, class, mobility, gender, educational attainment, and spatial location. This dynamic can be mitigated but is always present and is especially pronounced in situations in which the participants are from marginalized groups. As is typical with fieldwork in academic and, increasingly, artistic endeavours, researchers often travel to locations outside of their own place of origin. The editors of this volume note in the introduction that scholars who do work on rurality rarely do so while living in that rural place because, by and large, the educational institutions that employ them are in city centres. Even for researchers like me who had a rural upbringing, we cannot reside there now and maintain our professional lives. This metaphorical and physical distance from our study sites raises a number of ethical considerations about how our outsider status is to be negotiated and what it means for developing practices of solidarity with rural participants and lands.

The process of developing alliances with those with whom we do research has been mobilized by transnational feminist scholars. These theorizations are at once transnational, transhistorical, and transcultural. International connections between rural places are not new; they existed well before the contemporary globalization. Transnational history scholars have described how, through imperial conquest that began about 400 years ago, countries in the majority and minority world continue to be linked by the transfer of colonial practices related to race, land, migration, natural resources, and so on. For example, Angela Wanhalla (2015) has described how assimilation policies of the late 1800s – a set of often extreme physical, socio-economic, political, and cultural shifts – aimed at Indigenous peoples in Commonwealth countries were shaped by local conditions, yet evolved from practices and ambitions rooted in colonizing nations.

Canada and South Africa, although separated by great physical distance as well as significant cultural and demographic differences, share in a legacy of violent colonial legislation that isolated Indigenous peoples to rural areas. The similarities between the genocide and marginalization of Indigenous peoples were not coincidental. Forcibly removed and relocated, Indigenous people in both locations witnessed their tribal lands parcelled up by the government into reservations and the most valuable acreage given or sold to white settlers. As outlined by Saul (2010), from the Boer War onwards but particularly in the 1920s, South African leaders turned to the Canadian "Indian reservation" system as a blueprint for the "homeland" apartheid structure. The spatial control of Black people confined them to rural areas, or Bantustans (Gardiner, 2008; Lurie, 2000). Leaving the rural occurred only with special permission or if one had papers that allowed travel to urban centres for purposes such as employment. The South African Land Settlement Act of 1912 and 1913 was modelled after Canada's Dominion Lands Act of 1872. Canada's elaborate system of administrative and land-based segregation of colonized people was the most advanced and brutal at the time (see Bourgeault, 1988).

Transnational feminist scholar Leela Gandhi (2006) has argued for forging a form of hospitality that subverts borders and transcends the indifference of imperialism. Chowdhury and Philipose (2016) have described how they enact what they call a transnational analytic of care, "one that does not play into the politics of accommodation; it is not defensive, reactionary, or silencing; and is cognizant of 'local' and 'global' processes that create conditions of vulnerability" (p. 4). Nagar and Geiger's (2007) concept of situated solidarities helps to illuminate the processes of building alliances and friendships that often remain hidden or tacit. Situated solidarities are "attentive to the ways in which our ability to evoke the global in relation to the local, to configure the specific nature of our alliances and commitments, and to participate in processes of social change are significantly shaped by our geographical and socio-institutional locations, and the particular combination of processes, events, and struggles underway in those locations" (p. 273).

Historically, attentive transnational feminism interrogates the ways in which previous lives and events have been shaped by forces that exceed the borders of any one nation-state or territory. Understanding more fully what rurality means in the here and now requires an analysis of "processes and relationships that transcend nation states and that connect apparently separate worlds" (Curthoys & Lake, 2005, p. 5). Given the ongoing struggles faced by many of the world's rural people and the threat to rural lands created by corporate development and extractive industries, a transhistorical perspective helps to make visible how the legacies of past processes and relationships also continue to influence current political, economic, and sociocultural experiences. Such a reading of collective and individual pasts presents the possibility of alternative histories, ones that can unsettle the dominant narratives of the colonizer and create conditions that allow for mutual recognition between oppressed communities.

2. Extending the Global Countryside

Transrurality brings together theorizations that address political and geographical relationships in the era of globalization. Geographer Michael Woods (2007) describes a hypothetical, interrelated space articulated through rural locales in response to globalization that he calls the "global countryside." He suggests that "we need to recognize space as multidimensional able to be crumpled and folded to produce proximities that defy conventional geographical logic, but always dynamic and unstable. From this perspective, places are not static and containable points on a two-dimensional map but shifting assemblages of spatial relations that leak and smudge and seep between dimensions" (Woods, 2011, p. 168). Building on the work of Doreen Massey (2005), Woods articulates how globalization is not imposed from the top down but, rather, is reproduced through and within local places. Local peoples are therefore capable of influencing the results of globalization through initiating their own transnational connections by "capturing, manipulating, resisting, and subverting global networks and processes" (Woods, 2014, p. 35). The rural of the global countryside is emergent and consists of hybrid spaces constituted through a complex relational system of adaptation and negotiation between local and non-local actors. This so-called new geography of the global countryside presents a "rural realm constituted by multiple, shifting, tangled and dynamic networks, connecting rural to rural and rural to urban" (Woods, 2007, p. 491). Like scholars writing from a South African perspective (see Balfour et al., 2012; Balfour et al., 2008), Woods (2011) asserts that there is "no such thing as an objective definition of rurality" (p. 34). Different definitions result, at least in part, because of the use of different systems of measurement. But discrepancies can also stem from the varying systems of power and decision-making at play in a given location. As proposed by Jacqueline Edmondson (2003),

> someone or some group is always deciding how rural life should be; someone is in charge. The question is whether those decisions about rural life are arrived at collectively from the rural people in the community or whether someone else from outside the community is deciding. (p. 116)

Thus, there is significant variability and contradiction possible even within one rural area, depending on the use of, or resistance to, terms of reference. It is possibly this definitional elusiveness that enables points of convergence and particularity simultaneously between rural places regardless of proximity to another.

Many of the research participants had never travelled to Durban or seen the ocean. They lacked the means, mobility, and/or the necessary social relationships to travel to and stay in nearby cities. They were, however, tapped into national and international forces that they actively shaped in ways that reflected the particularities of their rural surroundings. One of the young men in the secondary group, Umculi, often came to the art workshops with his notebook of poetry and song lyrics, and drawings of album covers, murals, and graffiti. For about the equivalent of CAD$20 at what was known as a "recording container," he bought time and the use of equipment to record his own music for distribution. This shipping container outside Pietermaritzburg had been repurposed and designed to fit the needs of nearby communities and also to act as a point of contact with the larger globalizing network of the music industry. Equipped with his phone and earbuds, Umculi often played for the group his intricate hip-hop beats that reflected his own experiences and rural upbringing, yet were also informed by both North American artists and DJs, including what he called "old school" artists like 2Pac, The Notorious B.I.G., and Jay-Z. Umculi's music was, for him, "all about success, bars, and the life we live." He was not merely a victim of globalization or a passive consumer but was able to enter into hybrid spaces organized on a global scale. He navigated the local micropolitics and power dynamics to circulate in larger systems of ideas and representations.

The concept of the global countryside does not fully describe existing rural spaces but rather imagines new, future ones that reflect the impact of globalization. The concept is intended to both illuminate the multitude of ways by which the rural is restructured through forces of globalization and reveal the power dynamics at play in that restructuring (Woods, 2007). According to Woods, rural places can be transformed by new global connections. But this process is multidirectional, and the involvement of local agents, both human and non-human, in these networks produces new hybrid outcomes. Therefore, globalization is not solely produced through the disempowerment of the local by the global. Rural reshaping results "through processes of negotiation, manipulation and hybridization, contingent on the mobilization of associational power, and conducted through but not contained by local micropolitics" (Woods, 2007, pp. 501–2). As such the emergent global countryside is not a uniform space but is articulated differentially in particular rural areas. It also does not exist in any specific location in a whole and pristine form. Rather, it is in a constant state of becoming (Woods, 2011).

It was made clear to me that creating an ethical research practice with young people was necessarily specific and must be shaped by history, place, and ongoing relations. The young people whom I introduced earlier in this chapter clearly articulated what they felt to be transgressions and the ways in which their situations could be improved.

> South Africa remains a place of explicit disparity in terms of race, class, and gender. However, the young people could identify how their own experiences were different from those of other individuals even within the same community. For example, in her exchanges with me, Ntwenhle, a secondary student, repeatedly outlined the ways in which she refused to legitimize her experiences of violence and negative schooling

Figure 4.1. The little artists that are looking forward to the future. Courtesy of April Mandrona.

environments. Her narrative suggested that while aspects of her lifeworld had been routinized, they had not been normalized. But it was also against these realities that the young people were able to identify and create alternative ways of being in the world as well as entertain hope for their own futures. (Mandrona, 2014, p. 201)

Working in the school environment meant that we had to navigate various obstacles (Figure 4.1).

We could make art or not, and we chose the former. For me, making was the only real option since just being there as some kind of observer had no value. We moved through the schoolyard as a group dubbed by the young people the "Little Artists that Are Looking Forward to the Future," working within the context but also outside of it, poking at the holes, both concrete and abstract. In other words, art making with them was an exercise in our learning to inhabit the world in a better way together within our existing, intersecting realities. This ongoing process of articulating worlds, or microtopias, was hopeful yet grounded in the here and now. (Mandrona, 2014, p. 203)

3. The Creative Rural

The liminal state of the rural as a site of becoming that Woods (2011) has spoken of is exemplified by the notion of rural creativity or how rural sites generate specific forms of being in and responding to the world that trouble deficit and moralistic paradigms of rural development. Although there is an emergent body of literature spanning the social sciences and the humanities that describes a shifting global landscape of economic development and speaks about how rural places can overcome vulnerabilities, less attention has been given to the inherent creativity and innovation of rural places enabled by the intersections of people and place. Corbett (2013) has outlined how cultural imaginaries, particularly fiction and non-fiction writings, signal the precarity of human existence and its intimate relationship to rural space. However, he also noted that the trouble with many of the current visualizations, particularly those that dominate the mainstream media, is that they are reductionist and rely on stereotypes and do not provide us with the encounters we need. Specifically in relation to rural schooling (although a perspective that is more widely applicable), Corbett has called for an approach that embraces creativity and improvisation in rural areas as an avenue of drawing on ways of thinking and working that are embedded in marginal social locations. In the rural, in landscapes that exist on the fringes, the embroilment of place, time, and people produces powerful modes of understanding. According to Corbett, the conditions of the rural continue to generate an innovative creative class, but this class, for the most part, tends to operate under the radar. The constraints and opportunities of the rural feed a certain type of creativity that makes do, perhaps poetically, by adapting what the surrounding environment holds. Rural creativity is intrinsically material, grounded in the immediate but also simultaneously oriented towards possible futures, and imaginative regarding solutions, possibilities, and ways of people being with each other and the environment.

The area of Vulindlela is marked by constraining influences that directly affect the lives of young people. Travel is difficult (many students walk long distances to get to and from schools); the AIDS epidemic that is concentrated in rural areas means that it is not uncommon for orphaned children to live alone or as heads of households; and the migration of parents to larger city centres for work may also create situations in which children care for younger siblings and take on household responsibilities. Despite their significant roles in the maintenance of civil and domestic life, young people often talked about their experiences of being discriminated against and socially excluded by adults, such as teachers, in their lives. But it was also in these spaces of marginalization that the young people actively redefined the meaning of materials and of the rural landscape.

Like other rural locations, a lack of infrastructure means that garbage is part of the environment, unlike more urban places that have municipal collection and disposal. The legacy of apartheid era practices that relegated Black people to the least desirable (read rural) land persist. It is not that rural areas are necessarily dirty but that the waste stays there, since there are little or no funds for comprehensive waste management. That which does not get burnt is left in open pits to be buried later. Since the goal of the research was to create art practices using accessible materials, whenever possible we sourced those that were free or of little cost. There are major tensions and contradictions involved in the process of transforming waste; it is simultaneously a source of creativity and of hazard. In their daily navigation of the schoolyards, the young people with whom I worked often had to dodge the threats of bits of broken glass, rusted metal, and asbestos tile. As we know, waste, the amount and type we produce and our proximity to it, is a function of our social, cultural, and class positioning at both local and global levels, so it was often only when materials were deemed rubbish by others or on the way to this designation that the young people could gain access to them.

The isolation and corresponding creative response of the rural schoolchildren was brought into focus at one of the secondary schools. In what used to be the men's toilet, there was a large pile of discarded books and unused stationery. This outbuilding would come to be known as the "room of knowledge" by the participants, and it became one of our sources of art supplies (Figure 4.2).

> We go to the room of knowledge where previously one of the resident chickens had laid a nest of eggs. The door is now barred with a locked metal gate. The children conclude that the school administration put a lock on the room because the chicken was getting too smart from reading all the books ... We manage to reach through the metal bars and take several books away with us. (Fieldnotes, 7 September 2011)

The next time we meet, the young women have brought in the results of their experimenting with found items that were given purpose both utilitarian and decorative (Figure 4.3).

> Mondx has brought in a pencil holder, "Made from a CD and toilet paper brown rolls ... [T]he sparkles are from a CD [reflective coating]," she says. Another shows the group her creation, "I made this liquid soap by

Figure 4.2. The "room of knowledge." Courtesy of April Mandrona.

Figure 4.3. Butterfly made of old book pages. Courtesy of April Mandrona.

adding leftover pieces of a bar of soap to water and dissolving them." They then all start making things from the torn pages of the books we have collected. There are only three students and the room is incredibly quiet, but as each girl arrives, it gets louder. Then the singing starts, in a whisper at first, then becoming louder. I have some leftover watercolour paints that I brought with me, and shortly afterwards the room explodes in colour, reds and greens spill across butterflies and tiny paper houses. (Fieldnotes, 10 September 2011)

> The young people were probing creatively into sites of interconnection, between inner and outer selves, others, places, and things. In those instances, where multiple ideas, skills, and materials are brought together in the complex and contested rural space, past interpretations are resisted, and knowledge has the potential to be both restored and newly created. (Mandrona, 2014, p. 219)

Our investigations into ceramics involved the collection of raw river clay. It was freely available and easily collected. South Africa has a long history of pottery, an art form that is often still primarily associated with women. Clay is dug out of the environments where it settles, typically riverbeds (Figure 4.4). It is from these rural areas that young boys fetch the earth and shape it into forms like horned cattle. They then sell the unfired pieces to passersby and tourists.

> For the group, collecting, drying, shaping, and firing the clay represented a form of connection to the rural landscape that was different from what we had experienced with the other materials, such as the recycled and waste items. We had taken a medium directly from its original rural source and in the process tapped into localized aspects of community life and creative activity. (Mandrona, 2014, pp. 141–2)

> We walk along the edge of the river; it is murky and pale. There are other people walking along the well-worn paths, and we exchange greetings. "They are so beautiful," says Ntwenhle as she inspects the surfaces of pebbles. We find a small hole that has been dug into the bank, and from the hard-packed grey earth we can tell it is clay. When dipped into the river water, the substance feels smooth and elastic under our fingertips. (Fieldnotes, 24 September 2011)

It was others in the community, notably adult relatives of the young people, who then asked these artists to teach them how to make things

Figure 4.4. T-Girl digging clay from the riverbank. Courtesy of April Mandrona.

from clay. "There was considerable potential in these young people sharing what they had learned and in their continued revival and modification of clay forms that tap into tradition but also reflect their own lifeworlds" (Mandrona, 2014, p. 145).

The experiences described in my fieldnotes highlight both the possibilities and difficulties of solidarity between ruralities. My upbringing and relationship to rural places was, and remains, markedly different from that of the young inhabitants of Vulindlela. The room of knowledge quickly brought these disparities into view. I did not have to contend with severe barriers to education and creative expression rooted in a historically racist and classist policy. However, my creation with materials like clay and other natural materials was often a result of my physical embeddedness in the rural. The land holds creative potential that allows for joy and movements that resist alienation. Perhaps this is a form of solidarity that must be understood in the context of local and global hierarchies defined by relative privilege. While the persistent and evolving nature of difference is inescapable, solidarity is enacted by commonalities and shared experiences that may be fleeting or more enduring. Relations of solidarity between rural people must be deliberately built and rebuilt.

Conclusion

Transrurality involves an attempt to bring together discussions about the establishment of transnational solidarity between researchers, participants, and lands as articulated through the lens of rurality as a global network of connections across place. Transrurality is just the beginning of a conversation about the influence of rurality on cross-border support and understanding. It is an imagining of what the spatial, material interrogation of the settler responsibility to eradicate the continued marginalization of rural places and people might look like. This process aims to raise several questions about what it means to be hosted, both as researchers in the field and as people who are on Indigenous territories. Entering into these places involves taking up notions of relationality and place-specific contingencies in the era of globalization. Those researching rurality must engage in analysis that is attentive to place-based specifics and also considers how unique spatial experiences interact with global connections. It is in this movement between the shared and the particular that new pathways of collective resistance may be forged.

REFERENCES

Balfour, R., de Lange, N., & Khau, M. (2012). Rural education and rural realities: The politics and possibilities of rural research in Southern Africa. *Perspectives in Education*, *30*(1), i–ix. https://hdl.handle.net/10520/EJC87668

Balfour, R.J., Mitchell, C., & Moletsane, R. (2008). Troubling contexts: Toward a generative theory of rurality as educational research. *Journal of Rural and Community Development*, *3*(3), 95–107. http://hdl.handle.net/20.500.11910/4867

Barndt, D. (Ed.). (2011). *Viva! Community arts and popular education in the Americas*. SUNY Press.

Bindewald, J. (2021). "Just a stupid carrot farm, dumb bunny": A critical media analysis of rural representations in Zootopia. In L. Haas & J. Tussey (Eds.), *Disciplinary literacy connections to popular culture in K-12 settings* (pp. 69–92). IGI Global.

Bourgeault, R. (1988). Canada [and its] Indians: The South African connection. *Canadian Dimension*, *21*(8), 6–10.

Cheshire, L., & Woods, M. (2009). Rural citizenship and governmentality. In R. Kitchin & N.J. Thrift (Eds.), *International encyclopaedia of human geography* (vol. 2, pp. 113–18). Elsevier.

Chowdhury, E., & Philipose, L. (Eds.). (2016). *Dissident friendships: Feminism, imperialism, and transnational solidarity*. University of Illinois Press.

Corbett, M. (2007). *Learning to leave: The irony of schooling in a coastal community.* Fernwood.

Corbett, M. (2013). Improvisation as a curricular metaphor: Imagining education for a rural creative class. *Journal of Research in Rural Education, 28*(10), 1–11. http://sites.psu.edu/jrre/wp-content/uploads/sites /6347/2014/02/28-10.pdf

Cousin, G. (2010). Positioning positionality: The reflexive turn. In M. Savin-Baden & C.H. Major (Eds.), *New approaches to qualitative research: Wisdom and uncertainty* (pp. 9–18). Routledge.

Curthoys, A., & Lake, M. (2005). Introduction. In A. Curthoys & M. Lake (Eds.), *Connected worlds: History in transnational perspective.* ANU Press.

Edmondson, J. (2003). *Prairie town: Redefining rural life in the age of globalization.* Rowman & Littlefield.

Epp, R., & Whitson, D. (Eds.). (2001). *Writing off the rural west: Globalization, governments and the transformation of rural communities.* University of Alberta Press.

Fraser, N. (2013). *Fortunes of feminism: From state-managed capitalism to neoliberal crisis.* Verso Books.

Gandhi, L. (2006). *Affective communities: Anticolonial thought, fin-de-siècle radicalism, and the politics of friendship.* Duke University Press.

Gardiner, M. (2008). *Education in rural areas.* Centre for Education Policy Development (RSA).

Gorlach, K., & Foryś, G. (2003). Key issues in rural-urban relations in Poland: Between peasant past and European future. In A. Cristóvão & L. Omodei Zorini (Eds.), *Farming and rural systems research and extension* (pp. 289–98). ARSIA.

Hart, G.P. (2002). *Disabling globalization: Places of power in post-apartheid South Africa.* University of California Press.

Howley, A., Eppley, K., & Dudek, M.H. (2016). From ingenious to ignorant, from idyllic to backwards: Representations of rural life in six U.S. textbooks over half a century. In J.H. Williams & W.D. Bokhorst-Heng (Eds.), *(Re)Constructing memory: Textbooks, identity, nation, and state* (pp. 93–119). Brill Sense.

Latour, B. (1993). *We have never been modern* (C. Porter, Trans.). Harvard University Press. (Original work published 1991)

Lurie, M. (2000). Migration and AIDS in southern Africa: A review. *South African Journal of Science, 96*(6), 343–6.

Mandrona, A. (2014). *What can we make with this? Creating relevant art education practices in rural KwaZulu-Natal, South Africa* [Unpublished doctoral dissertation]. Concordia University. https://spectrum.library.concordia.ca/979094/

Mandrona, A., & Mitchell, C. (2018). Visual encounters and rural childhoods: An introduction. In A. Mandrona & C. Mitchell (Eds.), *Visual encounters in the study of rural childhoods.* Rutgers University Press.

Massey, C. (2017). The rhetoric of the real: Stereotypes of rural youth in American reality television and stock photography. *Discourse: Studies in the Cultural Politics of Education*, *38*(3), 365–76. https://doi.org/10.1080/01596306.2017.1306982

Massey, D.B. (2005). *For space*. Sage.

McEwan, C. (2001). Postcolonialism, feminism and development: Intersections and dilemmas. *Progress in Development Studies*, *1*(2), 93–111. https://doi.org/10.1177/146499340100100201

Mitchell, C., & Mandrona, A. (Eds.). (2019). *Our rural selves: Memory, place and the visual in Canadian rural childhoods*. McGill-Queen's University Press.

Nagar, R., & Geiger, S. (2007). Reflexivity and positionality in feminist fieldwork revisited. In A. Tickell, E. Sheppard, J. Peck, & T. Barnes (Eds.), *Politics and practice in economic geography* (pp. 267–87). Sage.

Rentschler, C., & Mitchell, C. (2016). Introduction: The significance of place in girlhood studies. In C. Mitchell & C. Rentschler (Eds.), *Girlhood and the politics of place* (pp. 1–18). Berghahn.

Robinson, G.M. (2019). Sustainable and resilient ruralities. In M. Scott, N. Gallent, & M. Gkartzios (Eds.), *The Routledge companion to rural planning*. Routledge.

Rofe, M.W. (2013). Considering the limits of rural place making opportunities: Rural dystopias and dark tourism. *Landscape Research*, *38*(2), 262–72. https://doi.org/10.1080/01426397.2012.694414

Saul, J.S. (2010). Two fronts of anti-apartheid struggle: South Africa and Canada. *Transformation: Critical Perspectives on Southern Africa*, *74*(1), 135–51. https://doi.org/10.1353/trn.2010.0019

Shucksmith, M. (2018). Re-imagining the rural: From rural idyll to good countryside. *Journal of Rural Studies*, *59*, 163–72. https://doi.org/10.1016/j.jrurstud.2016.07.019

Swanson, D.M. (2013). Neoliberalism, education and citizenship rights of unemployed youth in post-apartheid South Africa. *Sisyphus Journal of Education*, *1*(2), 194–212. https://doi.org/10.25749/sis.3635

Vally, S., & Spreen, C.A. (2014). Globalization and education in post-apartheid South Africa: The narrowing of education's purpose. In N.P. Stromquist & K. Monkman (Eds.), *Globalization and education: Integration and contestation across cultures* (pp. 267–84). Roman & Littlefield.

Walker-Gibbs, B. (2019). Rural "tourist" – rural "resident" – betwixt and between places and spaces. In S. Pinto, S. Hannigan, B. Walker-Gibbs, & E. Charlton (Eds.), *Interdisciplinary unsettlings of place and space* (pp. 69–85). Springer.

Wanhalla, A. (2015). State-sponsored photography and assimilation policy in Canada and New Zealand. In K. Dubinsky, A. Perry, & H. Yu (Eds.), *Within and without the nation: Canadian history as transnational history*. University of Toronto Press.

Woods, M. (2007). Engaging the global countryside: Globalization, hybridity and the reconstitution of rural place. *Progress in Human Geography, 31*(4), 485–507. https://doi.org/10.1177/0309132507079503

Woods, M. (2011). *Rural*. Routledge.

Woods, M. (2014). Family farming in the global countryside. *Anthropological Notebooks, 20*(3), 31–48. http://notebooks.drustvo-antropologov.si/Notebooks/article/view/182/157

PART TWO

Girlhoods and Rurality as Context

5 Picturing Rurality: Towards a Shared Understanding of What It Means to Study Rurality in Two Country Contexts

KATJA GILLANDER GÅDIN AND NAYDENE DE LANGE

Introduction

International research collaboration aimed at shared understanding, learning, and knowledge exchange is encouraged worldwide, as is collaboration between the Global North and the Global South. This practice often means collaboration between researchers in high income countries and those in low and/or middle income ones. Knowledge is situated and linked to the place in which it is produced, so collaboration that brings together the expertise from the North and the South could challenge the mainstream emphasis on what could be called "northernness" in trying to solve global problems (Connell, 2007, p. 378). A transnational project involving researchers in South Africa and Sweden on sexualized violence against young girls in rural areas in the two countries began in 2017. Our project, "Intersections of Rurality and Gender in Relation to Violence against Girls and Women: An Urgent Matter of Health in Relation to Health Inequalities in Sweden and South Africa,"[1] was developed to deepen our understanding of violence against girls and young women when issues of place and space, particularly rurality, are taken into account. Our aim was not to compare the problem in the two countries but to learn from each other and "(1) to develop theoretical constructs to address gender violence in relation to rurality, (2) to use participatory visual methodologies as a way of highlighting the experiences and critical engagement of girls and young women as well as stakeholders and community members in the two country contexts, and (3) to promote extensive, policy-relevant dialogue as it relates to gendered health inequalities" (Gillander Gådin & Moletsane, 2016, p. 2).

Violence against girls and women is most often a result of social, economic, and structural inequalities and therefore needs to be addressed from all possible vantage points. As researchers planning to learn from each other, we needed to start the project by contextualizing ourselves. We needed to review our own understanding of rurality and learn more about our own local contexts in order to ensure fruitful dialogue as we developed our transnational exchange.

Our shared starting point was a strength-based paradigm in which we acknowledged the challenges that exist in rural areas, while "recogniz[ing] that individuals and groups also have strengths, skills, knowledge and resources that can be used to develop and implement interventions for social change" (Kretzmann & McKnight, 1993, as cited in Moletsane, 2012, p. 1). In order to acquire nuanced understanding, it was necessary for us to theorize the relations between and among place, gender, and violence in relation to rurality. However, we thought that, before we could do such theorizing, we, as a team of researchers, should reflect on our own constructions of rurality to come to some shared understanding of what it means to study rurality. Since we have different experiences of rurality, coming, as we do, from different countries with their own cultures, we had to find a way to understand and then communicate both the similarities and differences between the two countries in relation to the project. This we did through a series of webinars in which we used photographs to explore our understanding of what it means to study rurality. The aim of the chapter, therefore, is to describe how the use of a participatory visual methodology (Mitchell et al., 2017) enabled us as researchers from the Global North and the Global South to explore our own understanding of rurality towards the attainment of a shared understanding of what it means to study rurality.

Sexual and Sexualized Violence against Women and Girls

Violence against women and girls is pervasive and remains a challenge in most countries. According to the World Health Organization (WHO, 2011), sexual violence is defined as

> any sexual act, attempt to obtain a sexual act, unwanted sexual comments or advances, or acts to traffic or otherwise directed against a person's sexuality using coercion, by any person regardless of their relationship to the victim, in any setting, including but not limited to home and work. (p. 2)

However, sexual violence often remains hidden and unaddressed, and warrants only a mention, mostly brief and momentary, when it becomes the headline in a newspaper. We have to keep in mind that violence against women and girls is not only sexual but sexualized.

Hustedt (2017) pointed out that "the motivation behind the crime [of sexual violence] is not necessarily of a sexual nature, but rather an instrument for suppression and the demonstration of power" (para. 9). It is this suppression of girls and women, and the exertion of power over them, underpinned by patriarchy in all countries of the world, that makes it difficult for girls and women to express who they are and to live the lives they could live. Girls' and women's experiences of sexualized violence reveal even more complexities when we take into account the intersectionality of sex, gender, sexuality, race, class, age, (dis)ability, culture, and religion. As bell hooks (1984/2014) put it, a woman's fate is not determined only by her gender.

When we look at sexualized violence in the context of place, we add another layer to an already complex dynamic. Addressing sexual and sexualized violence against women and girls living in rural areas has been the focus of several studies, pointing to the realization of the extent of the problem in many parts of the world. The project titled "Sexual Violence against Girls and Women in Rural Areas," funded by the European Commission through the Daphne Initiative, is aimed at increasing public awareness of sexual violence in rural areas in Europe and at educating specialist staff to assist girls and women who have experienced sexual violence (European Commission, 2020). In the United States, Lewis (2003), in speaking about the project called "Sexual Assault in Rural Communities," carried out in Pennsylvania, Oklahoma, Alaska, and Mississippi, makes the point that the previously accepted notion that sexual assault in rural areas is low has been challenged by her own study and by Ruback and Menard's (2001) study, "Rural-Urban Differences in Sexual Victimization and Reporting: Analyses Using UCR and Crisis Centre Data." The transnational "Networks for Change and Well-Being" project (funded by SSHRC and IDRC,[2] 2014–20) of Mitchell and Moletsane (2014) is also focused on addressing sexual violence against Indigenous girls and young women in various contexts, including the rural in South Africa and Canada.

Rurality

We focus on rurality in our respective countries and try to better understand it, bearing our specific contexts in mind. What is meant by the notion of "rural" is difficult to pinpoint in a single definition; "rural" and "rurality" are defined in various ways. Lewis (2003) has suggested that rural areas "have low population density and high acquaintance density" (p. 2); she cites Sims (1988), who noted that "perhaps rurality exists more as a state of mind and attitude than as an area on a map or a ratio of persons per square mile. Rurality may be best defined subjectively" (as cited in Lewis, 2003, p. 21). Weisheit et al. (1994) posit that "a rural area is not simply a physical place but a social place as well" (as cited in Lewis, 2003, p. 2). It is this physical and social space that is often presented as being deficient. Odora-Hoppers (2004) has argued that rurality is seldom conceptualized as dynamic or as valuable, independent of urban influences, and makes a thought-provoking point that the focus is more often on space than on people. She also points out how rural space is homogenized as we lose sight of the "multiplicity of variation, identity, behaviour, and nuance … against the immensity of space or the geo-economic landscape and its attendant politics" (as cited in Balfour et al., 2009, p. 97). It is therefore necessary to remain reflexive and to look and relook at the nuances we note in the sharing of our understandings. We have to be aware that we, as researchers, are active agents not only in producing and reproducing rurality but also in performing rurality (Dymitrow & Brauer, 2017), which for us means that we want to contest the hierarchy between the rural and the urban, between the North and the South, and to see rurality as a fluid and non-static concept. While we do not want to address rurality in relation to the urban, or in terms of a margin-centre dichotomy, it might be difficult to avoid reproducing such hierarchical relationships in some way since the dichotomies remain connected. When doing research across country contexts, it is therefore important to reflect on contextual variations. For example, in Sweden, rural areas are called *glesbygd* (sparsely populated areas), and the connotations here include parts of the country that are not idyllic but rather stagnating, backward, wild, empty, and underdeveloped, as Eriksson (2010) has pointed out. In South Africa, the notion of a rural area has many different connotations, which include areas that are vast and expansive; dotted with small villages or small towns; associated with the various homelands[3] to which Indigenous people were consigned under the apartheid regime and where many Indigenous peoples still find themselves; agricultural lands from which farmers ensure food security for the country; as well as idyllic places to which more affluent people go to escape the activity and noise of urban life.

A significant proportion of the population of both countries continues to live in rural areas, even though the world is becoming increasingly urbanized. For many, therefore, rurality is a feature of their everyday lives. Indeed, people who have migrated to cities come from (and bring along with them) experiences and biographies of the rural. Since rural-urban migration continues to occur within and across countries, these patterns are transforming the rural landscape (McCarthy, 2008; Paquette & Domon, 2003). This phenomenon changes the power relations between urban and rural areas, which has implications for the occurrence and study of gendered violence (Pini et al., 2014). The urban condition and life in the city in relation to migration, housing, social supports, and violence itself (including sexual violence) is typically taken up in research that ranges from focusing on townships and informal settlements in the Global South through to the study of urban sites in the Global North. However, while migration to urban spaces is increasing, rural life presents its own challenges and possibilities.

Theoretical Framing: Generative Theory of Rurality

Balfour et al. (2009) have pointed out that "in South Africa no sustained scholarship on the rural in education existed until perhaps the publication of the Emerging Voices Report (HSRC, 2005), in which attention was given to the challenges and problematics associated with rurality as a learned and lived experience" (p. 97). Since then, several scholars in South Africa have ventured into this field and tried to expand its knowledge base. Balfour et al. (2009), drawing on their work in the Global South, have contributed a framework called the generative theory of rurality, which has enabled scholars to theorize their rurality research beyond a deficit paradigm and to see that "rurality as a signifier is transformative" (Marsden, 2006, as cited in Balfour et al., 2009, p. 95). Balfour et al. (2009) argue that

> the rural is rural precisely in terms of its dispersion from three dynamic variables available to address its challenges, named here as forces, agencies, and resources. These three variables generate a paradox, which because of its nature is also a dynamic peculiarity (to borrow from Budge [2005]): that the very isolation of the rural makes for the intensity of lived experience in more or less proportion to the forces, agencies, and resources available for intervening in that experience. (p. 99)

We draw on this generative theory of rurality and pay heed to the point made by Balfour et al. (2009) that "a theory of rurality needs to take account of contemporary theories of globalization and society, drawing from the sociological as well as the postcolonial accounts of identity and environment" (p. 95).

There is no doubt that the term "rural" produces a variety of associations, as Moore noted as early as 1984, and that people have thought of the rural as related to "space, isolation, community, poverty, disease, neglect, backwardness, marginalization, depopulation, conservatism, racism, resettlement, corruption, entropy, and exclusion" (Moore, 1984, as cited in Balfour et al., 2009, p. 97). We, as researchers, are not immune to the attraction of these associations, but we are also aware that there are other possible conceptualizations of the rural that are more positive and dynamic.

We are a heterogeneous group of researchers in relation to rurality; some of us have lived in remote rural areas and some in rural areas, while others have experienced the rural, but all of us now live in urban areas or in the conurbations of major cities and attend to the rural only as researchers and as visitors and tourists.

We think that a dynamic and generative theory of rurality will, first, make it possible for us to analyse data emerging from our joint project and take into account the relationship between space, time, and agency. Second, we think that, as subjects and agents "able to resist or transform the environment, depending on the resources available" (Balfour et al., 2009, p. 98), we are in a good position to offer a critical self-analysis along with an analysis of the participants in our project.

With this in mind, we follow England (1994) who has argued for "a geography in which intersubjectivity and reflexivity play a central role" (p. 82). England points out that "reflexivity is self-critical sympathetic introspection and the self-conscious *analytical* scrutiny of the self as researcher" (p. 82; emphasis in original). While this idea is important in our research, Finlay's (2002) notion of "reflexivity as intersubjective reflection" is critical if we are to "explore our mutual meanings emerging within the research relationships" (p. 215). Gilgun (2008) adds that a more "connected knowing" is opened up through reflexivity (p. 183). Such reflexivity is necessary when we venture into the rural research fields in South Africa and Sweden, since it can ensure that we keep our own positioning in mind and enable us to be more open to the "challenges to [our] theoretical position that fieldwork almost inevitably raises" (England, 1994, p. 82). Therefore, in locating ourselves in our work and reflecting on how our location influences what we study, how we study it, and how we see and represent our findings, we can ensure the integrity of our research.

Methodology

Participants and Research Team Members

The participants were conveniently and purposively selected with the inclusion criterion being that they had to be working in the Transnational Gender and Rurality Action Network (TGRAN) research project. All six members of the research team, and the four doctoral candidates whose studies were located in the research project, participated. The all-women research team, including the doctoral candidates, were from different disciplines that included public health, political studies, sociology, education, curriculum studies, and gender studies. In addition, we were all visual researchers, ranging from senior lecturers to full research professors, who had been doing research with girls and young women either living in or coming from rural areas.

Photo-Elicitation Method

Since the research team members were from different continents, we wanted to explore the different understandings of the concept of rurality that we would be bringing into the research project. Following Pauwels (2011), we used an explorative participatory visual research design in working with found visuals and secondary research materials. We made use of webinars and asked ourselves to picture rurality, using the following prompts: What does it mean to study rurality? How do we approach rurality? What does it mean to study rurality both within and across countries? How can we go beyond images of a declining rurality? How is rurality gendered? We asked each member of the research team to find one or two photographs from their own collections that depict the way they see rurality, to write a caption for each, and then to explain the significance of the photograph(s) to the others during the webinar. In the first webinar, twenty-three captioned photographs were shown, explained, and commented on. This photo-elicitation process (see Harper, 2002) took about an hour and a half, and ended with the realization that there was more to be said. A second webinar was planned that required us to revisit the data generated during the first webinar and, once again, find photographs from our own collections that would extend what we had already offered and discussed about rurality. We decided to respond to the prompts: What is missing? What else do we want to add to our understanding of rurality? The second webinar did not materialize because of technical challenges, but when we had a face-to-face research team meeting in Sweden, we decided to show and explain our second set of found photographs. This discussion also took about an hour and a half, and twenty-eight more photos were shown. The photographs with captions were collected, and the explanations and discussions were recorded and transcribed. The analytic focus was the found visual, the captions, and the explanations. In other words, what was depicted and how was it depicted? What was revealed about the representational choices made by the participants? As mentioned above, the generative theory of rurality (Balfour et al.,

Figure 5.1. Themes and related photos from South Africa and Sweden. Courtesy of the authors.

2009) was our theoretical frame for the analysis, and we used Braun and Clarke's (2006) work on thematic analysis.

Findings: What It Means to Study Rurality

This photo-elicitation work enabled us to express our ideas verbally as we remembered our own histories and lived experiences of rurality. It prompted us to reflect on our understanding of, and our approach to, rurality. We were able to conceptualize a textured and layered picture of rurality, which would form the basis of our gender work in rural spaces. We developed six themes, with several subthemes, from our data to respond to what it means to us to study rurality. Figure 5.1 shows the themes and some of the photographs from the collection.

Seeing the Researchers' Position and the Urban Gaze

The first theme pertains to the awareness of one's own positioning as researchers who come from an urban area and are outsiders looking in. One of the things that we wanted to avoid was using our researcher position and its urban gaze to mediate a picture of rurality. Katarina, for example, chose a photograph that showed how urban media comically portray men living in rural villages as hillbillies by ridiculing these rural men as fat, stupid, less educated, and not as sophisticated as men from urban areas. Katarina used this photograph to raise the point that we should be aware of our own urban gaze and be willing to critique our own standpoint in thinking that we could present and represent rural areas and rural people authentically.

We came to realize that we see what we want to see. The choices we make as researchers about how we see rurality are informed by our own memories and by pre-conceived ideas. Sara reflected on a photograph she took on a field trip to a rural village and realized that the photo perpetuates a stereotypical image of rurality. The photograph is clearly sexualized in showing a man standing with a guitar in his hand alongside a scantily dressed woman sitting enticingly in a posed position on the floor. Sara said:

> The ... picture is about entertainment, and it's, like, [a] highly problematic picture, a highly sexualized picture about this duo that's going to come ... and do some entertaining, and I think that this also reflects the pictures of rurality that I carry [and] that made me take these pictures because they are so deviant [compared to the] urban. So, I think this is me perpetuating stereotypical images of rurality.

Sara realized that she took the photograph to show the difference between the deviant rural and the classy urban entertainment, and if she had not reflected on this choice, she would have contributed to upholding a clichéd image of the rural. Sara and Katarina demonstrate how reflection can change one's conception of rural areas and rural people.

In reflecting on our positioning as researchers, Claudia showed a photograph of four schoolgirls walking together, side by side, on a dirt road in a research site in South Africa. She reflects and cautions herself, as an outsider from Canada, that "it's also making me much more aware of which pictures I take in another country." She explained that the photograph can be interpreted in a positive way – girls walking to or from school with friends – or as something problematic in that schoolgirls run the risk of being in danger if they do not have friends to walk with them and have to walk alone. Claudia recognized her own position both as a researcher and as an outsider in having to be careful of what kind of photographs she is taking and noted that she has a choice to determine what she sees and how she represents rural areas.

As researchers in a team, we need to recognize our own positioning, critique it and that of the others, and learn from each other. This reflexivity, along with working with participants who live in rural areas, could contribute to presenting and representing them, as well as rurality, authentically.

Seeing Intersections of Class, Race, and Gender

The second theme relates to seeing the similarities and differences in rurality across borders and geographical locations in terms of class, race, and gender, and the intersectionality thereof. This theme is also based on the revelation of contradictory ideals and realities. The theme gave rise to four interesting sub-themes: difficult lives, being out of reach, getting an education, and the rural as deviant.

Rural areas that are sparsely populated, and mostly underserved, point to difficult lives and people struggling to make do with the little available. Nonhlanhla's photographs show "how the households are in rural areas and ... the kinds of schools that the kids are exposed to and obviously, with both environments, we can see how hard things could be." Katja, too, pointed out how "people are struggling to survive in the rural areas."

Yet, the photographs also reveal contradictions. In South Africa, for instance, poverty can be seen right next to great wealth. For example, the vineyards in the beautiful winelands of the Western Cape are bordered by areas of extreme poverty. In rural areas, the contrast between wealth and poverty might be even more pronounced than it is in urban areas. Relebohile drew attention to the relationship between race and class, and said about her photograph:

> I was trying to capture the contradictions in our country and ... I'm going to make up a word, the classness of rurality. And so, depending how moneyed you are, you can live a very luxurious life in rural South Africa, whereas if you don't have any money then the picture is like the extreme opposite of that.

The fact that the rural areas are sparsely populated means that many of the necessary services are out of reach or limited. This unequal provision of infrastructure such as roads, lighting, schools, and health-care centres, as well as the limited job opportunities, contribute to deepening inequalities in rural areas in both countries. One of Katja's photographs shows complete darkness during winter. She said: "For me, it is particularly hard during winter, it is this darkness, you don't have lamps on the streets, and if you live there, it's really, really dark." She, however, made it clear that almost all the people in Sweden, wherever they live, have access to electricity, running water, sanitation, and an internet connection.

When we are studying rurality across these different countries, and particularly when we are working with young people, we have to recognize that the playing field is uneven. Lotta juxtaposed two photographs, one of a road in rural Sweden and one of a road in rural South Africa, which look the same at first glance. Closer scrutiny and a discussion of the two contexts, however, reveal differences. The schoolgirls in the photograph from South Africa are walking, while the young people in the Swedish photograph are cycling. Swedish children who live far away from school are transported to and from school in a government school bus or taxi, so they have a much safer way of getting to school. In South Africa, schoolchildren in rural areas, like the girls in this photograph, have to make their own way to school, often walking long distances to get there or travelling in a *bakkie* (small truck), which might not be that safe. One linked similarity, however, is the difficulty of getting qualified teachers to teach in rural areas in both countries, making it harder for children in rural areas to access quality education.

Claudia's photograph of the barbed wire fence around a rural South African school shows the relationship between rural education and violence. About her photograph, Claudia noted: "Whether girls are locked in or locked out [is the question here], whether [they] are being protected from the outside or whether [they] are being kept inside in a really dangerous zone."

She also reflected on the realities of rurality in terms of the danger of being a girl in relation to violence in these areas. Being at school, and walking to and from the school, can be dangerous, and girls can experience violence in different forms. In Sweden, the schools are not fenced in, and most of them are not even locked, but the question about whether girls are at risk outside and inside the school area remains.

Naydene's photograph of a farm school classroom raised the issue that "the children from the rural area there really struggle to have teachers to teach them." This problem affects the quality of education, yet hidden pockets of excellence ameliorate the uneven quality of education when, for example, "a farmer's wife [takes] up teaching at the farm school, and her passion for education has really raised the level of education for the group of children there." It seems that schools in rural areas are often forgotten, have low status, and have to fend for themselves, making it difficult for the children to later get access to university.

In Sweden, most people of colour, along with immigrants of foreign background, live in urban or suburban areas, and the rural areas are almost exclusively white. Although there was a change in the Swedish rural landscape during 2015 when many refugees, mainly from Syria and Afghanistan, migrated to Sweden and were placed in refugee accommodation in rural areas, most of the people whose nationality is other than Swedish and those who belong to visible minorities live in suburban areas. In South Africa, most of the people in rural areas are Indigenous African people, who were located there by the apartheid regime in accordance with their separate development policy.

Given the ramifications of race, colour, and status, it is clear that, when we are researching rurality, we, as the research team, need to be conscious of who we are and what we might represent in relation to ethnicity and/or race.

Seeing Land, Livelihood, and Women

The third theme illustrates for us, as researchers doing work on gender, the significance of the relationship in rural areas between and among land, food security, and women. Although there are vast expanses of land as a potential resource, the unequal distribution of landownership contributes to inequalities between men and women, and boys and girls. From this recognition, three sub-themes emerged: violence on the land, violence on the body, and activism as resistance. In South Africa, the relationship to land and the significance of this relationship for survival seems more pronounced than in Sweden. Nonhlanhla took a picture of the significance of land to food security, even on a school property, and spoke about "the school's feeding scheme that uses the school garden and produce from the school garden to feed the children who come to school hungry."

Violence on the land shows how women who, in spite of being connected to the land, are denied access to and ownership of it. For example, succession rights ensure that sons inherit the land, and therefore men of all ethnicities still own most of the land. Naydene, showing a photograph of her grandfather's homestead and vineyards, pointed out that she, her mother, and her sisters lost the land in the early 1960s to the boys in the family. She linked this experience to the apartheid regime's appropriation of land from "African people, men and women, [who] lost their land as well [but] on a much bigger scale." The effect of such loss of land on making a living, especially for women and girls, is felt perhaps in particular in the rural areas. Having seen how Kenyan women who own a small piece of land take pride in it and live independently and respectably off it enabled Naydene to see that, "when African people ask for land, they are not asking for a huge piece of land to farm commercially, they want a piece of land on which they can live respectably."

Naydene also referred to how one of the young Indigenous African girls in a project on addressing gender-based violence saw how land in her rural town could be used not only to ensure work and earning a livelihood but also how an agricultural endeavour could serve as a space in which to facilitate discussion with other Indigenous youth about gender and gender-based violence.

> She tries to use agriculture and has written a proposal to get land, a little piece of tribal land where she can work with youth, and so while teaching them agricultural stuff, she also speaks about gender-based violence in her rural space ... So I thought about land and the different stories and how owning land brings respect.

Katarina referred to how her understanding of the meaning of land has changed over the past few years as a consequence of her awareness of the Sami,[4] the Swedish Indigenous people. They, too, lost their land and are fighting for the land they see as theirs. Young Sami women activists have raised their voices through different artistic and feminist endeavours.

Linked to being deprived of land and ownership thereof is women and girls' vulnerability and lack of safety. Claudia's photograph of girls walking together to school, and her explanation thereof, points to the danger girls experience. She reflected on the fact that it could be a positive picture showing girls walking to school with friends, but she went on to say:

> What if you don't have anyone to walk with ... [Imagine] the extent [of] the fear and the possibilities of harassment and attack and so on [that] are so present. So ... it raises a great deal of concern to me about what happens when you can only walk in groups, or why you [should] have to. [May] you only walk in groups, or [do] you have to walk in groups, or strategically must you walk in groups? This is something that as women, girls and women, we have adjusted to in the world.

Claudia's earlier photograph showing the fence around the school reinforces the notion of the lack of safety women and girls experience in and around schools.

Katja's photograph of Indigenous Sami women moved the violence from the school to the home, where it is experienced in the form of men's violence towards women. In most isolated rural communities, there is often little chance of finding help, which is possibly available only beyond the boundaries of their community. But, while the idea of violence on the body seemingly positions women and girls as victims, our photographs also revealed women and girls as activists.

Katarina's photographs speak of the rural as a "site of contestations, mobilization, and resistance," revealing the activism of the marginalized Sami women in rural areas. As Katarina put it, "many of the activists are young women who combine their activism with different forms of artistic expression, often incorporating feminist claims."

However, it is not only young Sami women who are activists but also other Swedish communities, as depicted in another of her photographs showing a maternity clinic that was to be closed down. Katerina explained that the whole village was involved in protesting to prevent its closure by occupying the clinic, thus "bringing together feminist movements with old labour movements such as *Ådalen*[5] *reser sig* (Ådalen rises) in order to stand against centralization." Katarina's selection of photographs demonstrated her acknowledgment that

> during the last two years, my thinking on rurality or ruralness has changed, both as a consequence of my own interest and knowledge but also as a consequence of a general increased awareness of, for example, Sami and the Swedish Indigenous population.

Seeing the inhabitants of rural communities as activists also means that they can defend not only themselves but also their resources.

Seeing Rural as a Resource

The fourth theme focuses on the rural as a resource to be harnessed but also viewable as a resting place and how we, as researchers, contest the deficit view of the rural. Our photographs include depictions of the rural from the idyllic tourist perspective of wealthy people, for whom rural and Indigenous people are exoticized as objects of their gaze.

Sara's photograph shows a snow-covered mountain to which she usually retreats. She said: "There's nothing dangerous there, there's nothing to be afraid of."

This comment is an example of how an idyllic tourist perspective can operate in seeing the beauty of a rural place but not the starkness of rural lives. It is an example of the outsider looking in and not having to struggle with everyday life in the rural. The photographs depicting the rural in both countries reveal endless expanses of beautiful nature, revealing open space but no people. Lisa, one of the South African researchers, pointed out that it is usually rich people from urban areas who go to rural areas for a vacation. They seem to choose not to see the struggles of the people, but instead romanticize what they see.

> So you see the beautiful mountains and the cloud formations and the rivers and stuff, but you don't see the people who are living there and their daily lives, and when you don't see the people then you don't see the struggle, but you also don't see what they are capable of.

This idyllic perspective also seems true in Sweden and in relation to the general picture Swedes have of the Sami people, thinking of them in isolated villages with seemingly endless rural space.

A photograph, titled "Resting in the country?" shown by Ann, a visitor, depicts some people's choice to make the final resting place of their ashes a site in which there is peace, quiet, and beauty. Ann's photograph shows a cove, near the beach used by an elite resort, filled with several small plaques, flowers, and other objects left there in remembrance of people who have died; it brings us back to the notion of the rural as idyllic and as evoking feelings of nostalgia in this quiet and beautiful resting place, away from the bustle of urban areas, for the ashes of those who have passed away.

Some photographs also revealed the rural as a resource to be reaped in showing natural resources – the assets of rural areas – being used for economic development and providing work opportunities, mostly for men. Traditional gender divisions of labour and the gender regime in rural areas might contribute to a more gendered division of labour, where women are employed, for example, in the tourist industry, and men do traditional men's work like fishing, hunting, and forest-related work. But, while natural resources are harnessed in rural areas and wind power and water power are generated, most of the resources are not used to develop the rural areas themselves but are distributed to urban areas.

Katja's photo of windmills in a mountainous area is an example of how the aesthetics of a scenic place are affected. Also, the noise pollution of the windmills is hazardous for animals as well as for people. Since tourists demand recreation, goods, and services, these rural conditions might improve, but they might also be exploited, as Katja pointed out in relation to seasonal workers.[6] "Seasonal workers go to these places and the young people ... young girls and boys [use] a lot of alcohol and ... a lot of drugs, and this is creating specific problems."

Seeing Rural as Tradition, Culture, and Religion

The fifth theme is related to our grappling with tradition, culture, and religion, which often merge into one, and the role they play in a rural context. We often envisage rural areas as the places where people hold on to culture, tradition, and religion. Since Sweden is the most secular country in the world, it is easy for us who are from the cities to overlook the pronounced role that religion might play in rural areas. Katja's photograph of the church at the centre of a little village prompted her to wonder about the role of religion in a rural research context and what happens "if you have other religions? What does happen in a rural area?" In rural South Africa, the church with its steeple visible from far, as seen in Naydene's photograph, also points to the important role religion played, and still plays, in the rural towns. While belonging to a particular church can provide spiritual sustenance for its congregants, it might lead to intolerance of people of other religions. Religious belief, often linked to taboos, might also make it difficult to report sexual violence, something which is often hidden. The Swedish Indigenous people, the Sami, have reported similar problems and have pointed out that trying to escape violence is difficult for all women, but for Sami women living in reindeer herding Sami villages, it is even more so because escaping means having to leave their villages and find refuge among people of a different culture, far away from family and friends (Burman, 2017). In rural areas in South Africa, Indigenous people hold on to both traditional religious practices as well as Christian ones that control their everyday living. The leaders of some Christian churches[7] have been the subject of media revelations about their coercive sexual activities, which put girls and young women in danger.

Jenny's photograph addressed her understanding of Zulu[8] culture.

> My only little stories that I ever had of the Zulu culture [were] from my mom, and it was her perspective of rurality which really stuck with me. She ... often spoke about stories about ... her experiences with Zulu girls and how they lived as one and how they were friends and ... the struggles of the land were very, very real to them ... So my only inkling or gleanings from rurality as it was in the late 90s or late 80s was the girls that I met at university, and it shocked my modesty because it wasn't the kind of girl that my mom depicted back in the day, it was a new sort of contemporary rural girl that I met ... very modernly dressed girl and with very [few] stories about rurality, and all I saw was this girl on a career path ... you know a total different idea of what I heard from my mom and what I had.

Most people in rural Sweden are not Sami, and their relationship to animals is, to our knowledge, less obvious, except as far as hunting and fishing are concerned. In rural South Africa, owning animals such as cows, goats, and sheep is important, not only as a means of livelihood but, as Relebohile pointed out, also for their use in mediating between the living and the ancestors. She said:

> Black rural people's relationship to animals [includes] their mediating between living people and dead people – ancestors – and so [these people] use animals to talk to ancestors.

Relebohile's found picture of a goat with a speech bubble asking, "Do I look like a data-bundle to send messages to your ancestors?" depicts such mediation with ancestors, albeit very humorously.

Seeing a New Rural

The final theme refers to the idea of a new rural and how looking through an intergenerational connection can reveal change in how one sees the space, place, and people. Even if we do not have our own memories and experiences of the rural, we still have imaginative notions of what it was like and what it could be. Jenny grew up in a city and had heard stories of rural people from her mother, and when she actually met rural girls at university, she was surprised that they looked just as any modern urban girl would.

> It was a new sort of contemporary rural girl that I met, and I often wondered was it really that she [my mother] was obscuring rurality or me.

Jenny's discussion about her surprise at seeing "a new kind of rural girl" at university, different from the kind that her mother had talked about, reveals her awareness of "the new contemporary, the new risings of a new girl."

Relebohile also reflected on the past, since her photograph reminded her of her mother's house and the safety of the surroundings then, in comparison with the new dangerous rural. She explained:

> It just reminded me of our house, of my mother's house and the expansive fields around where we used to play as children. On the one hand, like space for being happy and for being a child but also [on the other] now a space of danger for children, so it's no longer what it used to be, children cannot roam freely as we used to as children.

The collection of photographs also points to new possibilities (and new problems), as in Katja's photograph and Jenny's reference to new imaginings, and new thinking of what rurality is and who rural girls are.

Discussion

In this discussion, we focus on three important issues: how we co-construct our understandings of rurality, the value of feminist reflexivity, and the place of the visual in rurality and rural studies.

We, as a research team, found photographs of the rural areas of Sweden and South Africa in which our research sites lie to show how we see the rural, but it was hard for all of us to get under the skin, as it were, of our rural places through the photographs. The webinars and seminars, the discussions, and the photo-elicitation work were necessary and complementary to each other in furthering our understanding of the rural places since it meant that we visited them in a different way. This work also served to elicit our own prejudices about the rural in our own countries. In the process of producing rurality, we are all makers of rurality, and so, we argue, there is a need for us to engage in a more critical exploration of the power of pre-conceived constructions of the rural.

Feminist reflexivity enabled us to engage with our own autobiographies through the photographs (see Kirk, 2009), which became a starting point for the exploration of our relationship to the other and, in this instance, also to the others' constructions of rurality. England (1994) has pointed out that "fieldwork is intensely personal, in that the positionality [based on class, gender, race, and so on] and biography of the researcher plays a central role in the research process, in the field as well as in the final text" (p. 87). The reflexivity made us aware of our "own projections, attachments, assumptions, agendas, and biases – like an eye that sees itself while simultaneously seeing the world" (Probst, 2015, p. 38). The reflexive research process also enabled us to position ourselves, to see the positioning of others, to critique our own constructions, to revise them, and to pose further questions. Lynch (2000, as cited in Probst, 2015, p. 39) argues that something useful should come from the reflexivity; otherwise it has no inherent value. It seems that our reflexivity as researchers studying rurality might have primed us, as England (1994) has pointed out, to draw on more inclusive, more flexible, yet philosophically informed methodologies sensitive to the power relations inherent in fieldwork with women and girls. From a feminist perspective, we also want to challenge the picture of girls and women in rural areas as passive victims in rural macho cultures and, as Baylina and Rodó-Zárate (2020) claim, to put a focus on girls' and women's agency and action capacity to contribute to the survival of rural societies, without diminishing the magnitude and difficulties from boys' and men's sexual harassment and sexual violence.

We did not want to reinforce a picture of rural areas as places with only negative connotations such as "space, isolation, poverty, disease, racism, tribalism, corruption," as observed by Balfour et al. (2009, p. 101). Instead, we wanted to further our understanding of what it means to study rurality in a Global South and a Global North context. In the process of globalization and renationalization, researchers from the North tend to dominate (in African contexts) with their Western epistemologies and ontologies, making it difficult for African voices to be heard (Moletsane, 2012). Our photo-elicitation method aimed at a shared understanding of what it means to study rurality, takes that into consideration, and lays the ground for a dialogue in which no one's knowledge is seen as more important than another's.

Following Harper (2002) in linking rurality, rural studies, and the place of the visual, we suggest that our work with the photographs and our having to reflect on our own pre-understandings have reduced the areas of misunderstanding. The work with the photographs and the experiences of visiting each other's countries have also made us look at our own country in a different way during this project, including seeing things that we otherwise might have taken for granted. The photographs helped us to show each other what we meant by rurality, but they also helped us to make our own imaginations visible, even those that were prejudiced and narrow. Harper (2002) has described how a photo taken from a different angle than usual manages to "break-the-frame" (p. 20) and change the informant's views. We argue that we managed to break our own frames in looking at our photographs through the eyes of our collaborating research colleagues from a different context and a different culture. While photo-elicitation is a powerful method enabling an understanding of cross-cultural contexts, it is not the same as a visit to the rural space of the other to enable seeing, sensing, and feeling, for a short while, the realities of the other. This insight is clear from Katja's reflections:

> The work with our own pictures, discussing the pictures together that everyone had taken and presented, was an autobiographical method to elicit our own understandings of the rural and also [to] increase the understandings of rurality in our different country contexts. However, even if the pictures, captions, and discussions were abundant, it could not replace the experience of visiting each other's countries.

If we want to understand how a community or an individual acts (expresses agency) in rural areas, in relation, for example, to the prevention of violence, we have to take into account the complexities of rurality in both countries.

Conclusion

We, as a research team, have tried, through a photo-elicitation process, to draw out our own understandings of what it means to study rurality. We did so by drawing on found photographs that brought into play our own memories and autobiographies. We tried to elicit the knowledges we bring to the project and to develop a rich, nuanced, and multifaceted picture of what it means to study rurality. We have not come up with explicit answers as to what rurality is, or to questions about how to study it, but we have, through our reflexivity, become aware of the complexities that underpin the rural areas in which we are working in our collaborative research project and that contribute to what we think of as rurality. Although we discussed themes, we do not suggest that these constitute a static representation of rurality, since we realize there is much more that might be said. Rieger (2011) has used rephotography (of place, participants, activities, and processes) to document social change. We might consider taking new photographs depicting our new understandings of rurality, once the project is complete, to see what has changed for us and what new dimensions of rurality, and new methods of studying it, might have emerged.

We realize that we have several more questions for ourselves, such as, for example:

- How do we as researchers enter the rural space?
- How do we make women's significance visible within these rural realities?
- How do we address the significance of tradition, be it cultural or religious, in relation to the gender regimes within these rural realities?
- Is there a need to disrupt how rural people represent themselves to others, and have we disrupted our own representations of people living in rural areas?
- Being researchers, entering the rural space for a relatively short time and with a limited view and perspective, using participatory methods, how do we overcome the power asymmetries?
- How do we remain cognizant of the importance of picturing rurality in a nuanced way, recognizing our own positioning?

NOTES

1 K. Gillander Gådin and R. Moletsane led this Transnational Gender and Rurality Action Network (TGRAN) project, funded by Forte (Sweden) and South African Medical Research Council (SAMRC), from 2016 to 2018.
2 The project was funded by the Social Sciences and Humanities Research Council (SSHRC) and the International Development Research Centre (IDRC).
3 Ten territories were set aside in South Africa for Indigenous African people to which they were forcefully removed.
4 The Sami is an Indigenous group of people recognized by the United Nations. They are spread over four countries and about 20,000 to 35,000 Sami live in Sweden, most of them in the most northern part of the country (Sametinget, 2019).
5 Ådalen is a region close to the maternity clinic, which is strongly connected to protest movements, strikes, and demonstrations. In 1931, five people died in Ådalen when the military, for the first and last time in Swedish history, were called in to defeat a demonstration against strikebreakers. When people in the region protested against the closing down of the clinic, there were parallels drawn to the rallying after the disaster of Ådalen 1931.
6 In this context, we refer to seasonal workers in the tourism industry, working in ski areas during winter and in summer holiday camps the other part of the year.
7 The rise of new churches has led to speculation that churches in South Africa should be regulated in a bid to ensure the safety of their congregants.
8 The Zulu people are one of the many groups of Indigenous African people in South Africa, who live in the province of KwaZulu-Natal.

REFERENCES

Balfour, R.J., Mitchell, C., & Moletsane, R. (2009). Troubling contexts: Toward a generative theory of rurality as education research. *Journal of Rural and Community Development*, 3(3), 95–107. https://journals.brandonu.ca/jrcd/article/download/139/49/385
Baylina, M., & Rodó-Zárate, M. (2020). Youth, activism and new rurality: A feminist approach. *Journal of Rural Studies*, 79, 189–96. https://doi.org/10.1016/j.jrurstud.2020.08.027
Braun, V., & Clarke, V. (2006). Using thematic analysis in psychology. *Qualitative Research in Psychology*, 3(2), 77–101. https://doi.org/10.1191/1478088706qp063oa
Budge, K.M. (2005). *Place as problem or possibility: The influence of rurality and a sense of place on leaders in one rural school district* (Publication 3183343)

[Doctoral dissertation, University of Washington]. ProQuest Dissertations. https://www.proquest.com/openview/4bc8c49719baab4374dff002e6772b33/1?pq-origsite=gscholar&cbl=18750&diss=y

Burman, M. (2017). Men's intimate partner violence against Sami women: A Swedish blind spot. *Nordic Journal on Law and Society, 1*(1–2), 194–215. https://doi.org/10.36368/njolas.v1i01-02.18

Connell, R. (2007). The northern theory of globalization. *Sociological Theory, 25*(4), 368–85. https://doi.org/10.1111/j.1467-9558.2007.00314.x

Dymitrow, M., & Brauer, R. (2017). Performing rurality. But who? *Bulletin of Geography. Socio-economic Series, 38,* 27–46. https://doi.org/10.1515/bog-2017-0032

England, K.V.L. (1994). Getting personal: Reflexivity, positionality, and feminist research. *The Professional Geographer, 46*(1), 80–9. https://doi.org/10.1111/j.0033-0124.1994.00080.x

Eriksson, M. (2010). "People in Stockholm are smarter than countryside folks" – Reproducing urban and rural imaginaries in film and life. *Journal of Rural Studies, 26*(2), 95–104. https://doi.org/10.1016/j.jrurstud.2009.09.005

European Commission. (2020). The Daphne Toolkit – An active resource from the Daphne Programme. http://ec.europa.eu/justice/grants/results/daphne-toolkit/content/sexual-violence-against-girls-and-women-rural-areas_en

Finlay, L. (2002). "Outing" the researcher: The provenance, process, and practice of reflexivity. *Qualitative Health Research, 12*(4), 531–45. https://doi.org/10.1177/104973202129120052

Gilgun, J.F. (2008). Lived experience, reflexivity, and research on perpetrators of interpersonal violence. *Qualitative Social Work, 7*(2), 181–97. https://doi.org/10.1177/1473325008089629

Gillander Gådin, K., & Moletsane, R. (2016). Intersections of rurality and gender in relation to violence against girls and women: An urgent matter of health in relation to health inequalities in Sweden and South Africa. Transnational Gender and Rurality Action Network (TGRAN) project proposal.

Harper, D. (2002). Talking about pictures: A case for photo elicitation. *Visual Studies, 17*(1), 13–26. https://doi.org/10.1080/14725860220137345

hooks, b. (2014). *Feminist theory: From margin to center* (3rd ed.). Routledge. (Original work published 1984)

HSRC (Human Science Research Council). (2005). *Emerging voices: A report on education in South African rural communities.* Nelson Mandela Foundation. https://www.hsrcpress.ac.za/books/emerging-voices

Hustedt, C. (2017, 1 March). Sexual violence requires smarter policy-making. *The Governance Post.* https://www.thegovernancepost.org/2017/03/sexualized-violence-smart-policy-making-understanding-perpetrator/

Kirk, J. (2009). Starting with the self: Reflexivity in studying women teachers' lives in development. *Counterpoints, 357*, 115–26. https://www.jstor.org/stable/42980341

Kretzmann, J.P., & McKnight, J.L. (1993). *Building communities from the inside out: A path toward finding and mobilizing a community's assets.* ACTA.

Lewis, S.H. (2003). *Unspoken crimes: Sexual assault in rural America.* National Sexual Violence Resource Center.

Lynch, M. (2000). Against reflexivity as an academic virtue and source of privileged knowledge. *Theory, Culture & Society, 17*(3), 26–54. https://doi.org/10.1177/02632760022051202

Marsden, T. (2006). Pathways in the sociology of rural knowledge. In P. Cloke, T. Marsden, & P.H. Mooney (Eds.), *Handbook of rural studies* (pp. 3–17). Sage.

McCarthy, J. (2008). Rural geography: Globalizing the countryside. *Progress in Human Geography, 32*(1), 129–37. https://doi.org/10.1177/0309132507082559

Mitchell, C., De Lange, N., & Moletsane, R. (2017). *Participatory visual methodologies: Social change, community and policy.* Sage.

Mitchell, C., & Moletsane, R. (2014). Networks for change and well-being: Girl-led "from the ground up" policy making to address sexual violence in Canada and South Africa. Project proposal submitted to International Partnerships for Sustainable Societies (International Development Research Centre and the Social Sciences and Humanities Research Council).

Moletsane, R. (2012). Repositioning educational research on rurality and rural education in South Africa: Beyond deficit paradigms. *Perspectives in Education, 30*(1), 1–8. https://www.ajol.info/index.php/pie/article/view/77005

Moore, M. (1984). Categorising space: Urban-rural or core-periphery in Sri-Lanka. In M. Moore & J. Harris (Eds.), *Development and the rural-urban divide* (pp. 121–40). Frank Cass.

Odora-Hoppers, C.A. (2004). The cause, the object, the citizen: Rural school learners in the void of intersecting policies and traditions of thought. *Quarterly of Education and Training in South Africa, 11*(3), 17–22.

Paquette, S., & Domon, G. (2003). Changing ruralities, changing landscapes: Exploring social recomposition using a multi-scale approach. *Journal of Rural Studies, 19*(4), 425–44. https://doi.org/10.1016/S0743-0167(03)00006-8

Pauwels, L. (2011). An integrated conceptual framework for visual social research. In E. Margolis & L. Pauwels (Eds.), *The SAGE handbook of visual research methods* (pp. 3–23). Sage.

Pini, B., Moletsane, R., & Mills, M. (2014). Education and the global rural: Feminist perspectives. *Gender and Education, 26*(5), 453–64. https://doi.org/10.1080/09540253.2014.950016

Probst, B. (2015). The eye regards itself: Benefits and challenges of reflexivity in qualitative social work research. *Social Work Research, 39*(1), 37–48. https://doi.org/10.1093/swr/svu028

Rieger, J.H. (2011). Rephotography for documenting social change. In E. Margolis & L. Pauwels (Eds.), *The SAGE handbook of visual research methods* (pp. 132–49). Sage.

Ruback, R.B., & Menard, K.S. (2001). Rural-urban differences in sexual victimization and reporting: Analyses using UCR and crisis center data. *Criminal Justice and Behavior, 28*(2), 131–55. https://doi.org/10.1177/0093854801028002001

Sametinget. (2019). *Samerna i Sverige* [The Sami in Sweden]. *Sámediggi.* https://www.sametinget.se/samer

Sims, V.H. (1988). *Small town and rural police.* C.C. Thomas.

Weisheit, R.A., Wells, L.E., & Falcone, D.N. (1994). Community policing in small town and rural America. *Crime & Delinquency, 40*(4), 549–67. https://doi.org/10.1177/0011128794040004005

World Health Organization. (2011). *Violence against women: Intimate partner and sexual violence against women.* World Health Organization.

6 Drawing Myself into the Picture: What Does It Mean to Be a Rural-Origin Student in an Urban University?

SAMUKELISIWE KHUMALO

Introduction

Since the end of apartheid in 1994, South Africa has been undergoing a process of transformation in various sectors of society. For example, higher education has become generally accessible to students from all walks of life, which has led to increases in student enrolment across the system. According to the Department of Higher Education Training, student enrolment in public and private higher education institutions (HEIs) reached a total of 1.1 million in 2016. The majority of students enrolled in public HEIs were Africans (71.9 per cent or 701,482), followed by white students (15.6 per cent or 152,489), coloured[1] students (6.3 per cent or 61,963), and Indian/Asian students (5.2 per cent or 50,450; Department of Higher Education and Training, 2016). However, the well-documented slow completion and low throughput rates throughout the higher education system have been cause for concern to government and among the country's institutions. Scholars have argued that among the factors that have a negative impact on students' success in universities is the uneven quality of the schooling system, given the historical imbalances of apartheid and the inadequate preparation, by some schools, of students for university study (Swartz et al., 2018). For example, a report by the Council on Higher Education (CHE) estimates the failure rates among students in the system at 55 per cent, while only one in four students complete their degrees in the stipulated time (CHE, 2016). Among those who reportedly struggle to succeed in universities are students from many of the country's rural schools (Wilson-Strydom, 2010). Specifically, because of the legacy of apartheid education and its racialized resourcing of schools, the resources allocated to schools in undeveloped rural areas geographically located away from the city differ, as does the kind of personnel these schools attract, as well as the levels of school infrastructure development and school community support. For instance, under the Bantu Education Act of 1953, as Soudien (2002) has written,

> the state also required that … the curriculum "stress … obedience, communal loyalty, ethnic and national diversity, acceptance of allocated social roles, piety, and identification with rural culture." A slew of new regulations was passed which resulted in, *inter alia* … pegging the [financial] contribution of the state to the cost of teachers' salaries and so requiring communities to supplement them and withdrawing essential services, such as caretaking and maintenance, from schools and shifting these to the communities. (p. 213)

For many rural communities, including mine, which were characterized by unemployment, this act meant that our schools were not only poorly resourced but, as learners, we were taught a curriculum that was meant to keep us in the rural areas. We were given an education that was inferior and did not prepare us, as Black children, for secondary education.

The pace of redressing these inequalities in rural schools and communities has been very slow. As Masipa (2018) has noted, although South Africa has made strides in addressing inequalities that result mostly from the legacies of apartheid, the story of rural schooling in the country has not changed much. The legacies of apartheid have resulted in poor infrastructure, inadequate teaching and learning, and lack of access to technology in schools. As a result, schools in these areas struggle to attract adequately and appropriately qualified teachers (Maringe & Moletsane, 2015). Most qualified teachers are not keen to take up teaching employment in these parlous rural schools; neither the economic incentive like the rural allowance nor the limited infrastructure support or encourage this placement. Those who do take up teaching are sometimes compelled to commute from the urban areas where they reside to the rural communities where they work. That commute results in a lot of teaching time lost to travelling, and the rural school learners are the ones who suffer. It is no wonder, then, that rural schools are often characterized as dysfunctional compared to most schools in developed settings (Chikoko et al., 2015).

While widening access to higher education has been seen as a necessary step towards redressing the apartheid inequalities in higher education, the massive increase in the number of students and the diversity they bring into the university also means new challenges for the higher education system. For example, as I have already mentioned, rural-origin students struggle with underpreparedness for tertiary education (Nel et al., 2009), poor academic literacy (Kapp & Bangeni, 2011), and a very limited grasp of the requirements of independent learning that is basic to university level education (Moll, 2004; Nyamapfene & Letseka, 1995) because of their poor schooling experiences (Moletsane et al., 2015). Socially, the rural-origin students battle to attain a sense of belonging to the urban university community (Czerniewicz & Brown, 2018; Morton et al., 2018), and they come with limited cultural capital (Czerniewicz & Brown, 2018), since most are first-generation university students (Jacobs & Pretorius, 2016) and are likely to encounter financial pressures (Sader & Gabela, 2017).

Thus, in this chapter, I address the question of how the schooling experiences of rural-origin students shape their learning in largely urban spaces in universities. Following Lapadat (2009), I use autobiography to recount my personal life looking inwards and outwards, and to negotiate my identity. Using autobiography and memory-work to reflect on my positionality as a lecturer tasked with supporting students, I reflect on the question of how my positionality as a former rural-origin student in largely urban university settings has assisted or hindered my approach to supporting similar students. I look back at my own rural schooling, my experiences of studying at an urban university, and my professional experience as a lecturer in an urban institution.

Positioning Myself in This Study

Universities are endeavouring to respond to the issues of students' transition from school to university more broadly. For example, many institutions offer orientation programs, online information, increased staffing for information services, and first-year experience or transition programs for all their first-year students. However, the lack of readiness, the epistemological gap, and poor adjustment to a new environment constitute challenges to first-year students in university and more so for those from a rural schooling background (Timmis et al., 2019). For rural-origin students, these challenges are compounded by their sociocultural backgrounds, and unless all these obstacles are adequately addressed, their resilience and success in universities is threatened.

Between 2010 and 2015, I was the coordinator of the Academic Monitoring and Support program in the School of Education at a South African university. My role was to identify students who were at risk of academic failure. In this cohort, the majority were rural-origin students. At the beginning of each semester, I conducted interviews with students in order to understand the nature of their challenges as well as to provide academic advice, monitor their academic progress, and offer tailor-made academic interventions such as peer mentorship, workshops, and individual consultations. When the challenges were non-academic, I referred students to other university sectors like counselling, finance, housing, and so on. From individual consultations with students, I identified a range of challenges (academic and non-academic) with which they were confronted, some of which were similar to what I had experienced as a rural-origin student during my years as a university student. Furthermore, I learned that poor student performance is not always a result of academic challenges (for example, lack of adequate academic skills) but can also emanate from non-academic factors, including the difficulty of adjusting to a new environment, lack of financial resources, housing issues, and other concerns. This performance problem, for me, required not only academic interventions but more holistic student support. For example, while many rural-origin students studying to be teachers are funded by the National Student Financial Aid Scheme (NSFAS) and the Funza Lushaka Bursary Scheme, some often use their stipends to support their poor family members back home. Many of the funded students do not benefit from scholarships and loans, and I mention, in passing, that this issue resulted in protests in higher education. #FeesMustFall, a student-led protest movement that began in 2015, centred on the voices of those who cannot afford financial access to university (Edwin, 2016). The movement fought the financial discrimination suffered by poor students and aimed to increase access to higher education for those from poor socio-economic backgrounds, including rural-origin students.

One of the main challenges of university structured interventions was often related to the stigma associated with asking for and accepting support, so many students shied away from accessing and participating in the intervention programs. For example, in the early days of my job in the support program, very few students attended the workshops and group meetings compared to the number of students who showed up for individual consultations. Some students indicated that they felt the workshops and group meetings suggested they were being labelled as failures and as "those [who] will not make it." To address the stigma associated with this form of support, I opened the support program to all students regardless of their academic performance. In addition, during the meetings with students, it was clear that they were aware of what they thought their support needs were and how they were to be supported to meet these needs.

Methodology

To reflect on my positionality and the ways in which it influenced how I supported students in the School of Education, I draw on a personal history memory-work approach through what Samaras et al. (2004) might refer to as self-study/autobiographical approaches. To do this work, in line with Clift and Clift (2017), I use in my professional practice my memories of growing up rural in an area with limited social networks, my rural schooling, and my experiences as a rural-origin student in an urban university setting as ways of understanding and engaging with students, including those with similar backgrounds to mine. In particular, to generate data in this study, I use what might be termed visual memory to reflect on my past experiences, tracing how my past experiences influence my current duties as a lecturer and as the Academic Monitoring and Support program coordinator. Memory drawing engages the participant in drawing and writing about the meaning embedded in the drawing (Lyon, 2019). It makes sense of the present reality by looking forward through past experiences (Strong-Wilson et al., 2014). For me, it serves as a reflection of what was, what is, and what will be.

Drawing from my research question, "How do the schooling experiences of rural-origin students shape their learning in largely urban spaces in universities?," I use visual memory to reflect on what it meant for me to be a rural-origin student in an urban university learning environment. I embarked upon a project of picturing my experiences through drawing a set of sketches to help surface the memories of my life in a rural village, my experiences of rural schooling, and my time spent as a rural-origin student in higher education in an urban setting. The sketches prompted memories about which I then wrote. However, because my sketches were not polished, I decided to work with a real artist. I commissioned the artist Victor Tshindane to use the sketches and my notes to produce final visual products. Through WhatsApp, I sent both sketches and notes, and further explained what I meant by the sketches. We had back and forth communication about what I wanted to show through the sketches and notes until I was satisfied that the final drawings represented my memories and reflections as closely as possible. Using these reflections, in the second half of the chapter, I ponder, as I have articulated earlier, on how my personal history and positionality might inform how I address the needs of rural-origin students in my practice.

Drawn into Memory: Three Memories

In using memory drawings in this chapter, I aim to reflexively analyse how my early rural schooling and my experience as a rural-origin student in an urban university learning environment has influenced how I currently work with students. In this section, I analyse three memory drawings: (1) *Life in a Rural Village*, (2) *Being a Misfit in the University*, and (3) *Thriving: Success Is What We Make of It*.

Memory 1: Growing Up as a Girl in a Rural Village

In the first memory drawing (Figure 6.1), I reflect on how, as mentioned earlier in the chapter, I grew up in a rural community. The drawing illustrates a typical rural girl's experience and understanding of a rural context. It gives expression to my view of the connectedness of life in a rural village. Most of the people in my village were subsistence farmers. The drawing shows girls fetching water from the river. Much has been written about how such chores deny girls in particular adequate time to spend on educational activities (Levison & Moe, 1998; Nyatuka, 2015). For me, however, these chores were a way of life and an opportunity to spend time with my peers and big sisters. At the time, I did not experience them as challenges. As a girl, doing chores that included fetching firewood from the forest, working in the fields, fetching water from the river, and selling produce after school was the norm. Waking up at dawn to fetch water and then getting ready to go to school, along with doing other chores, taught me time-management skills.

Going to school was the most exciting part of my daily routine. I persisted because I had an internal drive towards success in my future endeavours. In the memory drawing, I have included the long distances we used to walk from home to school and back again, at times walking alone and at other times with friends. I remember that I used to take my shoes off when I was crossing the river (there was no bridge). During heavy rains when the river was full, we stayed home and missed classes. Linked to my rural schooling, the memory of a woman with a basket of pineapples on her head in the village market reminds me of how my family taught me business skills and the value of hard work. During particular seasons, every day after school I sold fruit and vegetables from our garden in the local market. This task generated an interest in business and made me realize the importance of working together as a family. In addition, selling fruit and vegetables contributed immensely to my confidence in learning mathematics in school.

Figure 6.1. *Life in a Rural Village*. Courtesy of Samukelisiwe Khumalo.

Importantly for me, looking back, my childhood and attending rural schools not only presented me with challenges; it also taught me resilience and engendered the drive to work hard. Looking back, I can see that I drew on these experiences to see me through school, university studies, and beyond. Reflecting on this journey makes me realize how the challenges taught me endurance, patience, and also contributed to my vision to not only change my life but that of my family too. The drawing graphically plots the triad of vision, hard work, and success despite the hardships in the life of chores, routine, and regimentation that defined my rural setting. It is a visual that also reminds me of how life was seen as a whole with life events, trials, and triumphs, not as parts of a split reality. My rudimentary everyday life also involved tastes of joy and moments of sadness. In these moments, it was possible to find harmony and less discontent in my rural life. Something that stands out in my memory of my life in the village as depicted in this visual is a life defined by rhythm. Perhaps it is this rhythmic thread that drives the resilience that I developed, as well as being the reason why the values with which I grew up as a schoolgirl have endured.

Memory 2: Struggling to Fit Into an Urban University Culture

I am the seventh of eight children in my family and the first to get a university degree. My teachers and other community members inspired me to dream of a university education. My being a rural-origin student, far from diminishing this dream, was, rather, instrumental to attaining it. I worked hard, pushed boundaries, and being a girl in no way halted my determination to always go the extra mile to succeed in school. Our teachers motivated us to perform well academically. For me, the healthy competition with my peers enhanced this dedication, along with providing the opportunities for hard work and the determination to succeed. I chose to study science subjects, but, as discussed in the preceding sections, the failures of apartheid resourcing and the unwillingness among teachers to work in rural schools meant that my rural school did not have a science teacher. Specifically, in my grade 10 class, we did not have maths and science teachers. Teachers from other schools used to come on Saturdays to assist us. In addition, my school did not have a laboratory. Instead, teachers would bring science videos to teach us particular concepts and show us experiments when they could. Thinking back, attending such poorly resourced primary and secondary schools did not prepare me for higher education. The curves I had to negotiate transitioning from rural life and schooling to life on a university campus were part of a drastic and sharp experience. The taste of life in the rural community and its enduring passions made me feel excluded in what was to me a brazen and exotic campus life. The university with its openness to almost anything was an enigma to me, and at first it led to a lot of discontent, as did the lecturer's accent and the language barrier.

The visual memory, *Being a Misfit in the University* (Figure 6.2), illustrates how disconnected I felt in my first year of university, with its high expectations, structured learning environment, and an institutional culture that was very different from that of my rural school and community. As a first-year student, I was expected to fit into an environment that was designed without taking into consideration the needs of students like me. At first, I was excited to be on campus because that had been my desire all my schooling life. However, I was soon disappointed, since I was confronted by many barriers that constructed me as a misfit in the university. I remember sitting in the lecture hall and looking around at my peers who seemingly knew how to use a computer mouse. As the drawing depicts, my lack of computer literacy as a pre-requisite competency meant that I was bewildered during my earlier semesters and classes, and whenever I had to work in the students' computer pools. Being underprepared and unable to fit into the neatly carved institutional culture with all its expectations, I felt inadequate and even scared to say that I did not know what to do. As one of those whom the university would see as being at risk of academic failure, I felt profiled and negatively labelled. I felt that my prospects

Figure 6.2. *Being a Misfit in the University*. Courtesy of Samukelisiwe Khumalo.

of succeeding and graduating were limited, and I felt unfit to study at university. This situation meant that navigating my way as a university student was never easy. University meant, for example, staying off campus in the cheapest accommodation I could find, limited interaction with my peers, and limited access to the library after classes. In addition, I had limited facility in the English language, the only medium of instruction in all my classes. My first year was a lonely experience, even in the midst of the sea of people I encountered on campus.

But then, as a student, I knew that I had only one chance, particularly considering my background. I knew that if I worked hard and did well academically, I would qualify for a scholarship. I decided to seek out students who were from a similar background as mine, were hard working, and shared the same vision. This decision would come to play a very important role in my resilience and success at university. Drawing from each other's strengths, we supported each other through the difficult classes and celebrated each other's successes.

Memory 3: Hard Work, Determination, and Resilience

The third visual memory (Figure 6.3) uses a metaphor of two seeds planted simultaneously in the same land and under the same environmental conditions. Yet, they germinate and grow unevenly. This image raises the question regarding what is critical for success: is it the environment or what is made of it? Rural-origin students like me who arrive at university with added challenges need additional and targeted support to succeed in their studies. I think of students as being like seeds that are expected to germinate and grow in the university environment. Universities base their understanding of students they enrol and their ability and competency for university level studies on high school marks. Based on this assessment, to carry my metaphor further, they determine the type of soil, the amount of water and sunlight, and the tending they provide for students to flourish. But what might be

Figure 6.3. *Thriving: Success Is What We Make of It.* Courtesy of Samukelisiwe Khumalo.

critically missing is investment in the knowledge of the seeds. This lack of knowledge leads to ignoring contextual factors, including their family background, what kind of school they went to, their socio-economic status, and so on, which have influenced who the students have become.

To illustrate, as a first-year student, my classes were always full of students from different backgrounds, racial groups, and schools. Unlike in my high school where teachers would guide us and explain some of the concepts in our own language, at the university English was the only medium of instruction. At botany lectures, I used to sit in the front of the classroom because not only was English a barrier but the lecturer's accent also made it difficult for me to understand what was being said. To try to catch up with class work, I would take my textbooks and underline what I thought were the keywords the lecturer had emphasized, and then read the chapter again after the lecture. I also used previous exam papers from the library to familiarize myself with the assessment language and to learn key points and attempt to answer questions. I remember that, for some of my classmates who did not have textbooks, life was harder, and most ended up failing the tests and examinations and/or dropping out of the course.

Apart from academic challenges, there were other issues with which I was confronted that I have already mentioned, such as having no funding for my studies and living in cheap private accommodation off campus. Also, I had to walk a long way to campus and back again to where I lived so was unable to access the library in the afternoons. However, I knew that if I worked hard and did well academically, I would qualify for a scholarship or be funded. Then I would not have to worry about money and could become focused and energized to attend to my academic challenges. This realization, for me, eventually became the motivating force that drove my firm resolve and further developed my resilience.

Looking Back

Using a personal history memory-work approach, and in particular memory drawing, I have addressed in this chapter the question about how my rural-origin schooling shaped my learning in the urban spaces of a university.

My experiences of primary and secondary school in a rural context hold bittersweet memories. I remember my excitement the first time I went to school, the teachers who went out of their way to support us to succeed, how I looked up to them and dreamt that I would one day be a teacher and be like them. However, I also remember the hard work that was linked to growing up rural, like the chores I had to complete before and after school as a girl growing up in a rural village. While I have not examined the rural lives of the girls who enrol in our university, available research suggests that, in spite of the human rights–informed post-apartheid policy framework, girls continue to carry the burden of care in rural and other low-income contexts. In her doctoral dissertation, *"It's Hard Work to Be a Girl": Adolescent Girls' Experiences of Girlhood in Three Low-Income Communities in South Africa*, Van Wyk (2015) showed that, in rural communities, people evaluate girls favourably based on their performance of household chores, but their having to do those chores has an unfavourable impact on their school attendance and performance. Having no such chores puts boys in an advantageous position when compared to girls. Linked to this issue, the long distances we travelled to and from school also added to the challenges that we faced as children in rural communities.

My experiences of accessing higher education as a rural-origin student have taught me that students bring diverse characteristics and needs to their studies at the university, some of which are linked to their schooling histories, while others are related to who they are as social beings, such as, for example, boys and girls who have grown up in poor rural households. Yet, university programs seem to be designed for an imagined ideal student, one who comes adequately prepared for the academic work and whose social needs are catered for by their family and close community. With the documented high failure and dropout rates across the higher education system in South Africa, a plethora of academic support programs, like mine, for example, are put into place in order to mitigate the challenges students face in universities. These programs tend to focus largely on the academic aspects and ignore the social integration (or non-integration) of students into the institutions. Further, my experiences as a rural-origin student in an urban university suggest that such programs may not be adequate to meet the diverse needs of students generally and, most certainly, are not adequate to meet those of students with social and academic histories like mine. As I have pointed out, all students are challenged by academic and non-academic issues during the transition from school to university. Morrow's (2009) work has alerted us to the ways in which students' background and context impact on their academic success in higher education. For example, for students having to navigate a space with huge buildings, a sea of people, attending lectures at different times, and a culture in which there is no school bell, the university environment presents very different challenges compared to the schools from which most students come. Yet, most universities tend to focus on academic interventions and ignore the external environmental factors that students bring into the institution, which nevertheless play a very important role in their academic success, as Pather and Chetty (2016) have reminded us. These factors have an impact not only on whether students are academically integrated but also on how well they are socially integrated into the life of the institution. As available literature suggests, feeling socially integrated into the life of the institution helps students to become academically integrated and to perform well in their studies. When students do not feel socially integrated, they become alienated, and their academic performance is threatened; some eventually fail and/or drop out (Pather & Chetty, 2016; Tinto, 1975). It is often those from poorly resourced rural schools and communities who tend to bring what Bourdieu (1986) thought of as lower social and cultural capital standing than do their more privileged counterparts who are socially or academically integrated into the life of the university. For rural-origin students in particular, like me, "education (or its absence) shapes success and life choices and chances at school and in higher education" (Swartz et al., 2018, p. 11). For example, were it not for the support I drew from other rural-origin students like myself, I would certainly have failed and possibly dropped out in my first year of study at university. The support I received from my friends, mostly those who came from a similar background, helped me cope with the academic and social challenges I confronted at the university. Our support for each other provided the necessary crutches that helped us to navigate the unfamiliar and challenging terrain of learning in an urban university.

My experience as a rural-origin student who lacked some of the requisite skills for university study, such as computer literacy and English language proficiency, has taught me that this deficiency can have negative implications for students in their university studies. As a result, I am acutely aware that students who lack these skills struggle to cope with academic work in university settings and struggle to adjust to the high demands of higher education, putting them at risk of academic failure and resulting in some of them dropping out of university. While universities have implemented interventions to support students, particularly at the first-year level, a good understanding of who these students are, including their schooling experiences and how these have shaped their learning in university urban settings, is needed. Unless their challenges are adequately understood and addressed, the success of these students in university is threatened. These experiences not only influenced my understanding of what it means to be from a rural background but also enhanced my understanding of the challenges that rural-origin students are confronted with in a cosmopolitan university. While higher learning institutions expect students to have the capacity to adjust instantly and transit to this new life in the university, for many it is a difficult process and, for some, a reason why they fail and even drop out of university.

Looking Now

Having been a rural-origin student and now an academic involved in an academic support program allows me to reflect deeply on the support structures or programs available to students. In essence, my positionality enables me to relate to the challenges with which students are confronted and to acknowledge the silent nuances of what they bring with them when they are consulting with lecturers. Having walked the same or similar route allows me to see their struggles.

A lot of things have changed in the university environment since I was a student. One issue I did not have to deal with during my first year at university was safety, in particular, the rampant gender-based violence today's students have to confront. In my role as the Academic Monitoring and Support program coordinator in my university, I came to realize that being a female student in higher education not only comes with academic demands but also presents other sociopolitical challenges, such as gender-based violence, particularly sexual violence against women, which have to be negotiated (Treffry-Goatley et al., 2018). The communal life in many rural settings does not adequately prepare students for entering the university for the first time and does not enable them to cope with the complex challenges they are likely to encounter, particularly in their first year of study. Leaving home and being away from parents' supervision and guidance for the first time, and the freedom this new situation provides, on the one hand, and the lack of critical decision-making skills, on the other, arguably render young rural-origin students vulnerable to risk in unsupervised urban university spaces with their different cultures. With reports of sexual harassment and gender-based violence on university campuses (Mitchell & De Lange, 2015), for example, and reports of violence by intimate partners in HEIs (Dranzoa, 2018), unless targeted interventions are developed, women students are likely to experience barriers to learning and success and be at risk of failure and dropout. Such interventions must seek not only to prevent such violence but also to create safe spaces in which victims might engage in understanding and addressing it.

Conclusion

Reflecting on my positionality as a first-generation rural-origin university student and, later, a student support program coordinator tasked with supporting students identified as being at risk of academic failure has unearthed a number of important lessons. First, already vulnerable because of their socio-economic status and poor-quality schooling, rural-origin students are often at risk of academic failure at university. Compounding this problem are institutional support programs that tend to be generic in approach and, by being focused on academic development, ignore the diverse needs of students transitioning from school to university, including those of rural-origin students. This narrow approach threatens students' persistence and success in their university studies and, from a social justice perspective, denies them their right to access higher education. If their right to education is to be upheld and realized through equitable opportunities, more needs to be done in and by universities to mitigate the barriers that rural-origin and other marginalized students experience in their learning at university. Effective student support programs require proactive initiatives that address both the academic and social challenges of students when they enrol in universities.

Second, my negative experiences in my first year at university, particularly my feelings of inadequacy related to, for example, my lack of computer and language skills, left me feeling labelled as being at risk, and I felt marginalized because of this stigma. In my current work of supporting students in the university, this issue has implications for how I choose the language I use to identify and address diverse students' needs. Reflecting on my practice in my personal history and my memory-work has helped me to understand how students might experience coming into the university for the first time and how my positionality as a former rural-origin student might assist me to better support them.

Moletsane (2012) has argued: "Reasons for poor [student] performance are complex and can be found in the home, the community, the school, and the society and its various institutions" (p. 3). While these reasons must be acknowledged and addressed, the strengths that students bring from their communities and schools must be harnessed for their own success in higher education. In the context of the lives of First Nations people in Canada, Ponting and Voyageur (2001) wrote: "Let us remember that even among those persons subjected to the trauma and hardships … many have derived strength and not [only] vulnerability from the experiences" (p. 3). By way of comparison, in many ways my success as a student was in spite of what the university did. I drew on the strengths I brought with me from my rural upbringing and schooling to confront the challenges I encountered in university. Thus, my reflection has also cautioned me to consider the strengths students bring with them and the ways in which these can be developed and harnessed to support them to succeed and not to focus exclusively on the gaps that rural-origin students bring with them to the university. Such strengths can be built upon and used to understand who our students are (Swartz et al., 2018) and to assist in developing programs that effectively support them.

NOTE

1 According to Brown (2000), "coloured refers to any person of 'mixed-blood' and includes children as well as descendants from Black-White, Black-Asian, White-Asian, and Black-Coloured unions" (p. 198).

REFERENCES

Bourdieu, P. (1986). The forms of capital. (R. Nice, Trans.). In J.G. Richardson (Ed.), *Handbook of theory and research for the sociology of education* (pp. 241–58). Greenwood Press.

Brown. K. (2000). Coloured and black relations in South Africa: The burden of racialized hierarchy. *Macalester International*, 9(1), 198–207. http://digitalcommons.macalester.edu/macintl/vol9/iss1/13

Chikoko, V., Naicker, I., & Mthiyane, S. (2015). School leadership practices that work in areas of multiple deprivation in South Africa. *Educational Management Administration & Leadership*, 43(3), 452–67. https://doi.org/10.1177/1741143215570186

Clift, B.C., & Clift, R.T. (2017). Toward a "pedagogy of reinvention": Memory work, collective biography, self-study, and family. *Qualitative Inquiry, 23*(8), 605–17. https://doi.org/10.1177/1077800417729836

Council on Higher Education (CHE). (2016). *VitalStats: Public Higher Education 2016.* https://www.che.ac.za/sites/default/files/publications/CHE _VitalStats_2016%20webversion_0.pdf

Czerniewicz, L., & Brown, C. (2018). The habitus and technological practices of rural students: A case study. In A.H. Normore & A.I. Lahera (Eds.), *Crossing the bridge of the digital divide: A walk with global leaders* (pp. 163–80). Information Age Publishing.

Department of Higher Education and Training. (2016). *Statistics on post-school education and training in South Africa, 2016.* https://www.dhet.gov.za /DHET%20Statistics%20Publication/Statistics%20on%20PostSchool%20 Education%20and%20Training%20in%20South%20Africa%202016.pdf

Dranzoa, C. (2018). Sexual harassment at African higher education institutions. *International Higher Education, 94*, 4–5. https://doi.org/10.6017 /ihe.2018.0.10553

Edwin, Y. (2016). South African higher education at a crossroads: The Unizulu case study. In M. Langa (Ed.), *#Hashtag: An analysis of the #FeesMustFall movement at South African universities* (pp. 123–31). Centre for the Study of Violence and Reconciliation. https://www.csvr.org.za/pdf/An-analysis-of -the-FeesMustFall-Movement-at-South-African-universities.pdf

Jacobs, M., & Pretorius, E. (2016). First-year seminar intervention: Enhancing first-year mathematics performance at the University of Johannesburg. *Journal of Student Affairs in Africa, 4*(1), 77–86. https://doi.org/10.14426 /jsaa.v4i1.146

Kapp, R., & Bangeni, B. (2011). A longitudinal study of students' negotiation of language, literacy and identity. *Southern African Linguistics and Applied Language Studies, 29*(2) 197–208. https://doi.org/10.2989/16073614.2011.633366

Lapadat, J.C. (2009). Writing our way into shared understanding: Collaborative autobiographical writing in the qualitative methods class. *Qualitative Inquiry, 15*(6), 955–79. https://doi.org/10.1177/1077800409334185

Levison, D., & Moe, K.S. (1998). Household work as a deterrent to schooling: An analysis of adolescent girls in Peru. *Journal of Developing Areas, 32*(3), 339–56. http://www.jstor.org/stable/4192776

Lyon, P. (2019). Using drawing in visual research: Materializing the invisible. In L. Pauwels & D. Mannay (Eds.), *The Sage handbook of visual research methods* (2nd ed., pp. 297–308). Sage.

Maringe, F., & Moletsane, R. (2015). Leading schools in circumstances of multiple deprivation in South Africa: Mapping some conceptual, contextual and research dimensions. *Educational Management Administration & Leadership, 43*(3), 347–62. https://doi.org/10.1177/1741143215575533

Masipa, T. (2018). South Africa's transition to democracy and democratic consolidation: A reflection on socio-economic challenges. *Journal of Public Affairs, 18*(4), e1713. https://doi.org/10.1002/pa.1713

Mitchell, C., & De Lange, N. (2015). Interventions that address sexual violence against girls and young women: Mapping the issues. *Agenda, 29*(3), 3–12. https://doi.org/10.1080/10130950.2015.1070467

Moletsane, R. (2012). Repositioning educational research on rurality and rural education in South Africa: Beyond deficit paradigms. *Perspectives in Education, 30*(1), 1–8. https://eric.ed.gov/?id=EJ977794

Moletsane, R., Juan, A., Prinsloo, C., & Reddy, V. (2015). Managing teacher leave and absence in South African rural schools: Implications for supporting schools in contexts of multiple-deprivation. *Educational Management Administration & Leadership, 43*(3), 386–99. https://doi.org/10.1177/1741143215574508

Moll, I. (2004). Curriculum responsiveness: The anatomy of a concept. In H. Griesel (Ed.), *Curriculum responsiveness: Case studies in higher education* (pp. 1–19). South African Universities Vice-Chancellors Association.

Morrow, W. (2009). *Bounds of democracy: Epistemological access in higher education*. Human Sciences Research Council Press.

Morton, T.R., Ramirez, N.A., Meece, J.L., Demetriou, C., & Panter, A.T. (2018). Perceived barriers, anxieties, and fears in prospective college students from rural high schools. *The High School Journal, 101*(3), 155–76. https://doi.org/10.1353/hsj.2018.0008

Nel, C., Troskie-de Bruin, C., & Bitzer, E. (2009). Students' transition from school to university: Possibilities for a pre-university intervention. *South African Journal of Higher Education, 23*(5), 974–91. https://doi.org/10.4314/sajhe.v23i5.48811

Nyamapfene, K., & Letseka, I.A. (1995). Problems of learning among first-year students in South African universities. *South African Journal of Higher Education, 9*(1), 159–67.

Nyatuka, B.O. (2015). Overcoming domestic labour among secondary school students in Kenya. *International Journal of Education and Practice, 3*(1), 1–16. https://doi.org/10.18488/journal.61/2015.3.1/61.1.1.16

Pather, S., & Chetty, R. (2016). A conceptual framework for understanding pre-entry factors influencing first-year university experience. *South African Journal of Higher Education, 30*(1), 1–21. https://doi.org/10.20853/30-1-548

Ponting, J.R., & Voyageur, C.J. (2001). Challenging the deficit paradigm: Grounds for optimism among First Nations in Canada. *Canadian Journal of Native Studies, 21*(2), 275–307.

Sader, S.B., & Gabela, N.P. (2017). Spatialities of widening participation: Narratives of first year students receiving financial aid. *South African Journal of Higher Education, 31*(1), 227–42. https://doi.org/10.20853/31-1-1056

Samaras, A.P., Hicks, M.A., & Berger, J.G. (2004). Self-study through personal history. In J.J. Loughran, M.L. Hamilton, V.K. LaBoskey, & T.L. Russell (Eds.), *The international handbook of self-study of teaching and teacher education practices* (vol. 12, pp. 905–42). Springer.

Soudien, C. (2002). Teachers' responses to the introduction of apartheid education. In P. Kallaway (Ed.), *The history of education under apartheid 1948–1994: The doors of learning and culture shall be opened* (pp. 211–23). Pearson Education South Africa.

Strong-Wilson, T., Mitchell, C., Morrison, C., Radford, L., & Pithouse-Morgan, K. (2014). Looking forward through looking back: Using digital memory-work in teaching for transformation. In L. Thomas (Ed.), *Becoming teacher: Sites for teacher development in Canadian teacher education* (pp. 442–68). Canadian Association for Teacher Education.

Swartz, S., Mahali, A., Moletsane, R., Arogundade, E., Khalema, E.N., Cooper, A., & Groenewald, C. (2018). *Studying while black: Race, education and emancipation in South African universities.* Human Sciences Research Council Press.

Timmis, S., Mgqwashu, E., Naidoo, K., Muhuro, P., Trahar, S., Lucas, L., Wisker, G., & de Wet, T. (2019). Encounters with coloniality: Students' experiences of transitions from rural contexts into higher education in South Africa. *Critical Studies in Teaching and Learning (CriSTaL), 7*(2), 76–101. https://cristal.ac.za/index.php/cristal/article/view/195/194

Tinto, V. (1975). Dropout from higher education: A theoretical synthesis of recent research. *Review of Educational Research, 45*(1), 89–125. https://doi.org/10.3102/00346543045001089

Treffry-Goatley, A., De Lange, N., Moletsane, R., Mkhize, N., & Masinga, L. (2018). What does it mean to be a young African woman on a university campus in times of sexual violence? A new moment, a new conversation. *Behavioral Sciences, 8*(8), 67. https://doi.org/10.3390/bs8080067

Van Wyk, S.B. (2015). *"It's hard work to be a girl": Adolescent girls' experiences of girlhood in three low-income communities in South Africa* [Unpublished doctoral dissertation]. University of Stellenbosch, RSA.

Wilson-Strydom, M. (2010). Traversing the chasm from school to university in South Africa: A student perspective. *Tertiary Education and Management, 16*(4), 313–25. https://doi.org/10.1080/13583883.2010.532565

7 "Beyond Getting Something": Reflections on Researching the Closure of a Rural Municipality's Maternity Unit

EMELIE LARSSON

Recently a close colleague, who had read a draft of an article I was writing, asked me: "Why are you interested in this at all?" It was not a question that asked me to define what I find interesting about my project but one that asked me why I care about it. I told her I had moved from Stockholm to Sundsvall because Mid Sweden University's sociology department has a centre for risk studies and a forum for gender studies, and I wanted my PhD project to be about how risk is communicated to pregnant women.

Then BB Sollefteå – a maternity unit at the hospital in a town of 8,000 inhabitants, located inland, about two hours from Sundsvall – closed the day I started at Mid Sweden University, and this closure made news headlines. One of my supervisors suggested that I focus my project on how risk and power matter for that particular closure. "I wanted to write about gender, class, and ethnicity," I told my colleague. "But it turned out that, for the people I interview, it is a lot about feeling unseen, so I had to go into so-called centre-periphery theory, which I had not heard of before I started here." My colleague, who is about twenty years older than I am, grew up in the northern inland, and has spent almost all her working life struggling to make visible the more peripheral Swedish history or, put another way, women's history, the history of the poor, of criminals, of the mentally ill, of rural and small-town Sweden, replied: "So it's not just something that they say then? People from Stockholm are really that ignorant?"

The conversation I had with my colleague summarizes how I arrived at this topic for my PhD project and came to do research on rurality and centralization. At the time we had that talk, I was two years into my PhD and had been analysing how newspapers write about risk in relation to the closure, as well as how expectant parents perceive risks, given the longer distance to maternity care (a 100 to 200 kilometre trip).

I had interviewed people living in Sollefteå, both men and women, who were expecting a child, although most of my interviewees were women, and I had just completed the last interview. As I was interviewing, I thought a lot about how geography determines my perspective and how it affects the maternity unit closure in Sweden's northern inland, which was the focus of my project. Growing up, the logic of the big city was something I took for granted, and having been raised in a (middle-class) suburb, for me, the inner city was associated with opportunities. I spent much time admiring the city centre. When I was thinking about moving to another town, I thought of foreign capitals but not that often about moving to a smaller town in Sweden. However, my perspective has changed somewhat over the past years. In this chapter, I describe my new perspective and consider how my position as an outsider has affected my fieldwork in Sollefteå and the way I understand and interpret the outcome. This chapter is also an attempt to recognize the complications of my position as an outsider as I explore the pattern of my intersecting identities, some of which are static and others more fluid.

Central Concepts in This Chapter

Before I dig deeper into how my position has affected my PhD project on BB Sollefteå, I want to illuminate some theoretical concepts that I use in the chapter. To begin with, I rely on the conceptual pair of centre-periphery – a theoretical field I was, as mentioned, not familiar with when starting the project but one that has grown to become an important part of it. Centre-periphery stems from Marxist theorizations of how the establishment of economic "core regions" also creates peripheries: places that are economically disadvantaged and overlooked (see, for example, Wallerstein 1974). The concept has also been used to address the discursive "othering" of regions, people, and practices. For example, Eriksson (2010) used centre-periphery to address the way in which northern Sweden is continuously peripheralized and othered in Swedish news media and popular culture. As Eriksson notes, the common narrative is that northern Sweden is traditionalist, rural, and struck by depopulation. In the chapter, I will address how centre-periphery power relations matter for the case of BB Sollefteå, how they influenced my initial understanding of rurality and Sweden's northern inland, and how I have been part of upholding them.

To closer explore this topic, I have leaned on feminist theorizations of positionality. Famously, Haraway (1988) stressed that knowledge can never be objective – instead, it is situated and dependent on the researcher's position. Although agreeing with this statement, I also recognize the problems associated with striving towards transparency when it comes to how one's own position influences the research, addressed, for example, by Rose (1997, p. 318), who noted that it is impossible to *fully* understand one's own position, the context of the research topic, and the power dimensions at work in it. Still, the best we can do is to acknowledge the worries we might have about the impact of our work and engage reflexively with these worries. In this chapter, I will focus specifically on my position as an outsider (not being from Sollefteå or northern Sweden) and how it has affected the project. Following Naples's (2003) notion that positions are fluid, I will explore different sides of outsiderhood, including the positive sides of it, how it can be neutralized, and how it changes over time. However, I will start by returning to the beginning of the project, when BB Sollefteå had just closed and I visited the town to do my first interviews.

Arriving in Sollefteå (and Why I Was Not Any Good at Interviewing)

BB Sollefteå closed on 1 February 2017, the same day I started my PhD studies, as mentioned in the introduction, and two days after I arrived in Sundsvall. This new home is both periphery and centre; it is the biggest town in the region of Västernorrland, so among the inland towns and the rest of the municipality, it is often viewed as a centre that takes basic resources from other smaller places. For example, health services have been relocated to Sundsvall, as well as some of the university's departments that used to be located in Härnösand, north of Sundsvall. I have often heard people say that Sundsvall does not even identify as Norrland, and Sundsvall sees itself as a mini-Stockholm. However, in relation to Stockholm, Sundsvall is seen to be peripheral; this position is clearly illustrated by the questions I am often asked: "What are you doing up there?" and "When will you be done so you can come home?" The idea that there is more to my life here than just earning my PhD does not seem to have occurred to them.

In many ways, Stockholm and the other big cities in the south of Sweden determine how the rest of the country should be. For a colleague who grew up and still lives in the countryside in northwest Sweden, "it sets the agenda for what a good life is, what you need to be surrounded with, and what culture is." For me, having grown up in Stockholm, the city was the middle both symbolically and geographically, since everything south of Stockholm was "The South," and everything north was "The North." Ironically, however, as seen on a map, Stockholm is located in the south of Sweden, yet it is not thought of as part of The

South. It is clear that, as McDowell (1999) has concluded, "places are made through power relations which construct the rules which define boundaries" (p. 4). While Stockholm is indeed located in the south, Sollefteå and Sundsvall are located in the middle (about which Mid Sweden University makes a point), yet I struggle with what to write when I am locating Sollefteå geographically. Would the description of Sollefteå as a town in the middle of Sweden make sense? Would it tell my readers anything of significance?

Needless to say, the power dynamic that constructs half of Sweden as The North is part of an ongoing colonization of Saepmie, the Indigenous Sami people's land, and indeed of all the northern part of Sweden, which is treated as a fount of natural resources. Notwithstanding its natural features and the goods that are extracted from it, Saepmie is often pictured as almost nothing but wilderness (Kuokkanen, 2007; Nilsson & Lundgren, 2015). During my childhood and teenage years, I was surrounded by environmentalists whose strongest argument against nuclear energy was that we have all the rivers in the north to use for hydroelectric power. I was a political child, but even though I was outraged over geographic power inequalities in general, I was barely aware of how such inequalities were manifested in Sweden. Still, I remember that I did vaguely realize that there were problems, but I did not know enough to have an opinion.

I conducted my first interview as part of my PhD study only a month after I moved to Sundsvall, a time when I did not know much about the region or the power conflicts in it. Sollefteå, the inland town that had suddenly become the focus of my project, is located in Ådalen, a valley area that was the centre of Sweden's lumber mill industry in the early 1900s. In 1931, big strikes and protests by the workers against poor working conditions were met with brutal violence by the Swedish military. During the protests, five people were shot to death, and today that event is memorialized as "Ådalen 1931," thus marking one of the saddest and most violent days in Swedish workers' history (Johansson, 2001). However, the protests in Ådalen are also remembered with pride; as the maternity unit closed in Sollefteå, the hospital entrance was immediately occupied by local people, one of whose leaders said: "We are used to standing up against injustice." The 1930s workers' protests and an ongoing resistance against oppressive national and regional politics are part of Sollefteå's and Ådalen's identity. Even though Sundsvall has been associated with centralization politics for a long time, the decision to close units at the hospital led to escalated distrust. In addition, it sparked a political identity crisis for the people in Sollefteå, since the closures were pushed through by the Social Democratic Party, which, along with having a very strong position in Sollefteå,[1] had promised to keep the hospital intact.

I knew little about this history when I arrived in Sollefteå, but the conflicts and inequalities were immediately made apparent in the few interviews I conducted at the beginning of 2017. The people I interviewed did talk about pregnancy and risk, but they also spoke about how "they" (the decision-makers) wanted to "close down Sollefteå." My interviewees spoke to me about how they felt unseen and how it was to live in a town where basic services are taken away. I started reading academic texts about centre-periphery theory in relation to power, different kinds of writings about Sollefteå's history, and material about the political process that led to the decision to close the maternity unit. I had had some feminist schooling, which made me highly aware of the implications of my lack of knowledge. I knew too well that power structures are at work in all kinds of encounters, including the interview process, as Staeheli and Lawson (1994), who have written about the importance of connecting power on a macro level to everyday interactions and meetings, have pointed out. The fact that I did not have any tools to deal with this situation was stressful. When I realized that I needed to test the proposed study ethically and put the interviewing on hold until I had the study approved by the ethical board, I was relieved.

My Relation to Rurality and Rural Perspectives Growing Up in Stockholm

When I was interviewing in Sollefteå, I realized that I did not know much about the reality of the people I interviewed, and I was embarrassingly unfamiliar with the power relations that were key to understanding the motivation behind the closure. That feeling of displacement and ignorance needed my urgent attention. Drawing on the feminist geographers' notion that place matters (McDowell, 1992; Rose, 1997) and on the recognition that the researcher's position (social and geographical) has an effect on what knowledge she produces, I continue on here to describe my relation to rurality, having grown up in Stockholm.

Yet, before I start outlining my own position, I want to address the fact that, even though I arrived in Sollefteå with the feeling that I was different from the people in the area, whom I read then as belonging to one group, there is a spectrum of place-bound perspectives represented in my interview data. Some of my interviewees lived in the countryside outside Sollefteå, in villages and/or in rural areas, and some lived in apartments in the town. One of the women I interviewed had moved to Sollefteå from a small town in southern Sweden, and another had grown up in a big city in the Middle East before moving to Sollefteå as an adult. Acknowledging the different perspectives of my interviewees, I want to highlight the point that, in my exploration of my position, rurality is not to be read as a direct representation of my interviewees' lived experience but rather as my own located ideas about their realities. Having noted this point, I now move on to describe my encounters (both actual and discursive) with rurality and the rural north during my upbringing in Stockholm.

Growing up in a suburb of Stockholm, I spent most of my time in the city centre or in the southern suburbs. In the summer and over weekends, I sometimes spent time in my family's summer house in the archipelago, where my parents, who are about to retire, now spend about half their time. My parents both like to be out of doors, so we have often been out picking mushrooms or just going for a walk in the forests right outside the city. As in most Swedish cities, nature and rural spaces are always reasonably close; from Stockholm, one can always go on a ferry or a bus and be out of the city in about an hour. However, the social distance is much bigger. Growing up in Stockholm, one can have some relation to rurality, such as having relatives who live outside town; one could have access to rurality through a summerhouse; or one could have no connection or access to the rural. For the latter group, just going on a ferry is not an easy option, illustrated by a recent initiative in Stockholm that sees girls and women with social access to the countryside bringing other girls and women to it. Even though all suburbs in Stockholm are located close to the countryside in terms of geography, it is mostly people from some of these suburbs who lack access. As a child growing up with access to the countryside, I nevertheless associated the summerhouse in the archipelago with loneliness, because I am an only child and was sometimes forced to spend time there, but also with peacefulness, because, as I got older, I saw it as a space to escape what I thought of as destructive in my normal life or a place to go when I needed to study.

The ambiguous feeling about rurality as something that could be either enjoyable or forced upon me continued through other experiences. Several times, I attended *kollo* (summer camp), an old Swedish custom of having children, mostly from the cities, go to a camp in the countryside to engage in outdoor activities, and once I stayed for ten days on a farm. Summer camp was partly for my benefit, to give me something fun to look forward to during the summer, and partly for my parents, who could not be off work for the whole summer vacation period. I remember these times as sometimes fun but also traumatic, since I was not very socially skilled as a child, and *kollo* meant being constantly surrounded by other children and forced to participate in all kinds of games and activities. When I was a child, I also spent every midsummer at my best friend's summerhouse and always loved it. But when we got older, we were sent to the same place as punishment for throwing a party.

I never thought of rurality as the negative opposite of urbanity, but early on I associated it with disadvantage. I think I saw rurality as having a lower symbolic status than urbanity because of my grandparents' fights, which I did not witness but were related to me by my mother. Sometimes, when very upset about something, my grandmother would tell my grandfather that he just did not understand. She referred to him as not knowing either the Swedish language or what she thought of as its culture well enough, since he was from a big city in Poland. My grandfather would respond by calling my grandmother a hillbilly, referring to her childhood in the countryside in the Swedish-speaking Finnish archipelago, and pointing out that, therefore, she could not understand culture any better than he could. They used ethnicity and rurality as what we might think of as weapons of othering in their fights to create a kind of balance in disadvantage.

I also remember conflicts between the summer guests and the local people on the island where my family's summerhouse is located. A farmer used to drive his quad bike on the private road that crosses the plots of the summerhouses and refused to stop doing so, even though he was told that the road was only for smaller vehicles. He continued to drive where he had always been driving and sometimes even knocked over one of the big garbage cans that were lined up along the road without stopping to return the can to its original position. My parents and those in the houses nearby used to say that he was just a grumpy old man. I thought so too until I started to reflect on the issue and realized that this particular road was his only way of getting to the centre of the island and not everyone can use a small vehicle for their purposes. A few years later, the restaurant on the island was sold to a restaurant owner in Stockholm's hipster area, and the food went from steak and fries to more expensive meals with smaller portions. A discount card was given to the local people so that they could still afford to eat at the restaurant.

A smaller version of the bigger conflict between the city and the countryside took place on that island. People from the city who used the rural spaces for recreation were in conflict with those who lived in these spaces and worked the land as their livelihood. The events also mirrored the historic conflict of who has the right to land in terms of long-time residents versus those who have the capital that allows them access.

Recently, I listened to a radio program about the forest and the different ways it can be understood. I did not know much about the particular countryside that is the reality for some of my interviewees. I knew very little about the northern inland, or about the role it has played in Swedish political history, or its significance to Sweden's cultural life and economy. I have always felt an attraction to the north, and on two occasions, I got to follow my godmother's family on a hike in the mountains, and I loved it. I also spent some time at a folk music school in a northern town, and I fell in love with the surroundings. However, I now see that my fascination was based on the romanticized idea about The North that Nilsson and Lundgren (2015) have addressed. I think the romanticized image of Norrland,[2] which was part of the reason I considered moving to Sundsvall, remains with me, but the more time I spend with my project, new fragments of understanding and ways of relating to Sollefteå and Ådalen are added to this image.

On Outsiderhood and the Different Sides of It

That break as I subjected my study to ethical testing gave me some time to read and learn more about the case and the region's history. I analysed newspaper articles reporting on the closure; I read about Ådalen's political history; and I studied theories based on centre-periphery, colonization, and decolonization. I also spent time talking to colleagues and other people who had grown up in Sollefteå and Ådalen. My first roommate in Sundsvall, who is from a smaller town in the region, told me about her childhood and why she moved, and about the culture clash when her German boyfriend's big-town parents came to visit her parents in her hometown. My colleague next door, who grew up in a village outside Sollefteå, told me about politics and class, and about how she felt misplaced in Sollefteå as a child because the children from the town had nicer and more expensive clothes. I also got some important wake-up calls from one of my supervisors who happens to be from the same village as this colleague and made me aware of my slippages, however accidental, when I wrote from a big-town perspective.

When the study was approved and I started interviewing again, I felt much more comfortable doing it. When interviewees talked about something related to the closure, I knew what they were referring to, and I was familiar with the bigger villages in the area, although I sometimes had to admit to them that I did not know where a certain place was. I was surprised to find that my interviewees did not approach me only as an outsider. Even though it was clear that they saw me as someone who had come from outside, the particular subject of childbirth, on which the interviews centred, became a space where connections were made. I have no experience of either pregnancy or childbirth, but my interviewees did not know that. Everyone I interviewed was in their twenties (my age), and most of them were women. Given societal reproductive norms, it was likely they would assume I might have small children or be planning to have them in the near future. The women I interviewed would say things like: "I'm the one reading and planning [for giving birth]; you know how it is. Men don't really understand." Given that I have never been in a situation where I needed to plan for childbirth, it would be more likely that their male partners (sometimes already fathers of previous children) would understand, yet the interviewees seemed to assume that we shared these experiences as women.

As feminists have pointed out, some topics have been associated historically with a so-called private sphere that should be left outside politics; reproductive health is typically one of those subjects, as Gavison (1992) has reminded us. In talking to people about my project, I have noticed that some expect me to have some personal reason for choosing such a subject as pregnancy and maternity care. My reason has to do with solidarity with other women and does not stem from personal experience of childbirth. Even though I cannot relate specifically to childbirth, I do relate to the governing of women's bodies, and I can see how it matters, both in politics and in feminist research. Because my interviewees and I did not share some experiences, yet could relate to each other on other points, I noted that my outsider position took different shapes during the interviews. Sometimes my position was brought to the fore, and sometimes it was bridged by (supposedly) shared experiences.

The notion that we are all both insiders and outsiders, members of some groups and communities and not of others, was addressed by Merton (1972) and has since been discussed by many critical scholars doing ethnographic work. When I started interviewing, I had a static view on place and position, which I thought of as actual location and environment. Over time, my understanding of position (both my own and that of others) has changed, and I now think of place and position as something more abstract, intertwined, and somewhat fluid. Madge (1993) noted that we all carry multiple selves, which we need to take into account when we are collecting data. Even though I was quite familiar with intersectionality as a concept and a theory underlying methodology, I did not think much about how these different positions of mine interact and, together with the intertwined identities of my interview subject, form the interview itself (Bowleg, 2008; Christoffersen, 2018). When I was doing the first interview in March 2017, I thought a lot more about possible problems and the need to keep checking my-self than about the things that my interviewees and I might have in common. After having that break, I began to pay attention to how my interviewees and I were simultaneously different and alike, and I realized that it is not possible to know beforehand how the interview will turn out. Feelings of sameness and otherness between us interwove and formed the interview differently each time; every now and then, I found myself connecting with someone when I had expected a tricky interview. I will always remember an interview I did with a woman with whom I got in touch via a Facebook group to which I had written a post requesting interviewees. She was the same age as me and was expecting her first child. From her Facebook pictures, I could tell that we were quite different in terms of clothing style and ways of present-ing ourselves. However, when we met, I immediately liked her, and she rapidly opened up to me about her experience of expecting a child as a single mother, her political opinions, and her engagement in an ideologically driven organization. Because we connected on a personal level, the interview turned out to be my most informative, despite the differences I had thought might prevent our connectedness.

I also discovered that power relations were not always what I assumed they would be. When I was reading about the construction of bigger towns as centre and smaller communities as peripheral, I thought of the power relations between Stockholm and smaller towns, between The North and The South of Sweden, and between urban and rural areas. However, the more I talked to people and the more I read about the closure in newspapers, the more I noticed that the power conflict appeared to be foremostly regional. When I asked the expectant par-ents I interviewed where they planned to give birth, some of them said: "Övik" (a small coastal town, which still has a hospital with a maternity unit), and added: "I would never go to Sundsvall." It was obvious that many of them viewed Sundsvall, the region's urban centre, as the em-bodied cause of closures in the inland. Considering this view, it might even have been an advantage, or at least not a disadvantage, that I was not from Sundsvall, since many of the researchers in my department are. Following Rose's (1997) outlining of power as a landscape, I can see that sometimes one needs to drop the books and go into the field to be able to see how power operates in relation to a certain issue. Further, as McDowell (1992) has noted, it is important, as a researcher engaged in ethnographic work, to know both oneself, in terms of position, and the context of one's research project. For me, these were now no longer sep-arate parts but came hand in hand. I know that, before learning about the context, I did not really know my position.

Another thing it took me some time to appreciate was the benefit of people feeling the need to thoroughly explain the context to me. The people I interviewed commonly took their time to describe the places that they talked about and the political decisions that had caused their distrust. Sometimes, they went into detailed descriptions of all the good things about the area that made them want to stay. To some extent, perhaps my not knowing any of the people about whom my interviewees spoke made it easier for them to give their opinions and talk about their feelings. As Simmel (1921) suggested, people may feel more secure talking to a stranger than to someone from the neighbourhood. The fact that I did not know many people from Sollefteå and had no opinion (positive or negative) about the decision-makers behind the closure was, I think, also a good thing for me as a researcher. People from the region do sometimes refer to the good things these same politicians have done, aside from closing the maternity unit, but I am not familiar with those things, so they do not affect my analysis of newspaper articles or my interviews.

Right after finishing the interviews with expectant parents, I was working on a positionality piece for a course I was taking at that time, and the way I positioned myself was still static; I described my class background (middle-class with non-academic parents), where I grew up, and noted how it might affect my interviews and how I interpreted them. Now, I realize how much my perspective on rurality (especially the rural north) has changed during the last two years. When I do interviews in Sollefteå, I will always be an outsider, but, as Naples (2003) has claimed, "outsiderness and insiderness are not fixed or static positions, rather they are ever-shifting and permeable social locations" (p. 49), and on such a range, I am no longer at the extreme end of it. For me, the journey of my PhD project has been about both knowledge and emotion: I needed to read and talk to people to be able to better understand, but I also needed to identify with the perspectives that my interviewees expressed. In the beginning, I did not care to know much, but now I do, and it has affected the way I interpret what I read and hear. When I am doing my interviews, I still sometimes have the feeling that I go to Sollefteå or the nearby countryside to get something, the same way as I have done so many times before. I think that, because of this habit, I feel a need to do it differently this time by making the participants' voices central in order to give something back. Still, it is not solely about giving voice, since the maternity unit closure does not exist in a vacuum; it is not just one closure affecting the people living in that particular town but rather an outcome of centralization politics that affect everyone on a personal and political level.

Conclusion

In this chapter, I have tried to give a picture of my position that is as fair as possible. I cannot help but think about how fast perspectives change and how I am different from my parents and grandparents in terms of relating to the urban and the rural. I found that being fair was the hardest part of writing about my reflections on my own position. It is far too easy to fall into the trap of writing something simplistic that reproduces differences and stereotypes. I have become more and more aware of how the personal position is multiple in its character and that we all carry different selves, which will be more or less visible in different contexts. I have tried to make the different sides of me visible, endeavouring not just to reflect on geographic position but also to highlight how other positions matter in feminist research.

Finally, this experience has been an opportunity for me not only to reflect on how I affect my research but also on how my research affects me. Over the last two years, Sollefteå has become a part of me; it is a place in which I like spending time and with which I, to some extent, do identify. It is love from a distance, of course, as I will (probably) ever only know about doing research in Sollefteå and not about how it is to live there, but I am always happy to be there. I have come to see that research positionality is something that needs to be

Figure 7.1. Ångermanälven, the river in Sollefteå. Courtesy of Emelie Larsson.

re-examined and continually addressed during a project's different phases.

Figure 7.1 shows a picture I took of Ångermanälven the second time I visited Sollefteå. The sign on the riverbank says: "All fishing forbidden." When looking at the picture now, I see how it captures things that I initially associated with Sollefteå – beautiful nature, snow, rivers and hydro energy, and fishing. When asked, my interviewees mentioned closeness to nature as one of the good things about Sollefteå, but they also mentioned things that this picture leaves out, such as social life, cultural activities, and good schools. Coming from outside and carrying ideas about the area, I was at first unable to see these things.

NOTES

1 In 2014, when the discussions on closing the hospital were on the table, 54 per cent voted for the Social Democratic Party, which had promised to keep the hospital open, compared to 34 per cent in the 2018 election.
2 Norrland is the northernmost and biggest of Sweden's three "lands," consisting of a little more than half of Sweden's territory.

REFERENCES

Bowleg, L. (2008). When Black + lesbian + woman ≠ Black lesbian woman: The methodological challenges of qualitative and quantitative intersectionality research. *Sex Roles: A Journal of Research*, *59*(5–6), 312–25. https://doi.org/10.1007/s11199-008-9400-z

Christoffersen, A. (2018). Researching intersectionality: Ethical issues. *Ethics and Social Welfare*, *12*(4), 414–21. https://doi.org/10.1080/17496535.2018.1541230

Eriksson, M. (2010). (Re)producing a periphery: Popular representations of the Swedish north. [Doctoral dissertation, Umeå University]. Skytteanska Samfundets Handlingar No. 66. Umeå: GERUM.

Gavison, R. (1992). Feminism and the public/private distinction. *Stanford Law Review*, *45*(1), 1–45. https://doi.org/10.2307/1228984

Haraway, D. (1988). Situated knowledges: The science question in feminism and the privilege of partial perspective. *Feminist studies*, *14*(3), 575–99. https://doi.org/10.2307/3178066

Johansson, R. (2001). *Kampen om historien: Ådalen 1931. Sociala konflikter, historiemedvetande och historiebruk 1931–2000* [The struggle for history: Ådalen 1931. Social conflicts, historical awareness, and the use of history 1931–2000]. Hjalmarson & Högberg.

Kuokkanen, R. (2007). Myths and realities of Sami women: A postcolonial feminist analysis for the decolonization and transformation of Sami society. In J. Green (Ed.), *Making space for aboriginal feminism* (pp. 72–92). Fernwood Publishing.

Madge, C. (1993). Boundary disputes: Comments on Sidaway (1992). *Area*, 25(3), 294–9. https://www.jstor.org/stable/20003310

McDowell, L. (1992). Doing gender: Feminism, feminists and research methods in human geography. *Transactions of the Institute of British Geographers, 17*(4), 399–416. https://doi.org/10.2307/622707

McDowell, L. (1999). *Gender, identity and place: Understanding feminist geographies.* Polity Press.

Merton, R. (1972). Insiders and outsiders: A chapter in the sociology of knowledge. *American Journal of Sociology, 78*(1), 9–47. https://doi.org/10.1086/225294

Naples, Nancy A. (2003). *Feminism and method: Ethnography, discourse analysis, and activist research.* Routledge.

Nilsson, Å., & Lundgren, A.S. (2015). Logics of rurality: Political rhetoric about the Swedish North. *Journal of Rural Studies, 37*, 85–95. https://doi.org/10.1016/j.jrurstud.2014.11.012

Rose, G. (1997). Situated knowledges: Positionality reflexivities and other tactics. *Progress in Human Geography, 21*(3), 305–20. https://doi.org/10.1191/030913297673302122

Simmel, G. (1921). The sociological significance of the stranger. In R.E. Park & E.W. Burgess (Eds.), *Introduction to the science of sociology* (pp. 322–7). University of Chicago Press.

Staeheli, L.A., & Lawson, V. (1994). A discussion of "women in the field": The politics of feminist fieldwork. *The Professional Geographer, 46*(1), 96–102. https://doi.org/10.1111/j.0033-0124.1994.00096.x

Wallerstein, I.M. (1974). *The modern world-system: Capitalist agriculture and the origins of the European world-economy in the sixteenth century.* Academic Press.

8 A Button Thief or an Urban Researcher? Entangled Selves, Positionality, and Knowledge Production

SARA NYHLÉN

Introduction

In this chapter, I explore different methods for examining researcher positionality and reflexivity, which I discuss in relation to my own research. I do this exploration by using fiction, memories, and the analysis of photos I took to position myself in relation to my research. I use the novel *Till flickorna i sjön* (To the girls in the lake)[1] by Elin Olofsson (2014) in order to explore my own memories of growing up in a rural area and to examine how this experience is linked to the research that I ended up doing later in my life. My reading of the novel mirrors ideas and imaginative constructions of what (deep) rurality and rural life are and can be. It also enables me to ask questions and to explore the subjective and autoethnographic elements in the research process and how these are linked to the formulation of research questions and the use of methodologies. The purpose of my chapter is to reflect upon how the self as a child in a rural area interacts with the self as a researcher with an urban gaze who travels to rural areas and studies aspects of rurality. I explore how the different subject positions affect the knowledge I produce.

The chapter takes as its point of departure the novel *Till flickorna i sjön* (To the girls in the lake), which is set in the northern mountainous part of Sweden, a sparsely populated rural area. The main character is Helena, who has been left by her husband and, at the same time, has lost her job in the local municipality. She then starts to work as a cleaner at the hospital, where she suddenly spots her cousin, known as the "Blue Boy," in a hospital bed, and her mother starts calling her on the telephone after many years of silence. It is a novel about what a young woman once promised herself by a lake in the forest and what she, now grown up, needs to do to fulfil that promise. As readers, we come to understand that Helena suffered sexual abuse – she was probably raped – on the edge of a village lake when she was a child. On the book's cover appear the two questions the novel interrogates: "Is it possible to forget what was once inscribed onto your body? Do you need to return to what has been in order to ever become free?" (Olofsson, 2014).

In research, much discussion takes place concerning how researchers participate in mediating the production of knowledge and on the roles and identities performed by the researcher in enacting the research process (Woods, 2010). In this chapter, I acknowledge subjectivity and seek to examine the impact of these factors on knowledge production (Acker et al., 1996; Harding, 1986; Waldby, 1995).

Memories, Reading Novels, and Analysing Photos

My approach in this chapter is in the tradition of autoethnography and autobiography by using my own memories of growing up in a rural place and becoming a researcher who specializes in research in and about sparsely populated rural areas in Sweden. The methodology can be divided into three parts: (re)reading a novel; analysing and discussing the memories that arose from the reading; and, finally, using photographs I took during my fieldwork in order to analyse my own understanding of the research sites and objects that I pursue.

Using memory-work is a way of departing from everyday experiences that shape the understanding of our social lives. I have reconstructed the stories in this chapter from incidents that occurred during my growing up and my time in academia, along with memories of these incidents. I place special emphasis on describing the context that gives meaning to each individual memory and the feelings to which the memory led. Using my own experiences as the point of departure is a way of acknowledging my presence rather than abstracting myself. The methodology is inspired by feminist methodologies whose underlying focus is on underscoring the complexity of the intersections of power hierarchies, specifically as they relate to the production of knowledge (Jaggar, 2008). In my case, this approach means paying attention to different intersections in my research practices and the research project, such as rural/urban and researcher/participant, for example. I remain aware that, as Burns (2003) has claimed, one can, at the same time, be constituted and regulated by the discourses of which one is critical. However, my studying of them and reflecting upon how the novel, the memories, and the photos make me feel and react illustrates the operations of power at the level of my own body.

Given that the reading of a novel led to the memory-work, my methodology is a combination of memory-work along with group readings of the novel and discussions of it during a seminar. The idea behind my using the novel was a research seminar in which the focus was a discussion about rurality and gender in an effort to broaden the picture of rurality and its gendered dimensions. All the participants in the seminar had read the novel, but three of us had also prepared presentations on how the novel had inspired us, what it meant to us as researchers, and the connections we could see between it and our research; this process could be described as a trialogue. For me, reading the novel was a very emotional experience, since so many memories from my childhood and my relation to the place in which I grew up were brought to the surface. Before reading the novel, and before discussing it during the seminar, I was truly unaware of how deep my relations to rurality were, and it made me think about how this relation to place has shaped my researcher identity. It brought up memories of my growing up in a rural area and feelings of pride, shame, belonging, and disidentification, as I show in more detail later on in the chapter. The reading also sparked a realization that the experience of reading and discussing this novel is connected to the research I do and the research questions I ask, but it is also connected to how I analyse and understand the narratives offered by the research participants.

The work in this chapter can be described as individual memory-work inspired by the work of Frigga Haug (1987) and others, such as Fahlgren (2005), Fahlgren et al. (2015), Mitchell and Pithouse-Morgan (2014), Onyx and Small (2001), and Widerberg (1995), because it is based on the memories and feelings that arose in me when I was reading and discussing the novel. The work on memory becomes significant since it deepens the insights into how everyday experiences, as the basis of knowledge, are closely connected to societal processes and are, in that way, linked to socially created norms and expectations (Onyx & Small, 2001). The researcher's body can become a part of what is researched if we are willing to ask questions about who we are and what we are studying (see Peters & Burbules, 2004). Memories or experiences are regarded as something that constantly produce and reproduce us as subjects rather than as something that we have had (Fahlgren, 2005; Scott, 1991). We are constituted as subjects in relation to the experiences that are written into us, and it is these constituting experiences that we need to analyse rather than the experiences themselves (Scott, 1991). Sparked by the reading of a novel, the memories of my childhood and also the memories of experiences, feelings, and thoughts that I had during my research fieldwork in rural areas can be seen as memories that together compose my situation as an urban-based researcher travelling to do research in rural areas. While they might be seen as single moments or memories, together they create a complex experience of wanting to be both rural and urban at the same time. The memories are connected to being both the little rural girl and the researcher with an urban gaze; they show me how my two selves are entangled in the research process.

The last step in the method presented in this chapter is analysing the photos I took during my fieldwork. These are not photos that I use in my research but private photos that I took of the rural places to which I travelled while doing my research. I analyse and discuss the photos in relation to the readings of the novel and the memories and feelings that this process awoke in me. This approach reminds me of what Falconer Al-Hindi and Kawabata (2002) have called "return the look" (p. 110), and I return the look to myself by using a combination of the three steps in order to understand who and what I am researching.

Where It All Began

In order to understand my own positionality, I need to acknowledge my own "intellectual autobiography" (Stanley & Wise, 1990, p. 47) and return to my childhood (see also Enloe, 2004; Pini, 2004). I grew up in the countryside located on the coast in the northern part of Sweden. This area is actually located in the middle of Sweden, but it is discursively framed as the northern part of the country. In fact, in public discourse, everything north of the capital Stockholm is framed as "Norrland." In Sweden, rural areas are rarely termed "countryside" but are instead called "sparsely populated areas." This description is not associated with being idyllic in the way that descriptions of the countryside often are. Instead, it refers to stagnating, backward, wild, empty, and underdeveloped places (Eriksson, 2010). The place where I grew up is 40 kilometres from the closest city and 7 kilometres from the closest town. I often refer to my home as a village, but it is not – it is just houses located along a country road (see Figure 8.1). I spent hours outside running free in the woods with my brother. There were no other children living close by, so my brother and I played together a lot (see Figure 8.2). I always found the forest magical with my own secret places, such as "the golden woods," and I made up different animals, for example, by turning trees into dragons that I could ride. When it was time to go home, my mother used to whistle in a particular way that we knew was her calling us back.

In this chapter, I discuss three different studies that I conducted together with colleagues in rural areas in Sweden: my PhD thesis on

Figure 8.1. Countryside road where I grew up. Courtesy of Sara Nyhlén.

Figure 8.2. Exploring nature. Courtesy of Sara Nyhlén.

regional development of a mountainous area in Sweden; a project about the organization of eldercare and its working conditions; and a project that focused on gender-based violence against high school girls. The projects were all conducted in rural, sometimes deep rural, sparsely populated areas in Sweden. Looking back at the projects, using the three components of the method presented above, I can see that three different themes arise: the so-called unproblematic regional development; being the one who got away and then travels back to do research; and the collective internalizing of stereotypical images of rural areas.

The So-Called Unproblematic Regional Development

Since political scientists often work with problematizing issues of democracy, equality, and power, one would think that ideas about positionality or reflexivity would be commonly discussed, but they are not (Jansson et al., 2009). For me, writing my thesis was unproblematic in the sense of positionality and reflexivity. I did not discuss my position as the researcher travelling to the research site or the position of the Indigenous population and Swedish coloniality in the thesis. Even though I was a qualitative researcher, I upheld the old traditions of what is known as "scientific objectivity." Subjectivity glided past me like an oil tanker on a foggy night, to paraphrase Enloe (2004). It is important to understand that, if we do not see the power structures, hidden by fog, our ideas about how the world works will be unreliable. Jansson et al. (2009) pointed to these problems, to the lack of reflection and the reproduction of science as objective, and related them to science in general and political science in particular. In order for something to attain the status of scientific truth in political science, a researcher is not supposed to be personally involved in the object of study. Instead, a certain distance should be maintained (Jansson et al., 2009). The knowledge must stand out as objective, dissociated, and neutral; real knowledge cannot be based on opinions or individual experiences. In academia, it is important for one to show that one's scientific knowledge is characterized by distance and control. Research of lesser quality is associated with closeness, emotionality, less structure, and less control. This hierarchy is also gendered in that the abilities linked to good quality research are attributed to masculinity and the others to femininity (Howie & Tauchert, 2002). This gendering is especially evident in political science, where the defined object of study – politics – is an object of male activity (Keränen, 1993).

In my PhD work, I wanted to understand how a small village in the northern parts of Sweden could become an internationally famous

Figure 8.3. Missing out on politics (landscape). Courtesy of Sara Nyhlén.

destination, thought of as the centre of regional development in the area. In those days, I did not think at all about reflexivity or that we are all a part of what we are studying, continually producing and upholding hierarchies such as the rural and the urban. Looking at the pictures I took of the destination, I see that they all, more or less, portray beautiful landscapes and wilderness from the outsider's or the touristic gaze, like Figure 8.3. I see now that they display touristic attractions without any recognition of the ongoing colonial processes in the region. The Indigenous Samis are never present in my pictures. At that time, I did not reflect upon this omission, which makes the photos I took a visual representation of the Swedish colonial practice of erasing Samis and Sami rights – it is as if they were never there. This practice also erases the ongoing conflict between large-scale touristic activities such as cross-country skiing, hiking, downhill skiing, and so on and the Samis' right to use the land for traditional reindeer herding, fishing, and hunting. Feminist scholars with whom I came to work taught me to listen to silences, and I now ask about the missing Samis in the pictures, which leads me to question why I have not seen before that they are not there. It was not until I analysed the photos retrospectively that I began to realize I was missing a lot; I was missing politics, and I was not asking enough questions about power and structures. Enloe (2004) has described these situations as feminist awakenings sparked by feminist curiosity. My pictures are completely missing the fact that the countryside is, and always has been, a multicultural space and that my cultural construction of rurality circles around white rurality and the appearance of culturally homogenous idylls (see Panelli et al., 2009)

When I took the pictures, I did not relate my research at all to the framing of Norrland as different. I compounded this oversight by taking pictures of the wilderness, a tourist destination, and by not showing the ongoing, everyday life of people living there. In other words, in my continuing to frame Norrland and the Arctic region as empty, even though millions of people live there, my gaze was that of a visitor. This othering is also evident in politics (upheld by science), since the colonization of parts of the region since Linnaeus's writings in the mid-1700s can be clearly seen in current regional politics (Nyhlén et al., 2018).

I continue to exert the touristic gaze when I relate to rural areas as having great natural resources and as places for recreation and vacationing but not places in which it is possible to live. Travelling through the sparsely populated north where there is forest and only forest, I see no factories, schools, shops, or towns, and only one or two houses for tens of kilometres, and I often wonder how people living here are employed. I contribute to the constructions of urban and rural when I define myself these days as urban, upholding ideas about the rural as backward, violent, and traditional while regarding the urban as modern, gender equal, and sustainably oriented.

I left the rural area where I grew up. In that sense, I am one of those who escaped, but at the same time, I am the rural girl, since the experience of growing up in a rural area is inscribed into my body (see Olofsson, 2014). I am becoming a part of the ongoing othering of rurality. Little and Panelli (2007) pointed to this phenomenon in their research about outback Australia. The authors emphasized that narratives about nature and masculinity and femininity are entangled and that these narratives contribute to reproducing each other. They also referred to popular culture in which boys are depicted as "trained in the great outdoors," while girls do not like the "paternalistic" rural outback and "once they escape, they rarely return" (p. 179). This feeling of belonging and not belonging can be understood through the concept of disidentification (Butler, 1993; Lykke, 2014), and here the unifying signifier is rurality. I am drawn to it by the unity that rurality as a signifier promises, but I become uneasy with the situation when I disidentify with many of the stereotypical meanings that I also attach to the concept.

In the process of disidentification, the feeling is ambivalent, but Butler (1993) has pointed to how this ambivalence creates the possibility for politicizing and, in this case, a move towards a more complex understanding of the researcher position in relation to rurality. I make this move by understanding my multiple selves in relation to my research; I am the rural girl and at the same time the urban-based researcher. Reading Olofsson's (2014) novel about a woman who left a rural area where she grew up made me realize that I relate to this experience of being a rural child who moved away to the more urban centre. The feeling of belonging and not belonging when I travel to rural areas is expressed in the novel:

> "You have known the whole time that I'm not from the city," Helena said.
>
> "I recognized you at first sight. Evelina Fjällborg forgets no one," she said.
>
> "Then why did you continue talking about what everyone from the city is like and saying that I was like everyone else, making a fuss about me?"
>
> Evelina dragged her tongue against her upper teeth several times while she planned her answer and continued to glare at Helena.
>
> "Because I wanted to see how long you could go on lying," she said then. (p. 132)

I relate to this excerpt because I am embedded in a system that teaches us that leaving the rural parts is what people do in an attempt to be thought of, however erroneously, as ambitious and outgoing. They do not get stuck or left behind. The research about rurality contributes to the notion that leaving rural areas for more urban centres equals success and staying equals failure (Farrugia, 2016). I have internalized this view, as I have explained above, and carried it with me into my research. The feelings and memories connected to this excerpt reveal that I feel like an alien, an outsider who does not know how to respond to questions about where I live and what I work on. I do not want to become what the character Evelina Fjällborg in the novel says people from the city are like. In my interpretation of Helena's situation in the book, I am enacting the position of the one who made an active decision to leave, placing people who stay their whole lives in rural areas as "the ones who never left," as many Swedes disparagingly describe such people. Cook and Cuervo (2020) have shown in their study that this assumption is very common, however untrue. The decision to stay may very well be a considerate one or one choice among many different options.

Being the One Who Got Away

> How do you change your pack? You just get on the bus, regional bus 154. You wait by the bus stop in the village, in the darkness since the municipality can't afford to have the street lights on. You wave with your

reflector when the bus comes so that the driver sees that someone is there. You get onto the bus and buy a ticket … You carry the bag in front of you and take a seat almost at the very back. You can't see anything because of the darkness, only your own reflection in the dirty window, but from time to time you see her – the girl whom you are going to get rid of. You shed her like a snake sheds its skin, push her down into a plastic bag, and throw it out when the bus stops in Krokom, halfway to the city. And when you get off the bus, at the bus square in the city, you are someone else. If you have done it once, you can do it again and again.

– Elin Olofsson (2014, p. 43)

I am one of those who has changed her pack, leaving the rural area where I grew up, becoming the outsider, always a stranger when I go back to my home village. When I was a child in the village, there were two grocery shops, a bank, a post office, a flower shop, a gift shop, and a fabric store. I stole a button there, when I was five. My mother found it and made me return it. I remember how the shame made me feel, how it felt in my body. I thought that now everyone would know I am a thief. I felt visible, exposed. When I changed my pack and moved to the city, I no longer had to identify as the little button thief. I got rid of that girl, and at the same time, I keep coming back as her. Is it, as Olofsson (2014) has written, that returning is the only way to become free?

In one of my research projects, I was doing fieldwork in a remote rural place in the most northern part of Sweden. I had never been this far north before, and I was planning to set up interviews with politicians, white-collar workers, aid assessors, and volunteer organizations. The rental car was waiting for me at the airport when the plane landed – I found it idling when I got out of the small airport building. I said to myself: "Well, of course, that's how it's done in rural places. There are no voters for the Green Party living here." Through this memory, it became apparent to me the way in which I contributed to the ongoing process of internal othering (see Eriksson, 2010) of Norrland and the people living there, since I hold as an accurate representation the pictures that have been transmitted to the public in mass media films and literature, like novels and plays about the rural. Norrland is described as characterized by out-migration and as economically supported from the centre, as being backward and xenophobic, according to Eriksson (2008) and the contributors to Öhman's (2001) edited collection, as well as having more traditional gender roles (Stenbacka, 2011). This portrait can be compared to how popular culture shapes people's perceptions about Norrland, just as movies shape people's perceptions of the US South, the outback in Australia, or the rural British countryside (Bosworth & Somerville, 2014; Cook & Cuervo, 2020; Jansson, 2005; Williamson, 1995). Instead of being grateful for a warm car when it is −30°C, I see the act of leaving the car running to keep it warm as another indication or proof of an unsustainable rural lifestyle compared to the city's modern way of living, where people heat cars with electric heaters. It is important to reflect on these ideas that I carry, since they easily stick to understandings of places and narratives.

I travelled to this remote rural place to study the planning and implementation of the care of the elderly. To study eldercare in Sweden is equivalent to studying the working conditions of women, since women constitute most of the planners and executors of eldercare; with this job comes lower status, lower pay, and fewer opportunities to speak up against bad working conditions in comparison to sectors where men are in the majority (Andersson, 2007; Forsberg Kankkunen, 2006). When there is no value attached to one's work and few opportunities to renegotiate the terms, exit becomes a valid choice. When one is being squeezed like a "hamburger" (as one of the informants put it) between the economic pressure of maintaining the budget and pressure from the elderly and their relatives to find solutions to giving them care, quitting the job might be the only way out. These women then become the ones who got away. The eldercare sector is often described as a drain on the public purse, which is both a description of the relations between private and public funding and also a reference to the perception that the rural areas are an economic drain on the urban (Giritli Nygren & Nyhlén, 2017).

During this research project, I visited three rural municipalities, and I heard stories about pride, weariness, anxiety, joy, solidarity, hope, and despair. During the twenty-seven interviews I conducted, I met not a single white-collar worker or needs assessor who said they definitely believed that they would be working there in a year's time. When I sent out by email the final report for the project, I got five autoreplies telling me that this person's "employment has ended," and I instantly felt that she got away, just as Helena in the novel got away and as I have too.

When I look at the pictures I took of the research sites I visited during this research project, it is evident that I like photographing a kind of emptiness; there are streets, houses, natural features, and forest, but these sites are always without people in them. These are photos of what I think of as otherness, of things that do not look as though they are in the city, things that are stereotypically demonstrative of out-migration and decline. Cloke (2006) has explained this concept in terms of how modernization theory depicts rural places as backward, lagging

Figure 8.4. Rundown shop at a research site. Courtesy of Sara Nyhlén.

behind, and the opposite of urban places, which are characterized by social progress and as having many opportunities for the people living there. Figure 8.4 displays a clothing shop in a rundown house in need of painting. Here, I reproduce the dichotomy between the urban and the rural, with the latter in decline.

The photo symbolizes how I see urban-based lives as the norm and implicitly position rurality and rural lives as the other (Cuervo, 2015). I realize that I took this picture because the shop does not look like shops in cities; I took it because it did not comply with my norm of what a shop should look like. The picture repeats the idea that rurality is empty, rundown, and deteriorating or, put another way, deviating. My pictures lack the messy, plural, and overlapping meanings of rural sites. Instead, they depict stereotypical political and material realities (see Panelli et al., 2009). The pictures show how I had internalized the stereotypical ideas about rurality that I carried with me into my research, but reading the novel and reflecting on positionality helped me see that the research participants also internalized different ideas and images of rurality.

The Collective Internalizing of Stereotypical Images of Rural Areas

"Do not worry about Evelina Fjällborg. I'll always make it," she said, and small pieces of apple fell out of her mouth and down onto the table.

"Are there bears there?" Aileen asked.

"Yeah, my dad has even fought one. He has scars from it, on the side of his head, so you know it's true," said Evelina and pointed to the side of her head.

– Elin Olofsson (2014, p. 66)

I want to use this excerpt as a way of discussing how we are all what I call doers of rurality and how identity is a negotiated site based on historical and cultural forces that shape and influence rurality and rural life. It could be a shared site for struggle against oversimplified or stereotypical images, but often it is an adaption of stereotypical images or an addition to them, just as Evelina adapts and adds to stereotypes of the north in the excerpt above. As we read the novel and come to better understand this character through her attributes, we realize that, although it is never made explicit, Evelina belongs to the Sami population. By using the stereotypical idea of Swedish rurality as being filled with bears, sometimes even polar bears (see Eriksson, 2010), which do not even exist in Sweden, Evelina adapts to the situation and takes on the stereotypical position of a bear-fighter's daughter. Can the adaption be a productive way of taking on an identity, a transformative power? I return to this question later, but first, I look at the internalizing processes among my research informants.

It is now clear to me that the informants in my research project internalized and adapted to the ongoing othering of rural areas. I illustrate this internalization by using a story from one of the projects. The context here is that it is very difficult to find people who want to work in eldercare, and the manager whom I interviewed earlier that same day cried during the interview when she talked about the pressure and the stress she felt while trying to find personnel. As I ended the later interview with the deputy mayor and turned the recorder off, he became relaxed, sank back in the chair, and said: "How did I do? I had decided before the interview that I would not be whining; the development of municipality is up to us, and only us. Here in the countryside we are used to working hard."

The deputy mayor framed the talk about structural problems upheld by politics between rural and urban areas as "whining." We can tell from his statement that he, too, has internalized the images and constructions of the rural regions as a drain on the public purse, as though regional economic development is not connected to New Public Management and the political system (see Giritli Nygren & Nyhlén, 2017). Here, as we can see, rural areas in Sweden are sometimes described as if development is not a consequence of politics. Economic growth is articulated as the main goal, and the rural is depicted in terms of out-migration and decline; the "new economic geography" (Westholm, 2003, p. 3) conveys the idea that rural areas can never produce economic growth, since proximity to the urban and population density are lacking. The situation with the deputy mayor is important because it speaks to how he has internalized the notion that declining rurality is non-political. But it also shows how important it is for a scholar studying power to be curious and to pay attention to all dimensions of power. In thinking about the significance of what the deputy mayor said to me after the recorder was turned off, I am reminded of Enloe's (2004) point that it is important to pay attention to informal, private, casual conversations, to the shared jokes, and to the gestures and rituals in order to understand how relationships are "glued" together (p. 5).

Examples from my research projects show that respondents who do not live in a rural area but work there also internalize ideas about rurality in their everyday work. In this case, in relation to gendered violence, the white-collar workers of the region could not believe that the reported statistics of violence in the region were as low as they were. They insisted during the interviews that the low rate must surely be a case of low reporting of violence. Behind this objection was the belief that this area is rural, and rural areas are, by definition, violent (Nyhlén & Giritli Nygren, 2019). These ideas are strongly influenced by popular culture and one-dimensional descriptions of rurality (Skott et al., 2021). These two situations are very different. In the first interview, the deputy mayor was not aware of my double position as both a rural girl and a researcher; he was performing the interview with someone he believed to be only a researcher from the city. I think that this assumption affected the interview situation for him and reinforced the need to describe rural people as, for example, "hard working." In the second interview, I benefitted from the fact that the informants knew that I came from the city and also that I was a feminist working at a gender research institute. Analogously, although it reinforces stereotypical images, being the daughter of a bear-fighting father, as Evelina presents herself in the novel, might be a productive position. For me as a researcher, I also benefit from being coded as a feminist from the city and therefore occupy a position that affords me legitimacy in the research context that I would not necessarily have otherwise enjoyed (see Pini, 2004). I become an ally of the white-collar workers who situated themselves as

Figure 8.5. Concert advertisement. Courtesy of Sara Nyhlén.

being not rural and thereby more aware of gender equality and more knowledgable than those from the rural areas where they work and where my research took place.

Sweden, as a country, is often presented as modern and progressive (Hannerz & Löfgren, 1994; Pred, 2000), but Norrland is defined in relation to what it is not. The urban/rural divide became very prominent, as Eriksson (2010) has pointed out, when a member of the Swedish Parliament stated that "people in Stockholm are smarter than countryside folks" (p. 95). Looking back at the research projects now, I can see how I had internalized this idea. When incidents of racism, xenophobia, or misogyny occurred, I realize now that I interpreted them as proof of the inherited backwardness of rural areas. When I saw these kinds of incidents occurring in urban areas, I did not put them down to evidence of backwardness because I did not think of cities as places where it was impossible to live. This prejudice is what I carried with me, however unintentionally. Perhaps it is also possible to say that I even trivialized these incidents when they occurred in an urban setting. I can also see in my own photos how I adapted to the idea of rural areas being less gender equal, and I can see this belief symbolized in Figure 8.5.

By photographing a concert advertisement poster that I consider to be sexist, with the woman Agneta in a sexy pose sitting down in front of Peter, I attach stereotypical gendered behaviour to those in a rural place. Added to this notion is the effect of the old dilapidated board on which is advertised the only event – the concert with Peter and Agneta – happening in the area (or, at least, the only event that is advertised). Instead of unpacking rural masculinities and femininities more generally, focusing on the construction and performance of identities (see Little & Panelli, 2003), I saw rural spaces and practices from a perspective that reinforces ideas about hegemonic heterosexual masculinity and submissive femininity. I framed the photo of Peter and Agneta within the practice of highly conventional heterosexual performance, and I connected it to being typically rural. In this way, I saw the photo as constructing rural spaces as being connected to stereotypical gendered practices.

Conclusion

In this chapter, I make a contribution to the literature on reflexivity by discussing how I explored the different positionalities I have as a researcher and as a child who grew up in a rural area, and how this dual position is linked to the knowledge I produce. To carry out this exploration, I use my own memories, the reading of a novel, and an analysis of the visual representations of the photos I took of the research sites as three processes that are related to my research.

This chapter is built on my recognition that the idea that knowledge must be objective, dissociated, and neutral is not only wrong but also very naïve. Traditional research divides the researcher and the researched, the object and the subject, and the producer and the recipient of knowledge (Pini, 2004). This division, however, limits the knowledge produced. When we pay attention to reflexivity, we enhance our research; the underlying power dimensions become visible, and the silences are made apparent.

To have left the village where I grew up means, in part, to have left behind who I was and to have created for myself a new identity. Evelina, in the novel, accuses Helena of lying when she presents herself as someone from the city; this lie is also true for me. I always feel that I am in a border position, neither the rural girl nor the urban researcher, but I am both. Both positions are mine, and when I turn my gaze towards myself, I understand more fully who and what I am researching (see Falconer Al-Hindi & Kawabata, 2002). I will not always and forever be the little button thief, but at the same time, I will always carry the experience of my rural childhood with me and within me. Again, I find the words in the novel that "no one is to believe that Evelina Fjällborg is infallible" (Olofsson, 2014, p. 238) pertinent. My experiences affect the research I do and the knowledge I produce.

This chapter has also been the story of my awakening as a reflexive researcher or, as Enloe (2004) put it, the creation of "a list of embarrassments" (p. 16). By using a critical retrospective look – combining memories, visual material, and the reading of a novel in the discussion about my research and my different selves – I now understand how my position as a reflexive feminist scholar has helped me see more clearly the way in which the dimensions of power operate. A lack of curiosity and/or being uncritical is "dangerously comfortable"; in the discipline of political science, it is put forward as being reasonable or exercising intellectual efficiency. Enloe (2004) explained: "*Un*curiosity is dangerously comfortable if it can be dressed up in the sophisticated attire of reasonableness and intellectual efficiency: 'We can't be investigating everything!'" (p. 3, emphasis in original). Like other political scientists before me, studying formal politics made me think that I was studying what I thought of as real politics; it was not until I became part of a feminist research group with colleagues and friends who were already feminists that I learned to take a more holistic approach to power. They taught me how to study more thoroughly, dig deeper, pay attention to the wider spectrum of political life, and also to see the absences and hear the silences.

The methods applied in this chapter have been a way of conceptualizing my own reflexivity and have helped me to see my different selves as the rural girl and the urban-based researcher. Applying these methods has improved my understanding of the self as precarious, contradictory, and always in the process of being shaped and reshaped (see Weedon, 1987). The process has been both challenging and rewarding, and will never be complete, but it is a process that needs to be ongoing. As Pini (2004) has pointed out, "the self-evident, knowable, transparent self is not 'out there' waiting to be revealed" (p. 170). These methods have enabled me to develop an understanding of how the performance of different identities as a researcher affects knowledge production. Performing identities such as the feminist researcher or the rural girl (or hiding these identities in the interaction with research participants) gives greater access to participants or to information that would not have been accessible otherwise (Lohan, 2000; McDowell, 1998). As Enloe (2004) has pointed out, travelling from the centre to the margins is not travelling on a horizontal plane but, rather, is travelling from the top of a political pyramid down to its base. Once you are aware of these hierarchies, you can also see how you, as a researcher, can use and adapt them, framing yourself as a feminist or as a rural girl, or both, as necessary.

By working with fiction, memories, and photos in relation to visual research methods, I argue that drawing on the methods explored in this chapter will contribute to increased awareness about researcher positionality and reflexivity as it has done for me. We need to understand that identity is never singular and that one's performance of different identities affects one's research and the knowledge one produces.

> You forget, you move on, but you never forget, you never truly leave.
> – Elin Olofsson (2014, p. 44)

NOTE

1 This novel is written in Swedish and has not been translated into English. The conversations between the characters in the novel are written in dialect typical of the northern regions of Sweden. I offer my own translation as necessary.

REFERENCES

Acker, J., Barry, K., & Esseveld, J. (1996). Objectivity and truth: Problems in doing feminist research. In H. Gottfried (Ed.), *Feminism and social change: Bridging theory and practice* (pp. 60–87). University of Illinois Press.

Andersson, K. (2007). *Omsorg under förhandling: Om tid behov och kön i en föränderlig hemtjänstverksamhet* [Negotiating care: About time, needs and gender in a changing home care]. [Doctoral dissertation, Umeå Universitet]. http://www.diva-portal.org/smash/get/diva2:140010/FULLTEXT01.pdf

Bosworth, G., & Somerville, P. (2014). *Interpreting rurality: Multidisciplinary approaches.* Routledge.

Burns, M. (2003). Interviewing: Embodied communication. *Feminism & Psychology, 13*(2), 229–36. https://doi.org/10.1177/0959353503013002006

Butler, J. (1993). *Bodies that matter: On the discursive limits of "sex."* Routledge.

Cloke, P. (2006). Conceptualizing rurality. In P. Cloke, T. Marsden, & P. Mooney (Eds.), *Handbook of rural studies* (pp. 18–28). Sage.

Cook, J., & Cuervo, H. (2020). Staying, leaving and returning: Rurality and the development of reflexivity and motility. *Current Sociology, 68*(1), 60–76. https://doi.org/10.1177/0011392118756473

Cuervo, H. (2015). Rethinking social exclusion and young people in rural places: Toward a spatial and relational approach in youth and education studies. In N. Worth & C. Dwyer (Eds.), *Handbook of geographies of children and young people: Identities and subjectivities* (pp. 333–50). Springer.

Enloe, C. (2004). *The curious feminist: Searching for women in a new age of empire.* University of California Press.

Eriksson, M. (2008). (Re)producing a "peripheral" region: Northern Sweden in the news. *Geografiska Annaler, Series B, Human Geography, 90*(4), 369–88. https://doi.org/10.1111/j.1468-0467.2008.00299.x

Eriksson, M. (2010). "People in Stockholm are smarter than countryside folks": Reproducing urban and rural imaginaries in film and life. *Journal of Rural Studies, 26*(2), 95–104. https://doi.org/10.1016/j.jrurstud.2009.09.005

Fahlgren, S. (2005). The art of living – or the order of the living room sofa. *NORA – Nordic Journal of Feminist and Gender Research, 13*(1), 59–66. https://doi.org/10.1080/08038740510030443

Fahlgren, S., Giritli Nygren, K., Granberg, M., Johansson A., & Söderberg, E. (2015). Having your cake and eating it? The "Painful Cake" incident of 2012 examined. *Konsthistorisk tidskrift/Journal of Art History, 84*(1), 55–70. https://doi.org/10.1080/00233609.2014.981206

Falconer Al-Hindi, K., & Kawabata, H. (2002). Toward a more fully reflexive feminist geography. In P. Moss (Ed.), *Feminist geography in practice: Research and methods* (pp. 103–16). Wiley-Blackwell

Farrugia, D. (2016). The mobility imperative for rural youth: The structural, symbolic and non-representational dimensions rural youth mobilities. *Journal of Youth Studies, 19*(6), 836–51. https://doi.org/10.1080/13676261.2015.1112886

Forsberg Kankkunen, T. (2006). *Könade verksamheter: En studie av hur stressande arbetssituationer för kommunala enhetschefer hanteras inom tekniska respektive omsorgs- och utbildningsförvaltningar* [Gendered work: A study of how stressful work situations for municipal unit managers are handled within technical, care, and education administrations, respectively]. Arbetslivsinstitutet, förlagstjänst.

Giritli Nygren, K., & Nyhlén, S. (2017). Mapping the ruling relations of work in rural eldercare intersections of gender, digitalization and the centre-periphery divide. *Journal of Rural Studies, 54*, 337–43. https://doi.org/10.1016/j.jrurstud.2017.07.002

Hannerz, U., & Löfgren, O. (1994). The nation in the global village. *Cultural Studies, 18*(2), 198–207. https://doi.org/10.1080/09502389400490391

Harding, S. (1986). *The science question in feminism.* Open University Press.

Haug, F. (1987). *Female sexualization: A collective work of memory.* Verso.

Howie, G., & Tauchert, A. (Eds.). (2002). *Gender, teaching, and research in higher education: Challenges for the 21st century.* Ashgate.

Jaggar, A.M. (Ed.). (2008). *Just methods: An interdisciplinary feminist reader.* Paradigm Publishers.

Jansson, D.R. (2005). "A geography of racism": Internal orientalism and the construction of American national identity in the film *Mississippi Burning. National Identities, 7*(3), 265–85. https://doi.org/10.1080/14608940500201797

Jansson, M., Wendt, M., & Åse, C. (2009). Teaching political science through memory work. *Journal of Political Science Education, 5*(3), 179–97. https://doi.org/10.1080/15512160903035716

Keränen, M. (1993). *Modern political science and gender: A debate between the deaf and the mute.* University of Jyväskylä.

Little, J., & Panelli, R. (2003). Gender research in rural geography. *Gender, Place and Culture: A Journal of Feminist Geography, 10*(3), 281–9. https://doi.org/10.1080/0966369032000114046

Little, J., & Panelli, R. (2007). "Outback" romance? A reading of nature and heterosexuality in rural Australia. *Sociologia Ruralis, 47*(3), 173–88. https://doi.org/10.1111/j.1467-9523.2007.00434.x

Lohan, M. (2000). Extending feminist methodologies: Researching masculinities and technologies. In A. Byrne & R. Lentin (Eds.), *Feminist research methods in the social sciences in Ireland* (pp. 167–87). Institute of Public Administration.

Lykke, N. (2014). Passionate disidentifications as an intersectional writing strategy. In N. Lykke (Ed.), *Writing academic texts differently: Intersectional feminist methodologies and the playful art of writing* (pp. 30–47). Routledge.

McDowell, L. (1998). Elites in the city of London: Some methodological considerations. *Environment and Planning A: Economy and Space, 30*(12), 2133–46. https://doi.org/10.1068/a302133

Mitchell, C., & Pithouse-Morgan, K. (2014). Expanding the memory catalogue: Southern African women's contributions to memory-work writing as a feminist research methodology. *Agenda: Empowering Women for Gender Equity, 28*(1), 92–103. https://doi.org/10.1080/10130950.2014.883704

Nyhlén, S., & Giritli Nygren, K. (2019). "It's about gender equality and all that stuff …": Enacting gender-based violence policy into everyday preventive work in rural Sweden. *Journal of Gender-Based Violence, 3*(3), 355–71. https://doi.org/10.1332/239868019X15627570242841

Nyhlén, S., Giritli Nygren, K., Olofsson, A., & Bergström, J. (2018). Human security, risk and sustainability in the Swedish policy for the Arctic. In K. Hossain, J. Miguel, R. Martin, & A. Petrétei (Eds.), *Human and societal security in the circumpolar Arctic* (pp. 76–99). Brill Academic Publishers.

Öhman, A. (Ed.). (2001). *"Rötter och rutter": Norrland och den kulturella identiteten* ["Roots and routes": Norrland and the cultural identity]. Umeå Universitet.

Olofsson, E. (2014). *Till flickorna i sjön* [To the girls in the lake]. Wahlström & Widstrand.

Onyx, J., & Small, J. (2001). Memory-work: The method. *Qualitative Inquiry,* *7*(6), 773–86. https://doi.org/10.1177/107780040100700608

Panelli, R., Hubbard, P., Coombes, B., & Suchet-Pearson, S. (2009). De-centring white ruralities: Ethnic diversity, racialisation and Indigenous countrysides. *Journal of Rural Studies, 25*(4), 355–64. https://doi.org/10.1016/j.jrurstud .2009.05.002

Peters, M.A., & Burbules, N.C. (2004). *Poststructuralism and educational research.* Rowman & Littlefield.

Pini, B. (2004). On being a nice country girl and an academic feminist: Using reflexivity in rural social research. *Journal of Rural Studies, 20*(2), 169–79. https://doi.org/10.1016/j.jrurstud.2003.08.003

Pred, A. (2000). *Even in Sweden: Racism, racialized spaces, and the popular geographical imagination.* University of California Press.

Scott, J.W. (1991). The evidence of experience. *Critical Enquiry, 17*(4), 773–97. https://doi.org/10.1086/448612

Skott, S., Giritli Nygren, K., & Nyhlén., S. (2021). In the shadow of the monster: Gothic narratives of violence prevention. *Critical Criminology, 29,* 385–400. https://doi.org/10.1007/s10612-020-09529-x

Stanley, L., & Wise, S. (1990). Method, methodology and epistemology in feminist research processes. In L. Stanley (Ed.), *Feminist praxis: Research, theory and epistemology in feminist sociology* (pp. 20–60). Routledge.

Stenbacka, S. (2011). Othering the rural: About the construction of rural masculinities and the unspoken urban hegemonic ideal in Swedish media. *Journal of Rural Studies, 27*(3), 235–44. https://doi.org/10.1016 /j.jrurstud.2011.05.006

Waldby, C. (1995). Feminism and method. In B. Caine & R. Pringle (Eds.), *Transitions: New Australian feminisms* (pp. 15–28). Routledge.

Weedon, C. (1987). *Feminist practice and poststructuralist theory.* Blackwell.

Westholm, E. (2003). *Leaving rurality behind: Re-orientation of spatial policies in Sweden.* Arbetsrapport 2003:12. Institutet för Framtidsstudier. https://www .iffs.se/media/1095/20051201133910filp36o5SUA2825XsyxOu14.pdf

Widerberg, K. (1995). *Kunskapens kön* [The gender of knowledge]. Norstedts förlag AB.

Williamson, J.W. (1995). *Hillbillyland: What the movies did to the mountains and what the mountains did to the movies.* University of North Carolina Press.

Woods, M. (2010). Performing rurality and practicing rural geography. *Progress in Human Geography, 34*(6), 835–46. https://doi.org/10.1177 /0309132509357356

PART THREE

Positionality and the Rural

9 "Hey, Mlungu!": Positionality in Participatory Visual Research in Post-Apartheid South Africa

LISA WIEBESIEK AND ASTRID TREFFRY-GOATLEY

Introduction

As we began to write this chapter as a pair of white South African women who have worked for several years in rural contexts in South Africa, we shared stories of our research experiences, including Lisa's story quoted below:

> In 2012, I was working on a project evaluating an intervention in a deep rural school district in the Eastern Cape province of South Africa. On my first day, there was a great commotion as my colleague and I walked through the school towards the administration block to announce our arrival, with chairs scraping, the sound of laughter, and little faces pressed up against classroom windows. Initially, I thought that it was the sight of two strangers walking through the school in the middle of the school day that had caused such a reaction, and that may well have been part of it. However, with the cries of "Hey, Mlungu!" (white person), I became aware that it was not just that my colleague and I were strangers that prompted the children's reaction to us, but my being white. I had never felt so noticed and visible before, certainly never because of the colour of my skin. Over the next two or so years working regularly in that district, I got used to being called or referred to as Mlungu by project participants, having strangers call out the term sometimes more as an observation than a greeting as I walked or drove past, and younger children coming up to me wanting to touch my skin and hair. Of course, language was another issue. I am a first-language speaker of English and spoke no isiXhosa, the local African language, at all when I started working on the project. People had different reactions to me: some individuals (usually older people, especially men) would politely dismiss me with an "Ewe (yes), Mlungu," even after I'd learned some isiXhosa and was able to make polite conversation;

others would treat me with a deference that I had not earned and did not deserve. I got used to being an outsider in this environment. Importantly, however, I experienced my outsiderness as gentle rather than the violent discriminatory othering Black South Africans experienced under colonial rule, during apartheid, and continue to experience. This experience was humbling, and this humbling was important and necessary for me as a person and as a researcher. (Lisa, personal reflection, 2018)

American feminist scholar and anti-racism activist Peggy McIntosh (see, for example, McIntosh, 1988, 1989) has argued that part of white privilege is that our race is normalized and is something white people rarely have to think about – which is true for us as white South Africans. Part of our racial privilege is that, in the urban areas in which we spend most of our time, we seldom have to think about race or the racialized power dynamics that persist in this country. Further, in a country with eleven official languages, as first-language speakers of English, we can participate in all aspects of life in the urban areas in which we reside without having to consider using another language. Yet, having worked as researchers in rural contexts in South Africa for a number of years, we have become used to hearing calls of "Hey, Mlungu!," or variations thereof, as we move through communities largely populated by Black South Africans.[1] As a greeting or an observation uttered by young and old alike, this isiXhosa and isiZulu term for a white person is generally considered innocuous by both parties. In these contexts, this friendly acknowledgment of obvious visible difference between ourselves and the communities with whom we work belies the significance of race as a marker of our identities in South Africa, where our whiteness encodes and symbolizes a history of violent racial oppression under colonial and apartheid rule, and persistent inequity and privilege. It was only when we entered what we might think of as the rural field that, for the first time in our lives, our race became our most important identity marker and the marker of difference from people with whom we wished to connect.

Closely linked in terms of privilege and access to information, services, and upward social mobility, race and language remain contentious issues in South Africa (McKinney, 2013). Astrid studied isiZulu at school and university, and yet, even if she were to learn to speak it with native-like fluency, her race would always mark her as an outsider in certain contexts. Being positioned in this way ensures that we will always be outsiders in the rural communities in which we work. This position is a small-scale flipping of the colonial and apartheid scripts, which worked hard to constitute Black South Africans as the other in their own land, scripts that were taken up by both white and Black South Africans.

In the rural context where our research is located, racialized power dynamics, including those involving language, are particularly salient since our whiteness and access to English remain symbolic of the country's history of racial oppression and inequity. Given apartheid-era legislation, including the Natives (Urban Areas) Act (No. 21 of 1923), the Group Areas Act (No. 41 of 1950), the Promotion of Bantu Self-Government Act (No. 46 of 1959), and the Bantu Homelands Citizenship Act (No. 26 of 1970), rural areas in South Africa are still largely populated by Black South Africans.[2] These pieces of legislation were intended to ensure a physical segregation of the apartheid-defined racial and ethnic groups in terms of living areas, limit the access of Black South Africans to areas designated for whites only, and ensure that the vast majority of the country's resources were reserved only for whites. The under-resourcing and underdevelopment of rural areas has endured in post-apartheid South Africa. These communities often lack basic services and resources, have poor infrastructure, and few opportunities for employment.

Focusing particularly on race and language, in this chapter we use three case studies to explore how our positionality affects our research and influences the research relationships we cultivate with our participants and their communities. More specifically, in light of our position as white, English-speaking outsiders from privileged urban backgrounds, we reflect on whether we should engage in this work or leave it for other researchers with different pasts and presents, and different subject positions. Developing the idea of being allies, we argue that, while acknowledging and being mindful of our positionality and power relations is a necessary component of ethical participatory research, our subject positions do not disqualify us from doing good research that can make a valuable contribution to social change and scholarship. We suggest that this chapter will be most relevant to other researchers involved in similar work who are crossing racial, linguistic, cultural, or national boundaries.

A Picture of Our Research: Using Participatory Visual Methodologies

With the qualitative turn in social science research, scholars increasingly recognize knowledge to be situated and subjective, and view the positivist ideal of fully impartial, objective research as both unattainable and undesirable. In this context, a more interpretive style of research, with partial accounts of social phenomena located in particular social and historical contexts, is gaining traction. In addition, scholars are cultivating alternative ways of doing research using approaches that not only allow us to acknowledge our role in the research process but actually require this acknowledgment. Proponents of feminist research (see, for example, Hesse-Biber & Yaiser, 2004; Ramazanoglu & Holland, 2002) and community-based participatory research (CBPR; Chambers, 1994; Collins et al., 2018; Cornwall & Jewkes, 1995; Mitchell & Sommer, 2016) have been at the forefront of these changes and call on us as researchers to acknowledge who we are in the research process, particularly with regard to the relationships that we form with people and communities in the field. This approach requires us to go beyond simply listing the differences and similarities between ourselves and our co-researcher participants (hereafter referred to as participants). It requires us to be reflexive about our past, our presents, and our identities, and it requires us to be aware of the assumptions we bring to our research relationships and to the research process, and the power dynamics inherent in these. England (1994) has argued: "We need to locate ourselves in our work and to reflect on how our location influences the questions we ask, how we conduct our research, and how we write our research" (p. 251). One such research methodology in which reflecting on researcher positionality is key is participatory visual methodology (PVM).

Our work is located within an ongoing, transnational interdisciplinary project that uses PVM to work with Indigenous girls in Canada and girls from rural areas in South Africa to address sexual violence in their communities. Since our research is located in the interdisciplinary field of girlhood studies, we employ PVM to drive a process of research and development that is *"about* girls, *with* girls and ... led *by* girls" (Mitchell & Reid-Walsh, 2008, emphases in original). PVM includes a variety of visual methods such as drawing, photo voice, participatory video, and digital storytelling. These alternative channels of communication are particularly useful in resource-poor settings. England (1994) has pointed out that "shifting a lot of power over to the research*ed*" can help to address "asymmetrical and potentially exploitative power relations" (p. 243, emphasis in original) that arise in research settings, particularly with marginalized people. We argue that PVM provides the opportunity to do this power shifting. In addition, visual media can help us to hear, as it were, marginalized voices that articulate information that may otherwise have been difficult to share because of illiteracy, language barriers, or topic sensitivity (Gubrium et al., 2016; Mitchell & Sommer, 2016).

We are members of a research team that is working with girls and young women in two rural South African communities. Our research team is comprised of the principal investigator (PI), a Black woman who is a professor fluent in isiZulu; a Black South African man who is a research assistant and a native speaker of isiZulu; our community partner in one of our research sites, a social worker who is a Black South African woman and a native speaker of isiZulu; and the two of us. Lisa is the project coordinator, while Astrid, until recently, was the project's postdoctoral research fellow but is now a research fellow. Each of us plays an important role in the team. However, while as researchers we are all outsiders by virtue of not being members of the communities in which we work, as white English-speakers, our outsider status is immediately obvious while our colleagues' status as outsiders is not. Further, as the rest of the research team share both race and language with our participants and their communities, the figurative distance between them and our participants (mediated also by age, geographic location, and where we work) is not as great. We suggest that, although we can never be insiders in these communities, we can be allies in efforts to address issues and stimulate social change.

Both research sites are located near the Drakensburg Mountains in KwaZulu-Natal, South Africa. Khethani is a rural township situated on the outskirts of Winterton, a small farming town. Established in the 1990s, this relatively young community is characterized by high levels of unemployment, substance abuse, and food insecurity. The second site, Loskop, is a deeply rural area governed by the Amangwe Traditional Authority. Traditional cultural norms, practices, and values are widespread in the area. Loskop is also characterized by high rates of unemployment, poverty, and food insecurity. We have worked in Loskop and Khethani since 2016, when we recruited a group of girls in each site. The group in Loskop named themselves the Social Ills Fighters (SIFs); the group in Khethani called themselves the Leaders for Young Women's Success (L4YWS). Over the years, we have had several PVM workshops with the members of the SIFs and the L4YWS. In these workshops, we have created a number of visual products including cellphilms, digital stories, participatory asset maps, photo voice posters, and drawings. Through our work, the SIFs have focused on the practice of forced and early marriage that they experience as violence. In Khethani, the focus has been on two issues – intimate partner violence (IPV) and homophobia and transphobia.

Our Theoretical Lens: Positionality, Reflexivity, and Power

When scholars engage marginal populations in CBPR, positionality, reflexivity, and power are of fundamental significance. These issues need to be addressed if ethical and meaningful research is to be conducted

(Collins et al., 2018; England, 1994; Katz, 1994; Muhammed et al., 2015; Nagar, 2002; Sultana, 2007). By positionality, we refer to the identities that are both ascribed to us by society and those that are achieved; these include race, ethnicity, gender, economic status, and education (Holmes, 2020; Muhammed et al., 2015; Oetzel, 2009). We acknowledge that research happens in shared, dynamic spaces that are influenced by the positionalities of both the researcher and the researched; these are spaces that are "mediated by personal life experiences, motivations and connections" (Muhammed et al., 2015, p. 1052). While we recognize the importance of positionality, we are also aware of the potential risk of essentializing ourselves or our participants with meanings assigned to "pre-defined social categories." Many of these categories are not only essentialist but are also seen to exist "prior to and isolated from specific interactions, rather than as created, enacted, transformed in and through those interactions" (Nagar & Geiger, 2000, as cited in Nagar, 2002, p. 183). Consequently, when we are thinking, writing, and talking about positionality, we attempt to go beyond listing details about ourselves to try, in a particular moment in time, to situate ourselves in dynamic relation to our work with participants.

Although it is often misunderstood as "mere navel gazing," and even "narcissistic and egoistic" (England, 1994, p. 244), we understand reflexivity, like Soedirgo and Glas (2020), as the practice of "engaging in the dynamic, continual, and fluid practice of interrogating our own assumptions of positionality, how positionality is being read by others, and the impact of these assessments throughout the research process" (p. 3). Importantly, we understand reflexivity as going beyond self-criticism to include a critical engagement with our knowledge, our understanding of and relationship with the context in which we work, and the ways in which we understand our actions and decisions throughout the research process (Wint, 2011). We view this understanding as critical to the conduct of fieldwork, not only because it induces self-discovery and can lead to insights and new hypotheses about research questions but also because it can make us more aware of our shifting positionalities and those of our participants, and of the power relations between ourselves as researchers and our participants. In our writing, we aim to transgress the norms of transparent reflexivity by moving beyond the ideal of a "transparently knowable self," which is "separate from its transparently knowable context" (Rose, 1997, p. 314). We do this by acknowledging the messiness of research and by recognizing that, as researchers, we are tangled in the research process in multiple ways. Moreover, rather than trying to understand or tidy up this messiness, we embrace research as a "process of constitutive negotiation"

(p. 316) and provide examples of how these negotiations played out in our research experiences and what we learned in the process.

Rose (1997) has reminded us that the crucial goal "of situating academic knowledge is to produce non-overgeneralizing knowledges that learn from other kinds of knowledges" and that we need to think beyond the "polarities of fusion or distance offered by transparent reflexivity to consider the possibilities of other sorts of reflexive research practice" (p. 315). For example, Smith (1996) has argued that it is the uncertainties and not the revelations of reflexivity that should be written into research and that differences, tensions, and conflicts ought to be explored in writing, "not as problems, but as spaces of conceptual and indeed political opportunities and negotiations" (p. 165). Following this argument, it is imperative to situate ourselves less in terms of surveying positions in a landscape of power and more in terms of a view of power as punctured by gaps precariously bridged. The authority of academic knowledge is called into question not by self-conscious positioning but by gaps that give space to, and are affected by, other knowledges. What this idea means for our research in general, and this chapter in particular, is that we actively attempt to recognize these gaps and seek and value other knowledges.

Power is a key concern for feminist researchers, with many showing acute sensitivity to the intersection of power with academic knowledge (Pillow, 2003) and to their positions of privilege in relation to the participants with whom they engage. Kobayashi (2003) has argued that all academic women are privileged to some degree, since they have "access to the middle-class luxuries, such as education and professional status, that are still relatively inaccessible for most women of all backgrounds" (p. 76). Gilbert (1994) has also commented on "the fact that [she has] the final power of interpretation" (p. 94) at the conclusion of any piece of research, and for McLafferty (1995), it is the interpretive act that is the key site of academic power. These privileges can be seen to separate feminist researchers from the participants with whom we work, particularly when we are engaging across economic and geographic boundaries. Staeheli and Lawson (1994) make this latter argument in the context of research in the so-called Third World, since Western researchers are in a position of power by virtue of their ability to name the categories, control information about the research agenda, define interventions, and come and go as research scientists. This analysis of academic power has been summarized by McDowell (1992) in her remark that "there are real dangers that are inherent in our own position within the powerful institutions of knowledge production" (p. 413). McDowell's use of the term "position" is key here, since many feminists have elaborated their own role in the complex relations of power by exploring their position. Yet, as Spivak (1988) observed, "making positions transparent does not make them unproblematic" (p. 6). Certainly, we cannot argue that our position as white, English-speaking academics from urban areas doing research with girls and young women in rural areas is unproblematic.

In this chapter, we attempt to engage reflexively with our positionality and to show how we have come to understand and have endeavoured to locate ourselves in our work with communities as allies. Being an ally, Kendall (2006) suggested, involves using one's "privilege, power and access to influence and resources to change the systems that keep people ... oppressed" (p. 148). Being an ally also means that we must be willing to make mistakes, be uncomfortable, and confront our own privileges (without necessarily being able to shed them at will; Aveling, 2013). As allies, we "become comfortable with the uncomfortable and uncomfortable with the too comfortable" (Kendall, 2006, p. 153). We are at times positioned as more powerful than our participants, obliging us to ensure that we do not intentionally or unintentionally exploit this power. At other times, we are positioned as less powerful, at which time we must be mindful of this status and step back. We attempt to do this even as we are aware that the messiness of research and the uncertain, shifting nature of positionality and identities will result in it being only a partial and situated account of our experiences.

Who Are We in the Picture? Three Case Studies of Research in Rural South Africa

We present three case studies through which we reflect on our positionality and the power relations that often impact our research in unintended and unanticipated ways. We reflect particularly on race and language as two of the most salient markers of our identity and markers of difference from the people with whom we work. Through these case studies, we explore our location as allies and illustrate the complex and ever-shifting nature of positionality in relationship with the research context and our research participants.

Case Study One: Putting White Privilege into the Picture

We began recruitment in Khethani in mid-2016. We invited girls who were interested in working on a project with the university about girls' safety in their community to a meeting during a lunch break at the school. About twenty learners came to the meeting. We explained the project, what the girls' participation would entail, and went through the consent form carefully. We stressed that participation in the project was entirely voluntary and that no one should feel obliged to participate. When we invited questions, one of the girls asked if only girls were allowed to participate in the project. She explained that, although Z was a boy, he spent all his time with the girls. She further explained that they would not be comfortable being in the project if Z was not included. Of course, the PI agreed, and Z is now one of the most active and dedicated members of the L4YWS.

When we first met him, Z identified as gay. Even then, for us to say that he was brave to be out living openly in a conservative rural community like Khethani was an understatement. On the last day of our first PVM workshop with the L4YWS, we encouraged them to come dressed up so that we could take photographs of them, which we would print (using our portable photograph printer) for them to keep. Z arrived in a short skirt and high heels, with a scarf wrapped around his head like long hair. He had walked through the community dressed this way to get to our workshop. We suspected then that he might be transgender but did not address his sexuality or gender identity with him directly until he reached out to us about some difficulties that he was having with his family.

In response, Lisa went to visit Z in the community to connect him with an LGBT organization, which was well placed to offer him support. It was during this visit that Z told Lisa that she identified as trans and asked that we use feminine pronouns. A few days after this visit, Lisa phoned Z to check in. Z informed Lisa that things had got better at home and that she was feeling much happier. She explained that it was partly because she was now in touch with the LGBT organization but also because, when Lisa had dropped her off outside her home, her family and neighbours had seen this white woman get out of the car to talk to Z and give her a hug goodbye. Z said that, because her family saw she was friends with a white person, who obviously accepts her the way she is, things had got better for her at home and in her community.

For us, this case study illustrates two important things about positionality and power. The first is that, in spite of the power that we could be seen to hold in our interaction with potential participants because of aspects of our identities including race, age, geographic location, and where we work, the girls also positioned themselves as powerful and exercised that power when they made it clear they would participate in the project only if Z were included. The second relates to Z's situation at home improving after her family became aware of her friendship with Lisa. While the latter's immediate reaction was relief, she also felt uncomfortable. Indeed, this situation was a reminder that ignorance about racial power dynamics is the privilege of white people in South Africa (McIntosh, 1989). As a result of the unequal racial power relations that persist in South Africa where whiteness has, in many circumstances, greater social capital, a favourable outcome had been achieved for Z. Lisa had not set out to deploy her whiteness and the social capital associated with it in this way. Perhaps it was naïve of her not to realize that it might happen. This situation was a deeply humbling experience for Lisa and reminded her to remain aware of the broader racialized power dynamics within which our research interactions take place.

Case Study Two: Knowing Our Place in the Picture

From our very first PVM workshop with the SIFs in early 2017, it was apparent that their main concern in relation to gender-based violence (GBV) was early and forced marriages in their community. Since then, this issue has gained increasing prominence in their visual work, including their cellphilms and digital stories (see Treffry-Goatley et al., 2018; Treffry-Goatley et al., 2017; Treffry-Goatley et al., 2016; Wiebesiek & Treffry-Goatley, 2017). This issue remains a real threat for our participants, with four of the SIFs having been personally affected by early or forced marriage in the past fourteen months since the time of writing.

In response to this development, in collaboration with our community partner, we called an urgent meeting with a representative from the South African Police Service (SAPS) and a counsellor from LifeLine[3] stationed at the local police station to devise strategies to address this issue. At the meeting, it was agreed that we would hold a stakeholders' meeting, ostensibly to provide feedback on the outcomes of our research. It was also decided that the invitations to this meeting would be issued by the research team, specifically our male isiZulu-speaking research assistant. In response to the invitation, the iNkosi (the traditional leader), the iziNduna (headmen), and representatives from SAPS, the local Department of Co-operative Governance and Traditional Affairs (COGTA), the Department of Health (DoH), the Department of Social Development (DSD), the ward councillor, and the principal of the high school that the SIFs attended agreed to meet at the Traditional Court building in February 2019.

The research team decided that the PI would be the only member of the research team to speak during the meeting and that the two of us would remain in the background. Initially defensive, the iNkosi came around as the school principal, the ward councillor, our community partner, and a representative from the DoH all gave evidence about the practice of forced and early marriage and spoke out against it. The outcome of the meeting was that the iNkosi suggested a second meeting during which all the stakeholders could strategize about how to address this issue. At this meeting, which took place in March 2019, we were asked to assist with the development of a protocol against forced and early marriage. In April 2019, we held a community dialogue on forced and early marriage attended by the iNkosi. This meeting was followed by another stakeholders' meeting in July 2019 during which we shared the draft protocol with the traditional leadership, members of the community, and representatives from SAPS, Legal Aid, COGTA, the DoH, and the DSD.

We view research as a dialogic experience that occurs in a shared, dynamic space and is mediated by shifting power dynamics, personal life experiences, motivations, and connections. For example, when we entered the community and asked the SIFs in what way(s) they felt unsafe, neither the research team nor our community partner knew the extent of the early and forced marriage practices in this context. In this situation, the girls held more power in terms of community knowledge. Our knowledge, in this case, of what the theory and research literature say about GBV was less valuable at this juncture in the research. This case illustrates how we engaged the girls as knowers of their own realities and with an "unequivocal acceptance that the knowledge of the person being researched (at least regarding the particular questions being asked) is greater than that of the researcher" (England, 1994, p. 243).

Power dynamics changed, however, when we began to engage with decision-makers and policymakers in the community. In this rural context, girls are positioned as children, and given the deeply patriarchal norms operating in this community, it was unlikely that their voices would be welcome in traditional community forums where these issues could be addressed. Therefore, it was at this point that power shifted back to the adults, the holders of a different kind of social capital and knowledge. We, as adult members of the research team, made the decision that the girls should not be present at the stakeholders' meetings to avoid compromising their safety and well-being. But, what of us as white, English-speaking members of the team? In this account, we argue that it was not our place to be actively involved in this critical project activity. As white, English-speaking women from the university, we had little to no power in this forum. Our research assistant liaised with the traditional leadership, the decision-making structure in this rural community. This choice was strategic since he is male and isiZulu-speaking, and therefore has more cultural capital. The PI, a Black African professor from the university and a fluent isiZulu speaker, as described above, presented the findings of our work. There is no way in which we can make claim to any form of insider status in this situation. As allies in this space, the research team made the decision that the two of us would be present as observers and supporters, rather than take an active role in the proceedings.

Nevertheless, we wonder if our outsider status as a research team might have allowed the girls to bring up this issue in the first place. As our findings suggest, the violence they experience in the form of forced and early marriage is often perpetrated by their own families and community members. Who could they then turn to in their community who would have taken them seriously and raised the issue with them? We are outside the politics and power dynamics of the community and are therefore more able to avoid becoming entangled in them and can offer a different framing, for example, in terms of human rights. As Vanner (2015) observes, "although [our] social position is a detriment to this research in some ways, [we] can use [our] position to leverage less powerful voices to speak back to the powerful" (p. 3). In this case, we harnessed the position of the research team to leverage the voices of the SIFs in speaking back to the powerful adults in their community. But this outcome was achieved because we are part of a research team, which includes a Black African professor, a Black African male, and importantly, our community partner, who has networks and influence in the community. Indeed, as two white women on our own, it is unlikely that we would be able to work with the traditional authority. This case illustrates how positionality matters in research and how power dynamics, hierarchies, and identities are constantly shifting.

Case Study Three: Interpreting the Picture – Language Matters

In April 2017, we travelled to Loskop to run a PVM workshop with the SIFs. Our objective was to use cellphilm making to explore what GBV looks like in this community. Cellphilming is a method that involves participants' use of cellphones or tablet computers to create short films (Dockney & Tomaselli, 2009). As Mandrona (2016) has explained, cellphilms aim to bring alternative experiences and perspectives to the fore through the production and dissemination of short videos, usually on a particular topic or in response to a prompt. They involve participants in planning, performing, and recording productions that address the aspect of the issue being investigated. In this account, we reflect on facilitating this workshop with our Zulu-speaking participants without an isiZulu-speaking member of the research team present.

Although we are both well experienced in these methods, we were immediately concerned when we learned that none of our isiZulu-speaking colleagues were available to assist with facilitation and that the workshop could not be postponed.[4] As mentioned above, Astrid studied isiZulu at high school and university, and speaks the language relatively well. Yet running a workshop for first-language isiZulu speakers without the help of an interpreter was a bit daunting. We were concerned that the girls might not understand us or we them. We were also concerned that, should an issue arise or serve as a trigger for any of the girls, neither of us would be able to debrief them adequately nor get them access to the support they needed.[5] We decided against bringing a stranger in to interpret for us, given the sensitive nature of the subject matter.

In the end, the workshop went smoothly, and the girls used their cellphilms to delve deeply into the issue of GBV in their community. We ran the workshop in a mixture of isiZulu, English, and "Zunglish" (a mixture of isiZulu and English), and, in general, communication was not a problem until we got to the discussion on the last day after the screening of the cellphilms and digital stories. Indeed, there were times during the discussion when we both felt quite lost, and we were unable to ask the participants for further explanations and translations without relying on the girls who were most confident in using English. Over the course of the project, we have continued to grapple with language issues, and it is something that neither of us feels very comfortable about.

The language issue in South Africa is pertinent, especially since it is closely linked with race (see, for example, Alexander, 2012; McKinney, 2013; Ntombela, 2016). This issue is one that cannot be glossed over when doing research with communities because, as Parmegiani (2012) has observed, "language is not a politically neutral medium of communication, but a social practice that determines power relations and shapes subjectivity" (p. 74; see also Kaiper, 2018; Kamwangamalu & Tovares, 2016; Mesthrie, 2021). We have, as a research team, come back to this issue again and again. Whenever possible, there is an isiZulu speaker with us to interpret and translate, and we always remind the girls that they can speak, write, or perform in whichever language they prefer. This position reflects the importance we place on the girls being able to express themselves in the language in which they feel most comfortable.

The language issue came up again at the end of 2017 during our annual focus group discussions (FGDs), which form part of our project evaluation. In these FGDs, we reflect with the girls on the past year, solicit their feedback on the project, and discuss plans for the future. As part of their feedback on the project, the girls explained that they would prefer to speak English with the research team, since they wanted to have the opportunity to practise speaking the language. They explained that it is an opportunity they do not often get, even at school with teachers, living as they do in a community of isiZulu speakers. In this way, the girls viewed us as a resource, helping them to achieve greater fluency in a language that remains important in their schooling as the language of learning and teaching, and beyond. As allies, we were able to provide an opportunity to our participants that they would not otherwise have had. In this way, they derived benefit from the research relationship.

Nevertheless, we are aware that, when we are writing about our experiences of engaging in this kind of research, it is tempting to become defensive, to highlight all the times it worked out well for us despite our outsider status as white women from urban areas working at the university. But that would be disingenuous and counter-productive because, while being English-speaking facilitators may have some benefits, not being fluent in the language of the participants is a disadvantage in many ways. If all the interactions between the research team and the girls were in isiZulu, the language in which all the girls feel more comfortable expressing themselves, we might obtain more nuanced data about the phenomenon under study. It is also a concern that meanings, particularly subtle ones, may be lost in translation. Another difficulty is that, in this dynamic, we have not done anything to disrupt the hegemony of English and have worked instead within these broader social power dynamics to help our participants achieve a positive outcome. This result is problematic because, in failing to challenge the hegemony of English in South Africa, we contribute to its perpetuation.

Researcher Positionality in Participatory Visual Research: Discussion

In this chapter, we selected the case studies because they offer a window into the messiness of research and illustrate how the positions and identities of the researcher and researched shift in an interactive and mutually transformative process (England, 1994). Writing about positionality is not an easy task. The research experiences that we discuss above and others have made us question whether we can do sound, ethical research in this context or whether we should rather leave it to other researchers with different pasts and presents, and different subject positions. Certainly, there are arguments in the literature that it is not the place of white researchers to "conduct research within Indigenous contexts," since our way of "being, knowing and doing emanate from a position of white privilege" (Aveling, 2013, p. 203) and are historically and culturally specific. While these concerns about (mis)representation and (in)authenticity are important to consider, they can lead to what Sultana (2007) has called a "withdrawal from fieldwork in the Global South, [since] fewer scholars are engaged in research that can be politically and materially useful for the poor in the Global South" (p. 375). Nagar (2002) has criticized this "impasse" (p.180) and has argued that "feminist social scientists located in the western or northern academy cannot choose to remain silent on marginalized women's struggles concerning sensitive issues such as domestic violence in the so-called Third World simply because there is a messy politics of power and representation involved in the fieldwork encounter" (p. 181). Rather, scholars should accept the challenge of figuring out how to engage productively with, and participate in, mutually beneficial knowledge production about those struggles. We are also encouraged by bell hooks (2003), who has maintained that, in situations of difference and inequality, "the will to form a conscious, cooperative partnership that is rooted in mutuality" is a principle of key importance. In addition, "striving to be mutual is the principle that best mediates situations where there is unequal status" (p. 63). Like hooks, we believe that, as allies, it is possible to have close, productive, meaningful relationships with people of different races even as we continue to live in societies divided by racism and characterized by persistent racialized inequality.

In the meantime, we cannot leave the work undone. Therefore, while we acknowledge our privilege in the racialized power dynamics in this post-apartheid context, we also know, as Applebaum (2010) has remarked in a different context, that this issue is not of our own individual making. Consequently, while we are ever conscious of our privileged positions, we choose not to be ashamed of our identities or our work. Again, we turn to hooks (2003), who contends that white people can and do choose to be anti-racist. "This does not mean that they do not listen and learn from critique, but rather that they understand fully that their choice to be anti-racist must be constant and sustained to give truth to the reality that racism can end" (p. 65). Therefore, we persevere with our work using PVM to try to create or facilitate safe spaces in which our participants can voice their concerns, be heard, and work towards social change. We are committed to social change to challenge unequal power structures and are willing to use our skills, knowledge, and social positions to advance these changes in partnership with the people who know most about these issues.

Conclusion

Through the accounts that we offer in this chapter of experiences of confronting and doing positionality, we are not seeking to offer examples of how we got it right. Instead, we seek to engage critically with the ways in which the power relations inherent in our work as academics impact our research. Writing about positionality is not an easy task, and questions that scholars need to address in these kinds of studies are often uncomfortable. Yet, as feminists who are committed to conducting ethical and meaningful CBPR, we have found that we need to embrace this sense of unease, and, following Kincheloe and Steinberg (2008), we have to approach our hurdles and discomforts as an integral part of being informed allies for the girls and young women outside of their local communities. In addition, because such research is so much about relationships between us and the people with whom we work, we must acknowledge as outsiders that we will not always be the most appropriate people to do the work. In order to do this work ethically and effectively, we must work in collaboration with insiders and be aware there will be times when we must take a step back. We also acknowledge that there will also be times when our outsiderness may be advantageous in the research context. In these cases, we must be willing to step forward and use our social position to foreground the voices of those who are positioned as less powerful, as Vanner (2015) has suggested. As noted in the introduction, we knew from the outset that our positionalities would be problematic and that we would always be outsiders. However, we endeavour to position ourselves in our work with communities as allies, all the time knowing that there is no perfect solution and that positionality is always contentious.

NOTES

1   Although problematic, in this chapter, we use the terms "Black South African" and "white South African," rather than, for example, "Black African," because, while these racial categories are socially engineered colonial and apartheid-era markers of racial identity, they continue to structure people socially, economically, and geographically. As McKinney (2013) has argued, "while race exists neither as a biological reality nor as an essentialist signifier of homogeneous experiences shared by social groups, it is pervasive in everyday discourse, as are its daily material effects" (p. 23).

2   The Natives (Urban Areas) Act designated urban areas in South Africa as white-only areas and required Black South Africans in urban areas to carry

permits or passes. The Group Areas Act was passed with the intention of eradicating integrated urban areas in South Africa in which different racial groups lived side by side. The act enabled the government to designate particular neighbourhoods as "group areas" in which only people of a particular apartheid-defined race group were legally allowed to reside. The groups were defined as "white, Black, Indian, and coloured." The effect of the law was to reserve the most developed, well-resourced areas for white South Africans. The Promotion of Bantu Self-Government Act established a number of so-called homelands or Bantustans. Far from the well-resourced urban centres occupied by white South Africans, the homeland areas were systematically and consistently under-resourced during the apartheid era. The Bantu Homelands Citizenship Act was a denaturalization law. Based on ethnicity often determined by language, through this act, Black South Africans become citizens of these self-governing homelands rather than citizens of South Africa.

3 LifeLine is a national non-profit organization that provides counselling services free of charge via face-to-face meetings and various hotlines.

4 Not all participants have access to a mobile phone, and those who do often share it with a family member. This situation can make communication challenging, and we have found that changing arrangements, particularly with short notice, is not a good idea. For example, when we have tried to postpone events in the past, a fair portion of the participants inevitably turned up and were rightfully upset when they waited for us in vain. Therefore, we try not to cancel events, and we travel, rather, to the research site regularly to communicate project updates to participants in person.

5 Fortunately, although she was not able to be at the workshop all the time, our community partner was able to drop by at least once every day. She shares a close relationship with the SIFs and could have provided them with any support they may have needed.

REFERENCES

Alexander, N. (2012). The centrality of the language question in the social sciences and humanities in post-apartheid South Africa: Revisiting a perennial issue. *South African Journal of Science, 108*(9/10), 1–7. https://doi.org/10.4102/sajs.v108i9/10.1443

Applebaum, B. (2010). *Being white, being good: White complicity, white moral responsibility, and social justice pedagogy*. Lexington Books.

Aveling, N. (2013). "Don't talk about what you don't know": On (not) conducting research with/in Indigenous contexts. *Critical Studies in Education, 54*(2), 203–14. https://doi.org/10.1080/17508487.2012.724021

Chambers, R. (1994). Participatory rural appraisal (PRA): Analysis of experience. *World Development*, 2(9), 1253–68. https://doi.org/10.1016/0305 -750X(94)90003-5

Collins, S.E., Clifasefi, S.L., Stanton, J., The LEAP Advisory Board, Straits, K.J.E., Gil-Kashiwabara, E., Rodriguez Espinosa, P., Nicasio, A.V., Andrasik, M.P., Hawes, S.M., Miller, K.A., Nelson, L.A., Orfaly, V.E., Duran, B.M., & Wallerstein, N. (2018). Community-based participatory research (CBPR): Towards equitable involvement of community in psychology research. *American Psychologist*, 73(7), 884–98. https://doi.org/10.1037/amp0000167

Cornwall, A., & Jewkes, R. (1995). What is participatory research? *Social Science & Medicine*, 41(12), 1667–76. https://doi.org/10.1016/0277-9536(95)00127-S

Dockney, J., & Tomaselli, K.G. (2009). Fit for the small(er) screen: Films, mobile TV and the new individual television experience. *Journal of African Cinema*, 1(1), 126–32.

England, V.L. (1994). Getting personal: Reflexivity, positionality, and feminist research. *Professional Geographer*, 46(1), 80–9. https://doi.org/10.1111/j.0033 -0124.1994.00080.x

Gilbert, M. (1994). The politics of location: Doing feminist research at "home." *Professional Geographer*, 46(1), 90–6. https://doi.org/10.1111/j.0033-0124 .1994.00090.x

Gubrium, A., Fiddian-Green, A., Jernigan K., & Krause, E. (2016). Bodies as evidence: Mapping new terrain for teenage pregnancy and parenting. *Global Public Health*, 11(5–6), 618–35. https://doi.org/10.1080/17441692.2016.1143522

Hesse-Biber, S.N., & Yaiser, M.L. (2004). *Feminist perspectives on social research*. Oxford University Press.

Holmes, A.G.D. (2020). Researcher positionality – A consideration of its influence and place in qualitative research – A new researcher guide. *Shanlax International Journal of Education*, 8(4), 1–10. https://doi.org /10.34293/education.v8i4.3232

hooks, b. (2003). *Teaching community: A pedagogy of hope*. Routledge.

Kaiper, A. (2018). "If you don't have English, you're just as good as a dead person": A narrative of adult English language literacy within post-apartheid South Africa. *International Review of Education*, 64, 737–57. https:// doi.org/10.1007/s11159-018-9733-y

Kamwangamalu, N., & Tovares, A. (2016). English in language ideologies, attitudes, and educational practices in Kenya and South Africa. *World Englishes*, 35(3), 421–39. https://doi.org/10.1111/weng.12207

Katz, C. (1994). Playing the field: Questions of fieldwork in geography. *Professional Geographer*, 46(1), 67–72. https://doi.org/10.1111/j.0033 -0124.1994.00067.x

Kendall, F.E. (2006). *Understanding white privilege: Creating pathways to authentic relationships across race*. Routledge.

Kincheloe, J.L., & Steinberg, S.R. (2008). Indigenous knowledges in education: Complexities, dangers and profound benefits. In N.K. Denzin, Y.S. Lincoln, & L.T. Smith (Eds.), *Handbook of critical and Indigenous methodologies* (pp. 135–56). Sage.

Kobayashi, A. (2003). GPC ten years on: Is self-reflexivity enough? *Gender, Place and Culture, 10*(4), 345–9. https://doi.org/10.1080/09663690320001533313

Mandrona, A. (2016). Visual culture, aesthetics, and the ethics of cellphilming. In K. McEntee, C. Burkholder, & J. Schwab-Cartas (Eds.), *What's a cellphilm? Integrating mobile phone technology into participatory visual research and activism* (pp. 183–98). Sense.

McDowell, L. (1992). Doing gender: Feminism, feminists and research methods in human geography. *Transactions of the Institute of British Geographers, 17*(4), 399–416. https://doi.org/10.2307/622707

McIntosh, P. (1988). *White privilege and male privilege: A personal account of coming to see correspondences through work in women's studies* (Working paper 189). Wellesley Centers for Women. https://www.wcwonline.org/images/pdf/White_Privilege_and_Male_Privilege_Personal_Account-Peggy_McIntosh.pdf

McIntosh, P. (1989). White privilege: Unpacking the invisible knapsack. *Peace and Freedom Magazine* (July/August), 10–12. https://psychology.umbc.edu/files/2016/10/White-Privilege_McIntosh-1989.pdf

McKinney, C. (2013). Orientations to English in post-apartheid schooling: A study of sociolinguistic and identity changes amongst adolescent girls in multilingual schools. *English Today, 29*(1), 22–7. https://doi.org/10.1017/S0266078412000491

McLafferty, S. (1995). Counting for women. *Professional Geographer, 47*(4), 436–42. https://doi.org/10.1111/j.0033-0124.1995.436_j.x

Mesthrie, R. (2021). Colony, post-colony and world Englishes in the South African context. *World Englishes, 40*(1), 12–23. https://doi.org/10.1111/weng.12469

Mitchell, C., & Reid-Walsh, J. (2008). Girl method: Placing girl-centred research methodologies on the map of girlhood studies. In J. Klaehn (Ed.), *Roadblocks to equality: Women challenging boundaries* (pp. 214–33). Black Rose Books.

Mitchell, C., & Sommer, M. (2016). Participatory visual methodologies in global public health. *Global Public Health, 11*(5–6), 521–7. https://doi.org/10.1080/17441692.2016.1170184

Muhammed, M., Wallerstein, N., Sussman, A., Avila, M., Belone, L., & Duran, B. (2015). Reflections on researcher identity and power: The impact of positionality on community based participatory research (CBPR) processes and outcomes. *Critical Sociology, 41*(7–8), 1045–63. https://doi.org/10.1177/0896920513516025

Nagar, R., & Geiger, S. (2000). Reflexivity and positionality in feminist fieldwork revisited. (Manuscript under review). [Later published as Nagar, R., & Geiger, S. (2007). Reflexivity and positionality in feminist fieldwork revisited. In A. Tickell, E. Sheppard, & J. Peck (Eds.), *Politics and practice in economic geography* (pp. 267–78). Sage.]

Nagar, R. (2002). Footloose researchers, "traveling" theories, and the politics of transnational feminist praxis. *Gender, Place and Culture, 9*(2), 179–86. https://doi.org/10.1080/09663960220139699

Ntombela, B.X.S. (2016). "The burden of diversity": The sociolinguistic problems of English in South Africa. *English Language Teaching, 9*(5), 77–84. https://doi.org/10.5539/elt.v9n5p77

Oetzel, J.G. (2009). *Intercultural communication: A layered approach.* Vango Books.

Parmegiani, A. (2012). Language, power and transformation in South Africa: A critique of language rights discourse. *Transformation: Critical Perspectives on Southern Africa, 78,* 74–97. https://doi.org/10.1353/trn.2012.0042

Pillow, W. (2003). Confession, catharsis, or cure? Rethinking the uses of reflexivity as methodological power in qualitative research. *International Journal of Qualitative Studies in Education, 16*(2), 175–96. https://doi.org/10.1080/0951839032000060635

Ramazanoglu, C., & Holland, J. (2002). *Feminist methodology: Challenges and choices.* Sage.

Rose, G. (1997). Situating knowledges: Positionality, reflexivities and other tactics. *Progress in Human Geography, 21*(3), 305–20. https://doi.org/10.1191/030913297673302122

Smith, F. (1996). Problematising language: Limitations and possibilities in "foreign language" research. *Area, 28*(2), 160–6. https://www.jstor.org/stable/20003653

Soedirgo, J., & Glas, A. (2020). Toward active reflexivity: Positionality and practice in the production of knowledge. *PS: Political Science and Politics, 53*(3), 527–31. https://doi.org/10.1017/S1049096519002233

Spivak, C.G. (1988). Can the subaltern speak? In C. Nelson (Ed.), *Marxism and the interpretation of culture* (pp. 271–313). University of Illinois Press.

Staeheli, L., & Lawson, V. (1994). A discussion of "women in the field": The politics of feminist fieldwork. *Professional Geographer, 46*(1), 96–102. https://doi.org/10.1111/j.0033-0124.1994.00096.x

Sultana, F. (2007). Reflexivity, positionality and participatory ethics: Negotiating fieldwork dilemmas in international research. *ACME: An International E-Journal for Critical Geographies, 6*(3), 374–85. https://acme-journal.org/index.php/acme/article/view/786

Treffry-Goatley, A., Moletsane, R., & Wiebesiek, L. (2018). "Just don't change anything": Engaging girls in participatory visual research to address violence against women and girls in rural South Africa. In C. Mitchell & R. Moletsane (Eds.), *Disrupting shameful legacies: Girls and young women speak back through the arts to address sexual violence* (pp. 47–64). Brill Publishers.

Treffry-Goatley, A., Wiebesiek, L., de Lange, N., & Moletsane, R. (2017). Technologies of nonviolence: Ethical participatory visual research with girls. *Girlhood Studies: An Interdisciplinary Journal, 10*(2), 45–61. https://doi.org/10.3167/ghs.2017.100205

Treffry-Goatley, A., Wiebesiek, L., & Moletsane, R. (2016). Using the visual to address gender-based violence in rural South Africa: Ethical considerations. *LEARNing Landscapes, 10*(1), 341–59. https://doi.org/10.36510/learnland.v10i1.737

Vanner, C. (2015). Positionality at the center: Constructing an epistemological and methodological approach for a Western feminist doctoral candidate conducting research in the postcolonial. *International Journal of Qualitative Methods, 14*(4). https://doi.org/10.1177/1609406915618094

Wiebesiek, L., & Treffry-Goatley, A. (2017). Using participatory visual research to explore resilience with girls and young women in rural South Africa. *Agenda: Empowering Women for Gender Equity, 31*(2), 74–86. https://doi.org/10.1080/10130950.2017.1362898

Wint, E. (2011). Reflexivity in practice: Developing a new attitude as part of teaching and engaging in participatory research and development. *Journal of Progressive Human Services, 22*(1), 68–83. https://doi.org/10.1080/10428232.2010.523678

10 Acting Like a Skank: Reflections on a Researcher's Involvement in the Production of Participatory Visual Research Texts in a Rural Area

KATIE MACENTEE

Skank, n.

Chiefly *derogatory*. A person regarded as unattractive, unpleasant, or disreputable; *esp.* a woman who has many casual sexual encounters or relationships.[1]

1 A slutty person who doesn't know how to say no to sex.
2 Derogatory term for a (usually younger) female, implying trashiness or tackiness, lower class status, poor hygiene, flakiness, and a scrawny, pockmarked sort of ugliness.[2]

Introduction

In this chapter, I reflect on my experience of being photographed by a participant in a photovoice project. The photograph depicted me as a skank and was taken while I was conducting research on the contributions and challenges of using photovoice, and other participatory visual methodologies, in preparing teachers to teach about HIV and AIDS in rural South African schools.[3] I describe the events leading up to the taking of the photograph and its production and dissemination in order to explore two questions: What do these reflections tell us about the use of photovoice in preparing teachers to teach in rural areas? When we are using the photovoice method, what can be learned from a researcher literally being in the picture? To answer these questions, I conduct a reflexive analysis. I argue that photovoice can offer a compelling insight into the complexities of preparing teachers to address HIV in rural schools, but I acknowledge that the method also has its limitations. Beyond issues of rurality, I contend that there are methodological challenges related to a researcher being depicted in photovoice images as well as some possibilities.

Photovoice Method

Photovoice is a participatory visual method developed by Wang and Burris (1997) when they were working with rural women farmers in China. Drawing on feminist theory, education for critical consciousness, and documentary photography, the method involves participants taking photographs that describe personal and community concerns and potential solutions. Participants work collaboratively or independently to take photographs and then come together to consider the images and write short captions about their significance. The participants' discussion can be recorded and, together with the photographs and captions, analysed as data. These materials can also be exhibited as part of the project's knowledge translation activities to engage a wider audience in a discussion about community challenges and solutions. Evans-Agnew and Rosemberg (2016) summarize Wang and Burris's seminal work as empowering and enlightening for participants. Women working with Wang and Burris developed an awareness of community needs, reflected on structural constraints on achieving these needs, and gained a desire to act on this awareness for political and social change. Malherbe et al. (2017) explained that "much of the methodology's liberatory potential ... rests on its ability to elevate participant voice, catalyse material enactments of social justice, and privilege endogenous knowledge" (p. 167). For O'Donovan et al. (2019), it is a highly democratic research method because it provides participants with greater means of expression and control in data production and research trajectories. The method's emphasis on community-based social change has made it popular among community-based and participatory researchers interested in a range of social issues globally, as Catalani and Minkler (2010) have previously observed. Its developmental roots in rural contexts make it particularly compelling when we are working with pre-service teachers in addressing HIV and AIDS in rural schools.

Inspired by Wang and Burris's (1997) work, as well as that of Lykes (2001) and photographers like Ewald (2000), colleagues at the Centre for Visual Methodologies for Social Change (CVMSC) started employing photovoice (and other participatory visual methods) to address the AIDS epidemic in South Africa (De Lange et al., 2010). Much of their work was with community health-care workers, young people, and teachers in rural areas of KwaZulu Natal, where rates of HIV and AIDS were, and continue to be, among the highest nationally and globally (UNAIDS, 2021). They adapted Wang and Burris's (1997) photovoice method by having participants work collaboratively in small groups to take photographs in the workshop context (Mitchell, de Lange et al., 2005;

Mitchell, Moletsane et al., 2005). This work demonstrates the adaptability of the method and has highlighted the potential of photovoice to give access to spaces and perspectives that are inaccessible or previously overlooked by researchers (Mitchell et al., 2006). The influence of visual media made in rural communities has been discussed as especially influential for its ability to centre the ideas of the community members and young people who are often overlooked and marginalized in urban-based educational initiatives (Balfour et al., 2008).

Reflexivity and Photovoice

There is an ethical imperative for researchers using the photovoice method to be reflexive. According to Guest (2016), reflexivity is necessary to make visible how a researcher guides the interpretation of images. McLeod and Guillemin (2016) have demonstrated in their reflexive analysis of their participatory visual interpretative process that a participant's photograph has its own agency through which it can affect a researcher's physical and emotional well-being. Likewise, Suffla et al. (2015) have argued that a researcher's reflexive practice is tethered to the participatory forms of knowledge construction and the commitments of a research approach to consciousness raising and transformation. Guided by this imperative, I examine critically how being in the picture has influenced my understanding of the photovoice process and how pre-service teachers are prepared to address HIV education in rural South African schools.

The Research Context

The story begins with research I conducted in 2010 and continues in relation to a study that took place in 2012. In both instances, I was studying pre-service teachers' use of participatory visual methodologies (photovoice as well as collage, participatory video, and cellphilms) to address HIV and AIDS in rural KwaZulu Natal (MacEntee, 2016, 2017, 2020). Over 12 per cent of the population in KwaZulu Natal are living with HIV (Be in the KNOW, 2021). Girls and young women between the ages of fifteen and twenty-four are especially vulnerable to contracting HIV because of sociodemographic vulnerabilities such as gender roles that disempower girls and women in relation to their sexual agency and stigmatize boys' and men's use of condoms. Social inequalities like poverty, lack of access to condoms and other birth control methods, barriers to education and employment, and consequent involvement in transactional sexual relationships, as well as concomitant high rates of gender-based violence and rape are all factors driving the South African HIV and AIDS epidemic among young women (Maughan-Brown et al., 2018). Girls living in rural areas experience further challenges in accessing services (Chimbindi et al., 2018). In the rural area of Vulindlela, young women in their early twenties are four times more likely to contract HIV when compared to their male counterparts (South African National AIDS Council, 2017).

Teachers in rural schools are well situated to address the complexities of the ongoing epidemic. Unfortunately, they encounter barriers that inhibit them from taking advantage of their position of influence. Francis (2016) has pointed out that some teachers refuse to educate their students about HIV because they fear talking about sex in their classrooms. Young people report that teachers who take an authoritarian position in the classroom when talking about sexual health make them seem "unapproachable on matters related to sex and sexuality in the same way as conservative parents" (Mayeza & Vincent, 2019, p. 480). Higher education programs should be supporting teachers to acquire HIV and AIDS competencies (Higher Education and Training HIV/AIDS Programme, 2018). However, previous research has questioned whether these competencies are adequate and applicable for teachers who will be working with diverse students and communities (Francis & DePalma, 2015). As a result of these challenges, students may not be receiving important information about their health and well-being.

The Research Projects

My research, both in 2010 and 2012, was connected to the "Youth as Knowledge Producers" (YAKP) project, which was a Social Sciences and Humanities Research Council of Canada (SSHRC) and National Research Foundation–funded project conducted in connection with the CVMSC in the Faculty of Education at the University of KwaZulu Natal (UKZN). YAKP was headed by Jean Stuart with overlap into a portion of a related project called "Every Voice Counts," which was led by Naydene de Lange. The YAKP project had three main goals: (1) to engender a practice of self-study and reflexivity in relation to pre-service teachers' approaches to HIV education; (2) to provide training for pre-service teachers in participatory arts-based methodologies for HIV education; and (3) to provide opportunities for pre-service teachers, as peer educators, to gain practical experience facilitating these methodologies in rural settings (CVMSC, 2010). Over the course of four years, the project recruited a total of forty-two students from the Faculty of Education at UKZN to be HIV peer educators. In 2010, I was invited by the research team to conduct collage training with pre-service teachers. This event was a two-day training session that was attended by twenty-six students. Having completed their training, five students and I co-facilitated a collage workshop attended by eighteen high school students in Vulindlela. In the week following the workshop, members of the research team, two of the pre-service teachers, and I returned to the rural area to attend a presentation of the learners' collages during school assemblies and at a community event organized for World AIDS Day (MacEntee, 2011).

In 2012, as part of my SSHRC-funded doctoral research, I returned to South Africa and conducted a follow-up project that looked, in part, at the impact of pre-service teacher involvement in YAKP. I conducted one-on-one interviews with three pre-service teachers about their experiences with YAKP. After the interview, each participant produced five photovoice images and captions that responded to the prompt, What difference do the arts make for youth to address HIV and AIDS? Then participants attended a participatory analysis workshop during which we engaged in several activities to interpret the photovoice data.

Situating Myself in the Research

I have been dealing in one way or another with questions around HIV and AIDS education and participatory visual methods for more than a decade. My training in this area began in Western Canada where I worked with young people in housing crises, and I volunteered with a youth-run organization that provided HIV and AIDS peer education in schools and community centres. My master's research was an exploratory case study of five youth-centred HIV and AIDS education interventions in Canada that were integrating participatory visual methods into their programming (MacEntee, 2009). My research focus turned to South Africa in 2008, when I had the opportunity to visit the country as an intern with the Rural Teacher Education Project (RTEP).[4] As part of this project, my role was to support pre-service teachers during their four-week practicum at two schools in Vulindlela.[5] Before, during, and after this month-long internship, I learned more about how these experiences impacted me and my self-understandings. I also continue to wonder what I contributed to the project and how my presence impacted the project and people whom I met. This chapter is a continuation of this questioning, which I see as my ongoing responsibility to trouble, disrupt, ask questions, and think productively about what it means to be a Western white cis-gendered female urban academic conducting community-based and participatory research on gender and sexuality in rural sub-Saharan contexts.

Method: Reflexivity

A reflexive practice includes a critical examination of how identity and power come together in context and in relation to others to inform research process and outcomes. Following this method, identity is understood to be representational, multifaceted, situated, and relational, and thus shifting, as well as, at times, fraught, as Muhammad et al. (2015) have observed. Depending on the setting, aspects of my identity may change in relation to different identities both physically and/or symbolically present. In my reflexive practice, therefore, following Sultana (2007), I foreground the intersubjectivities and the physical, political, emotional, and social spaces that we inhabit in the moment to better understand how we construct and represent knowledge.

According to Rose (1997), who draws on Foucault's definition of power as saturated and fluid, rather than seeing power as fixed in the hands of one group over the other, we need to recognize that it is exercised and resisted dynamically by individuals and groups. Power affects the researcher, the participant, the research process, and the research outcomes. Rose has explained that "we are made through our research as much as we make our own knowledge" (p. 316). This understanding of power within a reflexive method requires that I reject any oppositional binary that would situate the researcher as expert and the participant as other. Furthermore, a reflexive analysis cannot mitigate power inequities between people. Rather, it signals a contextual reading of how individual positions are negotiated and how this negotiation impacts the partiality of any knowledge claim advanced by the research findings.

My reflexive analysis is further influenced by England (1994) and her analysis of her "failed research" (p. 84) on lesbian women living in Toronto. While discussing her role as a researcher conducting a study on a socially marginalized group, she highlighted the dialogic exchanges between her and the participants. She argued that "we do not conduct fieldwork on the unmediated world of the researched, but on the world *between* ourselves and the researched. At the same time this betweenness is shaped by the researcher's biography, which filters the 'data' and our perceptions and interpretations of the fieldwork experience" (p. 86, emphasis in original). Her reflexivity or, put differently, her awareness of and sensitivity towards power differences is not a way of transcending the impact of these differences on the research outcomes. She has argued that the research process is inescapably steeped in relational power dynamics, which results in partial knowledge claims that are tethered to the betweenness of research interaction. Making explicit the ways in which the researcher is integrated into the research process helps indicate how their presence informs, constructs, and distorts knowledge claims. In applying this reflexive method to my analysis of the skank photograph, I am interrogating my relationship with a photograph, its maker, my research participant group, and with power.

Findings

There are unexpected moments in research. For me, some of these moments come up again and again, and as I revisit them over time, I construct meaning about them. This reflective process was certainly the case for the photograph that is the focus of this chapter. What I thought was going to be a description of a single photograph ended up being a reflection on interactions that happened two years before the photograph was even created. After many starts and restarts, I have ended up representing the findings in three sections, or what I have come to think of as three stories. The first story is based on my memory of how the topic of skanks entered the research space. The second story draws on transcripts to recount how the photograph was made. The final story has integrated excerpts from my field notes to illustrate my initial uncertainty about how to engage productively with the photograph in the participatory research space.

The Backstory

The following memory was elicited by engaging with the photograph of the results of the brainstorming activity (Figure 10.1) from a multi-day workshop conducted with pre-service teachers in 2010.

Early one evening in May 2010, I started a collage workshop with pre-service teachers at the University of KwaZulu Natal. It was attended by about twenty students. They were all sitting in a semicircle chatting among themselves and waiting for the workshop to begin. They were mainly Black and coloured[6] students, which reflects the racial diversity of students who were living on campus at the time. I did not ask about the participants' ages, but I guessed that most of them were in their early twenties. To get the evening's activities started, I walked to the front of the room and wrote in big letters on the blackboard: HIV and AIDS. The group stopped chatting and focused their attention on me. I turned to face them and asked: "What do these words make you think about?" I was not surprised that the group was a little reticent to answer my question. I had used the same activity many times before in my HIV and AIDS activist work and knew to expect this response. As the first exercise of the workshop and with HIV being a taboo topic for many, I could sympathize with their hesitance to speak out in front of the whole group. The intention of the brainstorming activity was to help break the ice, disrupt this taboo, and for me to hear how people were thinking about HIV and AIDS.

One participant tentatively suggested that the terms reminded them of sickness. I praised their suggestion and wrote it on the board. Someone else contributed ARVs (anti-retroviral treatments). I nodded and wrote ARV on the board as well. At this point, the session began to gain momentum. They started to call out their ideas more quickly: VCT (voluntary counselling and testing), immune system, condoms, and sexuality. I thought to myself: "OK, we are getting somewhere." The group's answers revealed to me that they had a good understanding of HIV and AIDS as an illness in relation to medical treatments and prevention methods. This knowledge led me to wonder if the group had ideas about the social determinants of HIV vulnerability, so I prompted them with another question: "How does society think about the virus?" The room was silent again as people thought. I prompted again: "What are some stereotypes that we have about HIV?" One female participant took a big breath and said loudly: "Skanks!"

The room erupted into laughter. As I waited for the laughter to die down, I wondered if this participant was testing me. I felt she was waiting for me to respond to see if she had shocked me and to find out if I would chastise her for using a sexist term. I wrote the word on the board alongside all the other contributions. While I was writing, I asked her to explain what she understood to be the connection between HIV and AIDS and skanks. She answered: "Skanks are women who sleep around with men. They are responsible for spreading the virus through their promiscuity." I thanked the young woman for her explanation and then asked if it was only girls who are skanks and responsible for the spread of HIV. The group responded in chorus: "No." After this, another female participant suggested adding rape to the brainstorming list "because sometimes people do not have a choice about whom they have sex with." Someone else said: "Discrimination." Then the contributions continued again one after the other: myths, stereotypes, unsafe sex, hopeless, patriarchy, polygamy, stress.

I intended to introduce pre-service teachers to using collage to reflect on, and teach about, HIV and AIDS. I remember feeling that the brainstorming activity was successful at getting the participants to open up and think about the wider impact of HIV and AIDS on people's everyday lives and on society. The feeling of being tested by the young woman and the notion that she was looking to get a laugh from her

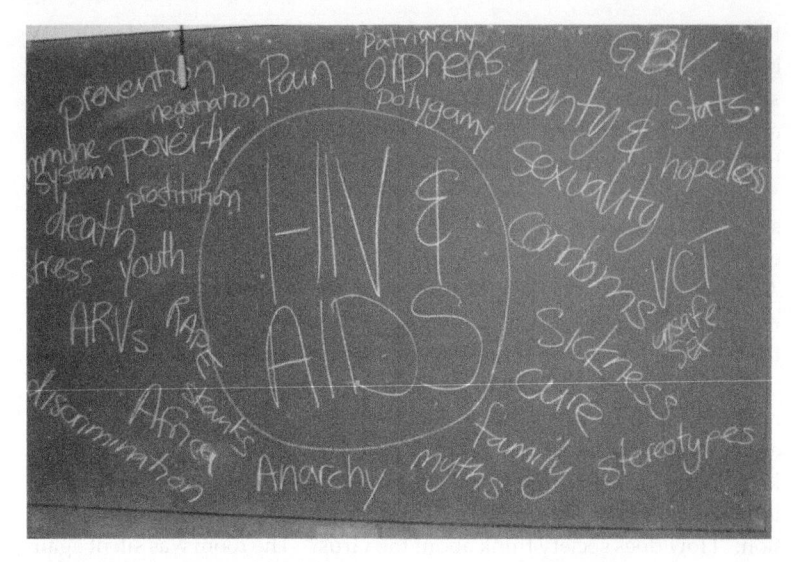

Figure 10.1. The HIV and AIDS brainstorm conducted in 2009 as part of YAKP. Courtesy of Kathrine MacEntee.

peers is also a vivid memory for me. My response to her at the time was guided by my training as a peer-based HIV and AIDS educator, which had taught me not to automatically shame people's use of offensive language but to encourage the group to unpack the term and question the assumptions behind it. Asking participants to expand on how a word typically connects to HIV and AIDS, as I felt it did in this example, spurs the group to take up alternative viewpoints and disrupt the problematic stereotypes that might be tied to these kinds of terms. What I did not expect at the time of this workshop was to have this particular word reappear two years later. And when it did, I started to reconsider my facilitation of this activity and reflect on how I could have responded differently.

The Making of the Photograph

In 2013, I was in South Africa conducting my doctoral research. The young woman who had contributed "skank" to the brainstorm was now volunteering as a participant in my research. I was using photo elicitation as a way of engaging participants in an interview about the impact that having used participatory visual methodologies had had on their understanding of HIV and AIDS education in rural schools. Some of the photographs that I used to elicit participants' responses were taken at the first workshop back in 2010, including the photograph of the HIV/AIDS brainstorming activity (Figure 10.1). The participant's reactions to this photograph were varied.

> PARTICIPANT: Yes! You were writing about it, weren't you? And you were saying all the things that are, I don't know, associated with HIV and AIDS or that link to HIV and AIDS. And we were giving the answers.
>
> KATIE: Right, so it was a sort of "What does HIV and AIDS make you think of?" brainstorming [activity].
>
> PARTICIPANT: Yes.
>
> KATIE: Yeah, this was one of my most impressive brainstorms I've ever done. This is something I do quite a bit in workshops, and I have to say that I was very impressed with some of the stuff that came up here. Like a real range of, like, you've got the immune system and ARVs, and the medical sorts of things.
>
> PARTICIPANT: Skanks. I think I gave that answer.
>
> KATIE: Yeah!
>
> PARTICIPANT: Skanks! [laughs]
>
> KATIE: Yeah, I think that might be my first memory of you! Your saying to me, "skanks." But it made me really excited because you sort of opened a door for people to go there.
>
> PARTICIPANT: And we were all laughing.
>
> KATIE: Yeah.

The participant's reaction to seeing the photograph confirmed for me that, in contributing the word "skanks," she was, first and foremost, looking to get a reaction. Likely, she had been less interested in my reaction (as a test) than she was in eliciting laughter from her peers. When I returned to this interview transcript in preparation to write this chapter, I was struck by my own response to the participant's memory, which was to try and turn the conversation to focus on how her including this word was highly generative for the group's thinking. However, this idea was not picked up by the participant, who returned again to mention her peers' laughter.

The interview progressed for about another hour, and the participant told me more about her life (she was, at the time, pregnant), her subsequent training in education (she was just one term away from graduating), and how her ideas about participatory visual methodologies and HIV education in rural schools had developed since the workshop (she found it highly generative and hoped to use the methods in her future teaching).

After the interview, the participant engaged in a photovoice activity. She took five photographs that responded to the prompt, What difference do the arts make to working with youth to address HIV and AIDS? The participant asked me to be in three of these photos with her (while a bystander snapped them). In one photograph, she used my scarf to tie our legs together, and we stood smiling with our arms around each other's shoulders at the bottom of a flight of stairs. In another, we sat at a table, smiling at each other with a laptop and pad of paper in front of us. In the third, the participant told me to pose "acting like a skank." When I asked how I should do it, she directed me to sit in a sexually provocative way, so I leant back on a chair with my feet up on a table. I pursed my lips and looked directly at the camera. She struck a similar pose on her own chair, and the bystander took the photo. I remember feeling ridiculous and uncertain about posing in this way for this last picture. I was especially uncomfortable about being asked to look sexually provocative in a photograph that was to be part of my doctoral research, but I consented to be in the photo nonetheless.

After the photographs were taken, I downloaded them onto my laptop, and the participant scrolled through the photographs and wrote one short caption about each of the five photographs. The participant was in a hurry to get to another appointment, so we parted without having had the chance to talk about the photographs and captions together. When I looked through the data on my own, I was surprised to see the caption for the photograph of the two of us acting like skanks read: "[Participatory visual methods in HIV education] help learners become aware of [skanks] and try to help eradicate the number of them in society by making people aware of what they do in society." I felt ill.

My Initial Reflections on the "Skank" Photograph

In the days following the meeting with this participant, whenever I looked at the image of me acting like a skank, I felt an immense sense of regret. I felt (and still feel) that the photograph stigmatizes women who have sex. My work has always been politically motivated to resist gender inequality and challenge the stigmatization of women's sexualities. How did I not see at the time the path this image would take? What would happen if I showed this photograph to other people in the research project? What if I showed it to my doctoral committee or to the public and to young people? What harmful stereotypes had I been party to reproducing while posing for this photograph?

As I mulled over these (and other) questions, I was preparing for a participant analysis workshop. This event was a two-day workshop held at UKZN, which brought together different groups of participants from my PhD project – youth, pre-service teachers, and researchers/lecturers at UKZN – some of whom knew the participant who had created the skank photograph. I wondered if any of the lecturers were teaching her that year. At the workshop, we were going to analyse the photovoice data in a collaborative fashion, and activities would include having everyone look at all the photovoice images and captions in order to interpret their meaning. Prior to engaging in the photovoice activity, everyone had signed a consent form releasing the photographs and captions for public display, but I considered excluding this particular image from the analysis process. As I prepared for the workshop, I wrote in my fieldnotes:

> I am not sure, exactly, how I want to deal with this picture. It makes me angry, and I want to know what the rest of the participants might think of it. But I also wonder if I should worry about displaying it. What will the researchers say? Will they attack [the participant]? Did [she] really understand, even though I explained it to her before we started the activity, how the pictures were going to be used? At the time she took it, I was more worried about putting up a picture called "Skanks" when I knew [that] learners would be looking at it. But now I'm more worried about the flack [the participant] might get from saying what I think she is saying about who is responsible for spreading HIV. Part of me is really excited about putting up what might be a very controversial image. Another part of me worries that I might be putting [the participant] in an unfair position and whether she has really thought about what she is saying with this photo. And, if I contact her beforehand, how do I raise the issue without just persuading her to not show it but just maybe making sure that she understands how the message might be understood and the risks associated with this in the audience attending and participating in the workshop. (Fieldnotes, 2013)

It is evident that I saw several risks associated with exhibiting the photograph during the participant analysis workshop. There were risks to the participants, such as a chance that someone in the group would find the caption offensive and uncomfortable. There was a risk to the participant who made the photo in the form of a negative backlash from the other participants, and especially from her lecturers, for having taken the photograph. There was also a risk to me of experiencing a backlash from the participant group, which would negatively impact my standing within the communities with which I was working and potentially negatively impact my doctoral research project. I also saw a risk to young women who may experience further stigma based on this message perpetuated via the data.

So why, recognizing these risks, did I end up including the image and caption in the participatory analysis process? Honestly, my curiosity over the other participants' reactions to the photograph outweighed what I saw to be the risks to the participant and to myself. I hoped that the collective agreement of respect and generosity that we had created prior to the analysis process would help us, as a group, deal with any negative backlash in a respectful manner. I also hoped that, in the participatory analysis space, we would engage closely with the visual data to unpack the image with the caption, and it would be a generative and learning opportunity for everyone. Indeed, I worried that, if I did not include the photograph in the analysis workshop, the myths and gender oppressive sentiment surrounding how girls and women are responsible for HIV and AIDS might go untouched in the research data.

Surprisingly, the image did not garner as much reaction from the other participants as I had expected. During an initial walk-about of the collection of images and captions, a couple of the participants laughed at the image, and one or two others made noises of shock or distaste. During other activities, participants were invited to work first individually and then in small groups with one or more pictures. But no one chose to work with the skank photograph, and none of the participants ever brought up for discussion the ideas depicted in the photo. One part of me was relieved that there was no (explicit) judgment of the participant or me for making the image. Another part of me was disappointed that it was not given more attention. I worried that the participants' silence meant that the message of "eradicating skanks" was accepted uncritically. I wondered if I had imposed greater meaning on this photograph because I was in it and/or because it conflicted with my personal morals. A big regret is that I did not ask the participants directly about the photograph, so the impression it left on the group is unknown to me.

Discussion

In following a reflexive methodology, I am motivated by the epistemic belief that the researcher should make visible the relational and contextual power dynamics that inform the research process and outcomes. The methodology invited consideration of how personal relationships informed the knowledge process and my assumptions about what makes good quality photovoice research (England, 1994; Guest, 2016; McLeod & Guillemin, 2016). This chapter contributes to reflexive methodology by demonstrating how a photovoice image and caption can serve as an entry point for reflexive ruminations on how the photovoice method is a relational and iterative process that can, in my experience, involve multiple encounters between researcher and participants over time. In the following discussion, I seek to avoid what Pillow (2003) describes as "reflexive transcendence." By this term, she is referring to nullifying differences in privilege or shortcomings in the research process. This chapter is not my effort to explain away or excuse my participation in the photograph's problematic message and my discomfort about the participatory analytic process. Rather, I will explore my experiences in relation to a sociocultural interpretation of the term "skank." I also consider what I have learned and how I might respond differently in future to the participatory analysis workshops.

Unpacking the Term "Skank": Three Dimensions

I began the chapter with reference to the *Oxford English Dictionary* (*OED*) definition of "skank," which articulates how the term is gendered as well as its connection to the social construction of beauty. The *Urban Dictionary* supports the *OED* definition and contributes a further distinction of lower class. It also includes a reference to poor hygiene or to being dirty, which links to vectors of disease. In the following discussion, I look more deeply into the contextual understanding of this term. Specifically, I consider what the term means from my perspective as an urban white researcher appearing in a photograph about addressing the AIDS epidemic in rural South Africa.

When I saw myself in the photograph, I was confronted by my pose and how I unquestionably moved my body to look like a skank. What was I thinking? For me, "skank" is a misogynistic slang word that aims to control young women's sexuality and sexual rights. The vilification of female sexuality is not a problem only in South Africa. In Canada, from the early 1920s to the 1970s, economically disadvantaged women (and some men) were sterilized without their consent in an effort to control "syphilis, epilepsy, alcoholism, prostitution and sexual promiscuity" (Amy & Rowlands, 2018, p. 127). Despite international human rights law that makes it illegal, racism in the Canadian health-care system at large has meant turning a blind eye to the forced and coerced sterilization of Indigenous women (Collier, 2017). As a researcher working in the area of rural education and sexual health, I knew that this sexist colonial violence is linked to the myth that marginalized and racialized women are often associated with so-called promiscuity and considered to be vectors of disease, but still I consented to being in that photograph. I am ashamed that my posing in the photograph makes me party to reproducing these harmful histories.

The strong sentiment of the photovoice caption advocating for the "eradication" of "skanks" echoes the popular social sentiment favouring sexual abstinence that is promoted throughout South African schools. Young people are encouraged to abstain from all sexual contact until after marriage. "Abstain, be faithful, and condomise" is a slogan made popular in work on trying to help eradicate sexually transmitted infections (STIs) and on HIV prevention in the early 2000s, and the mantra can still be heard being advocated by teachers in the rural schools where I have worked. Indeed, it is a common refrain across sub-Saharan Africa, even though this approach to HIV prevention is known to be ineffective at reducing HIV rates among young people (Lo et al., 2016). These types of slogans contribute to the accusatory eye that is cast on young women, who are stigmatized because of their gender and age (as well as their sexuality, race, socio-economic status, and so on) as vectors of disease, as Campbell et al. (2006) have reminded us. The AIDS epidemic has fueled the myth that adolescent sexuality and sexual pleasure is inherently dangerous and irresponsible (McFadden, 2003). Therefore, while women and girls are increasingly becoming leaders in the response to the epidemic, as Wickremsinhe et al. (2019) have pointed out, this legacy continues to shape racialized young women students' experiences in schools.

These sentiments of restriction, shame, and risk are even more pronounced for young women living in rural areas. Sennott and Mojola (2017) explained that, recently, a diversification of pathways into adulthood has emerged for rural young women. Traditional markers of transition, such as the development of the body through puberty, interest in the opposite sex, marriage, and motherhood, coincide with modern markers of adulthood, such as completing higher education and maintaining gainful employment. However, while the diversification of pathways introduces new ideas of womanhood to girls, there are structural constraints in the rural context that limit the viability of the more modern pathways. Limited access to higher education and employment can leave rural girls feeling trapped into upholding traditional cultural values that honour what is thought of as respectability, along with virginity above all else (Sennott & Mojola, 2017). As a result, girls in rural areas find themselves in contexts of high levels of gender inequity and close surveillance (Moletsane & Mitchell, 2018; Van Wyk, 2015).

Preparing pre-service teachers to address HIV and AIDS in rural schools is complex. It requires teachers to reflect on their deep-seated and sometimes intersecting social norms around gender and rurality. Teachers from urban areas, such as the participants in this study, may not realize how their biases can permeate their educational messages. It is not expected that one participatory visual intervention will bring about long-term transformation on these matters, but it does have an impact. The participatory visual approach followed in this study (the brainstorming activity and the follow-up photovoice work) was highly effective at drawing attention to this participant's understandings and presented a starting place from which to unpack her and my assumptions and ideas as they intersect with HIV education in rural contexts.

Making Sense of an Audience's Lack of Reaction

Despite my awareness of the possible contention of the photograph, I struggled to address these tensions in the participatory analysis workshop. The participants' reactions to the skank photograph left me wondering if including the image perpetuated stigma towards rural young women as an impact of the project. It is similar to Call-Cummings and Martinez's (2016) experience during a photovoice project with Latinx students in the United States. Those young people exhibited photographs about their family and home life with the intention of confronting racism and developing a more enlightened perspective among their white peers and teachers. Unfortunately, they reported that the exhibit may have left the opposite impression on the audience. They wrote that, "although created for empowering and emancipatory purposes, photovoice has the potential, if not used in very specific, reflexive ways, to allow criticism of the Other but not reflection on oneself" (p. 808). In response, they argued, and I agree, that space must be created and time dedicated to engaging producers and audiences in critical reflection on the knowledge produced through exhibitions.

When the skank image and caption did not engage the audience as I had hoped it would, I struggled to respond during the workshop. I have since learned about Mitchell and De Lange's (2013) work with rural teachers and their response to participants' cellphilms, some of which suggest problematic responses to HIV education. To address their concerns, the researchers developed the "Speaking Back" method. It included viewing photovoice images about HIV stigma made by youth, having the participants rewatch their own cellphilms and identify each video's ideal audience, and then creating another set of cellphilms that included a message or learning for a specific audience. The intention of these activities was to encourage participants to "critically engage with their own work and 'speak back' to dominant images"

(p. 7). While the Speaking Back method was not entirely successful at countering the problematic content of the teachers' cellphilms, the research team observed the teachers shift their thinking on some issues. When reflecting on the skank photograph, I have considered how the Speaking Back method might have been adapted and implemented in the participatory analysis workshop for photovoice data.

The intention of the participatory analysis workshop was to make space for critical reflection on collaborative engagement through the analysis of the photovoice data. On the one hand, I see the potential of the Speaking Back method. It would have provided a means to directly elicit participants' responses to the skank photograph within the context of the workshop and in relation to HIV education in rural schools. On the other hand, I see this method as potentially taking away from the participatory, community-driven commitments of the analysis workshop by imposing a direction on the analysis that was researcher-driven in its focus on disrupting problematic social norms. There are any number of reasons why the participants may have avoided critiquing the image, including a concern that doing so would have been interpreted by me as a personal criticism. It may be that I have imbued the image with more significance than it deserves. The skank photograph was one of sixty-two images with captions that were collected during the project. During the analysis workshop, participants made meaningful contributions to the interpretation of several of the photographs in the collection but not to all of them. Why am I not focusing in a similar reflexive way on another photograph to which the participants did not respond? Perhaps the most salient learning for me regarding these questions about what I could have done differently and where I could have focused my and the participants' attention during the workshop points towards the need for more scholarship on the techniques of participatory analysis of participatory visual data, which includes deeper investigation into the role of the facilitator/researcher in supporting a participant-led process.

Conclusion

I conclude that there are benefits and challenges to the researcher being, literally, in the picture of participants' photovoice images regardless of the setting. At the same time, though, and returning to the theme of this book in looking at what the rural has to do with it, my reflexive analysis demonstrates the complexities of using participatory visual methods in preparing teachers to teach about HIV and AIDS in rural schools. I recognize that there are limits to the capacity of one intervention to transform deep-seated and pervasive social norms surrounding young rural women's sexuality. However, I am hopeful about the use of these methods and their capacity to bring forward pre-service teachers' assumptions and bias about the intersections of rurality and gender. In preparing teachers to address the dynamic social drivers of the epidemic, participatory visual methods offer a very promising means of teacher preparation, especially considering the complexities of rural contexts.

Conducting a reflexive analysis of being in the picture has required me to think more substantially about how I might be more present and accountable to the messages and learnings that come from participants' creative outputs. This interpretation of events leads me to agree with Sarah Switzer's (2019) assertion that the researcher-as-facilitator of the participatory visual process is always involved in a co-production of participant's media. Being pictured in the skank image is just visual evidence of this involvement. The reflexive process has made me more conscious of the risks a participant takes when she chooses to identify herself in photovoice images and how, when a photograph is taken out of the context of its production, it might carry a very different meaning than it had when it was produced. Thus, being in the picture contributed to the outcomes of the research because it made me more attuned to, and more accountable for, how meanings are interpreted throughout the photovoice process. Being in the picture may have influenced my sense of ownership. I operationalized this ownership by choosing to present the photograph in the participatory analysis workshop despite the foreseen risks to the participant (and myself). I further highlight the challenges of facilitating participant engagement in the visual analysis around this photograph. I am uncertain why participants did not choose to focus more on the photograph, and my being in the picture may have influenced their reticence to take up the photograph's problematic message. I see potential in the Speaking Back method to overcome some (but not all) of these tensions. I advocate the need for further development in participatory analysis methods and for further research that critically interrogates the role of the facilitator in directing the participatory visual process.

NOTES

1 Oxford English Dictionary. (n.d.). Skank. In *Oxford English Dictionary*. Retrieved 17 June 2023 from https://www.oed.com/view/Entry/246662?rskey=KBzifR&result=1# eid.

2 Urban Dictionary. (n.d.). Skank. In *Urban Dictionary*. Retrieved 17 June 2023 from https://www.urbandictionary.com/define.php?term=Skank.
3 I have not included the image in this chapter because the participant is also identifiable in the photograph, and I want to avoid any potential negative feedback on the chapter or the image and its caption to be linked back to this participant.
4 My internship with RTEP was funded through Partnerships for Change (PI: David Dillon). RTEP organized teacher practice for pre-service teachers in two rural high schools in the Vulindlela region of KwaZulu-Natal. Submersed in the project for a month, during the week I lived alongside eighteen South African students, three international students, and three other Canadian interns, and on weekends I stayed on the UKZN Faculty of Education campus. For more information about RTEP, see Islam and Mitchell (2011).
5 I was one of four white Canadian interns, and we worked as a team to organize activities and take care of the administrative side of the pre-service teachers' experiences while in the rural area.
6 Coloured is an ethnic category that persists in South Africa post-apartheid and refers to people of mixed racial heritage.

REFERENCES

Amy, J.-J., & Rowlands, S. (2018). Legalised non-consensual sterilisation – Eugenics put into practice before 1945, and the aftermath. Part 1: USA, Japan, Canada and Mexico. *European Journal of Contraception & Reproductive Health Care*, 23(2), 121–9. https://doi.org/10.1080/13625187.2018.1450973

Balfour, R., Mitchell, C., & Moletsane, R. (2008). Troubling contexts: Towards a generative theory of rurality in education research. *Journal of Rural and Community Development*, 3(3), 95–107.

Be in the KNOW. (2021). At a glance: HIV in South Africa. https://www.beintheknow.org/understanding-hiv-epidemic/data/glance-hiv-south-africa#

Call-Cummings, M., & Martinez, S. (2016). Consciousness-raising or unintentionally oppressive? *Qualitative Report*, 21(5), 798–819. https://doi.org/10.46743/2160-3715/2016.2293

Campbell, C., Nair, Y., & Maimane, S. (2006). AIDS stigma, sexual moralities and the policing of women and youth in South Africa. *Feminist Review*, 83(1), 132–8. https://doi.org/10.1057/palgrave.fr.9400285

Catalani, C., & Minkler, M. (2010). Photovoice: A review of the literature in health and public health. *Health Education & Behavior*, 37(3), 424–51. https://doi.org/10.1177/1090198109342084

Centre for Visual Methodologies for Social Change (CVMSC). (2010). *Center for visual methodologies for social change: Annual report, September 2009–December 2010* University of Kwazulu-Natal. http://cvm.ukzn.ac.za/Libraries/Annual_Reports/Annual_Report_2009_-_2010.sflb.ashx

Chimbindi, N., Mthiyane, N., Birdthistle, I., Floyd, S., McGrath, N., Pillay, D., Seeley, J., Zuma, T., Dreyer, J., Gareta, D., Mutevedzi, T., Fenty, J., Herbst, K., Smit, T., Baisley, K., & Shahmanesh, M. (2018). Persistently high incidence of HIV and poor service uptake in adolescent girls and young women in rural KwaZulu-Natal, South Africa, prior to DREAMS. *PLoS One, 13*(10), e0203193. https://doi.org/10.1371/journal.pone.0203193

Collier, R. (2017). Reports of coerced sterilization of Indigenous women in Canada mirrors shameful past. *CMAJ: Canadian Medical Association journal, 189*(33), E1080–1. https://doi.org/10.1503/cmaj.1095471

De Lange, N., Mitchell, C., Relebohile, M., Balfour, R., Wedekind, V., Pillay, D., & Buthelezi, T. (2010). Every voice counts: Towards a new agenda for schools in rural communities in the age of AIDS. *Education as Change, 14*(S1), S45–S55. https://doi.org/10.1080/16823206.2010.517916

England, K.V.L. (1994). Getting personal: Reflexivity, positionality, and feminist research. *Professional Geographer, 46*(1), 80–9. https://doi.org/10.1111/j.0033-0124.1994.00080.x

Evans-Agnew, R.A., & Rosemberg, M-A.S. (2016). Questioning photovoice research: Whose voice? *Qualitative Health Research, 26*(8), 1019–30. https://doi.org/10.1177/1049732315624223

Ewald, W. (2000). *Secret games: Collaborative works with children, 1969–99.* Scalo.

Francis, D.A. (2016). "I felt confused; I felt uncomfortable … my hair stood on ends": Understanding how teachers negotiate comfort zones, learning edges and triggers in the teaching of sexuality education in South Africa. In V. Sundaram & H. Sauntson (Eds.), *Global perspectives and key debates in sex and relationships education: Addressing issues of gender, sexuality, plurality and power* (pp. 130–45). Palgrave Macmillan.

Francis, D.A., & DePalma, R. (2015). "You need to have some guts to teach": Teacher preparation and characteristics for the teaching of sexuality and HIV/AIDS education in South African schools. *Journal of Social Aspects of HIV/AIDS, 12*(1), 30–8. https://doi.org/10.1080/17290376.2015.1085892

Guest, C. (2016). Cultivating reflexive research practice when using participants' photographs as research data. In D. Warr, S.M. Cox, M. Guillemin, & J. Waycott (Eds.), *Ethics and visual research methods: Theory, methodology, and practice* (pp. 75–88). Palgrave Macmillan.

Higher Education and Training HIV/AIDS Programme (HEAIDS). (2018). *University narratives: HIV curriculum integration – A unique strength in the national HIV response.* https://higherhealth.ac.za/wp-content/uploads/resources/publications/10830_heaids_hei_case_studies_web_1.pdf

Islam, F., & Mitchell, C. (2011). *School-university partnerships for educational change in rural South Africa: Particular challenges and practical cases.* Edwin Mellen Press.

Lo, N., Lowe, A., & Bendavid, E. (2016). Abstinence funding was not associated with reductions in HIV risk behavior in sub-Saharan Africa. *Health Affairs, 35*(5), 856–63. https://doi.org/10.1377/hlthaff.2015.0828

Lykes, B. (2001). Creative arts and photography in participatory action research in Guatemala. In P. Reason & H. Bradbury (Eds.), *Handbook of action research: Participative inquiry and practice* (pp. 363–71). Sage.

MacEntee, K. (2009). *Where are we now? Qualitative evaluation of participatory arts-based sex education in Canada* [Unpublished master's thesis]. McGill University. https://www.collectionscanada.gc.ca/obj/thesescanada/vol2 /002/MR61556.PDF?oclc_number=791129994

MacEntee, K. (2011, 1–5 May). *Participation in leadership: A critical analysis of participation in a youth-based collage workshop on HIV and AIDS in rural South Africa* [Paper presentation]. Conference of the Comparative and International Education Society, Montreal, Canada.

MacEntee, K. (2016). Two years later: Preservice teachers' experiences of learning to use participatory visual methods to address the South African AIDS epidemic. *Educational Research for Social Change, 5*(2), 81–95.

MacEntee, K. (2017). *Can participatory visual methods make a difference? Responding to HIV and AIDS in rural South African schools* [Unpublished doctoral dissertation]. McGill University. https://escholarship.mcgill.ca /concern/theses/9p290d22n

MacEntee, K. (2020). Participatory visual methods and school-based responses to HIV in rural South Africa: Insights from youth, preservice and inservice teachers. *Sex Education, 20*(3), 316–33. https://doi.org/10.1080/14681811.20 19.1661833

Malherbe, N., Suffla, S., Seedat, M., & Bawa, U. (2017). Photovoice as liberatory enactment: The case of youth as epistemic agents. In M. Seedat, S. Suffla, & D.J. Christie (Eds.), *Emancipatory and participatory methodologies in peace, critical, and community psychology* (pp. 165–78). Springer International Publishing.

Maughan-Brown, B., George, G., Beckett, S., Evans, M., Lewis, L., Cawood, C., Khanyile, D., & Kharsany, A.B. (2018). HIV risk among adolescent girls and young women in age-disparate partnerships: Evidence from KwaZulu-Natal, South Africa. *JAIDS Journal of Acquired Immune Deficiency Syndromes, 78*(2), 155–62. https://doi.org/10.1097 /QAI.0000000000001656

Mayeza, E., & Vincent, L. (2019). Learners' perspectives on Life Orientation sexuality education in South Africa. *Sex Education, 19*(4), 472–85. https:// doi.org/10.1080/14681811.2018.1560253

McFadden, P. (2003). Sexual pleasure as feminist choice. *Feminist Africa*, 2, 50–60. https://www.jstor.org/stable/48724975

McLeod, K., & Guillemin, M. (2016). The impact of photographs on the researcher: An ethical matter for visual research. In D. Warr, S.M. Cox, M. Guillemin, & J. Waycott (Eds.), *Ethics and visual research methods: Theory, methodology, and practice* (pp. 89–100). Palgrave Macmillan.

Mitchell, C., & De Lange, N. (2013). What can a teacher do with a cellphone? Using participatory visual research to speak back in addressing HIV & AIDS. *Journal of Education*, *33*(4), 1–13. https://doi.org/10.15700/201412171336

Mitchell, C., De Lange, N., Moletsane, R., Stuart, J., & Buthelezi, T. (2005). Giving a face to HIV and AIDS: On the uses of photo-voice by teachers and community health care workers working with youth in rural South Africa. *Qualitative Research in Psychology*, *2*(3), 257–70. https://doi.org/10.1191/1478088705qp042oa

Mitchell, C., Moletsane, R., Stuart, J., Buthelezi, T., & De Lange, N. (2005). Taking pictures/taking action! Visual methodologies in working with young people. *Children First*, *9*(60), 27–30.

Mitchell, C., Stuart, J., Moletsane, R., & Nkwanyana, C.B. (2006). "Why we don't go to school on Fridays": On youth participation through photo voice in rural KwaZulu-Natal. *McGill Journal of Education*, *41*(3), 267–82. https://mje.mcgill.ca/article/view/740

Moletsane, R., & Mitchell, C. (2018). Researching sexual violence with girls in rural South Africa. In H. Shapiro (Ed.), *The Wiley handbook on violence in education* (pp. 433–48). Wiley and Sons.

Muhammad, M., Wallerstein, N., Sussman, A.L., Avila, M., Belone, L., & Duran, B. (2015). Reflections on researcher identity and power: The impact of positionality on community based participatory research (CBPR) processes and outcomes. *Critical Sociology*, *41*(7–8), 1045–63. https://doi.org/10.1177/0896920513516025

O'Donovan, J., Thompson, A., Onyilofor, C., Hand, T., Rosseau, N., & O'Neil, E. (2019). The use of participatory visual methods with community health workers: A systematic scoping review of the literature. *Global Public Health*, *14*(5), 722–36. https://doi.org/10.1080/17441692.2018.1536156

Pillow, W. (2003). Confession, catharsis, or cure? Rethinking the uses of reflexivity as methodological power in qualitative research. *International Journal of Qualitative Studies in Education*, *16*(2), 175–96. https://doi.org/10.1080/0951839032000060635

Rose, G. (1997). Situating knowledges: Positionality, reflexivities and other tactics. *Progress in Human Geography*, *21*(3), 305–20. https://doi.org/10.1191/030913297673302122

Sennott, C., & Mojola, S.A. (2017). "Behaving well": The transition to respectable womanhood in rural South Africa. *Culture, Health & Sexuality, 19*(7), 781–95. https://doi.org/10.1080/13691058.2016.1262062

South African National AIDS Council (SANAC). (2017). *Let our actions count: South Africa's national strategic plan for HIV, TB and STIs 2017–2022.* https://sanac.org.za//wp-content/uploads/2017/06/NSP_FullDocument_FINAL.pdf

Suffla, S., Seedat, M., & Bawa, U. (2015). Reflexivity as enactment of critical community psychologies: Dilemmas of voice and positionality in a multi-country photovoice study. *Journal of Community Psychology, 43*(1), 9–21. https://doi.org/10.1002/jcop.21691

Sultana, F. (2007). Reflexivity, positionality and participatory ethics: Negotiating fieldwork dilemmas in international research. *ACME: An International E-journal for Critical Geographies, 6*(3), 374–85. https://acme-journal.org/index.php/acme/article/view/786

Switzer, S. (2019). Working with photo installation and metaphor: Re-visioning photovoice research. *International Journal of Qualitative Methods, 18.* https://doi.org/10.1177/1609406919872395

UNAIDS. (2021). Country factsheets: South Africa. https://www.unaids.org/en/regionscountries/countries/southafrica

Van Wyk, S.B. (2015). *"It's hard work to be a girl": Adolescent girls' experiences of girlhood in three low-income communities in South Africa* [Unpublished doctoral dissertation]. University of Stellenbosch. http://scholar.sun.ac.za/handle/10019.1/97926

Wang, C., & Burris, M.A. (1997). Photovoice: Concept, methodology, and use for participatory needs assessment. *Health Education & Behavior, 24*(3), 369–87. https://doi.org/10.1177/109019819702400309

Wickremsinhe, M., Little, M., Carter, A., Sullivan, K., & Lyerly, A. (2019). Beyond "vessels and vectors": A global review of registered HIV-related clinical trials with pregnant women. *Journal of Women's Health, 28*(1), 93–9. https://doi.org/10.1089/jwh.2017.6857

11 Positioning Girls in Rural Contexts: Then and Now

NTOMBOXOLO YAMILE

We don't know where we're going ... Please Lord, protect us and give us strength and wisdom to face any challenge we might encounter ... We are forcibly removed from our home to an unknown place.

– My father's prayer, 1979

Introduction

I was born at the Committees Drift police station in Grahamstown District, Eastern Cape, South Africa, in 1983. When my mother went into labour, my father and grandmother hurriedly hired a van to take her to the police station where she was to wait for the ambulance from Grahamstown to take her to hospital to give birth. They waited in vain, and after eight hours, my mother ended up giving birth with my grandmother's assistance. My parents named me Ntomboxolo, which means "a girl bringing peace." According to my parents, the name signified that they had made peace with the unusual place in which I was born and with living in our rural township, a place to which the apartheid government had forcibly moved them in 1979.

I moved to the city after high school to study at the university. It is here that I am learning to become a researcher. It is here that, as an emerging researcher, I work with a group of young girls in a nearby rural township to understand and address sexual violence. In this chapter, I reflexively connect myself to my father's story and to those of the Young Girls Leading Change (YGLC),[1] a group of girls with whom I am currently working in a nearby rural community to better understand their experiences of sexual and other forms of violence. In particular, I use memory-work to look back at my father's story and my own childhood. Then, I look at my current work as a researcher documenting and analysing the girls' experiences of sexual violence in their rural community and working with them to develop strategies to address it. Finally, I look forward to the future without sexual violence that we (the girls and I) imagine. To do this work, I draw on the research of Haug (1999) and others. Haug describes memory-work as an "emancipating learning project" (p. 28). She further explains that "memory-work was developed with and for the feminist movement" and that her "writing method is written and designed as it applies to women's groups" (p. 2). Feminist researchers like Frost et al. (2012) describe memory-work as a qualitative research method developed as a means of exploring experience in the context of social change. Focusing specifically on memory-work in South Africa, Mitchell and Pithouse-Morgan (2014) explore its use to bring together the researcher and the researched in order to understand women's identities and the social structures in which women live.

Using autobiographical writing by looking back at my own story and considering the girls' stories, in this chapter I reflect on how being a girl in a rural village has changed over time and how, compared to what I look back on as a relatively carefree childhood, today's girlhood is splattered with violence, particularly sexual violence. Brockmeier (2001) has referred to autobiographical writing as "a story, or part of it, that refers in one way or another to one's life history" (p. 247; see also Lapadat, 2009). Autobiographical writing helps one to understand a person's life, but it is, according to Domecka et al. (2012), also a privileged way of approaching individual social reality. This technique has enabled me to reflect on and write about my life as a girl growing up in a rural township in a rural district in Eastern Cape, South Africa. To begin with, I visited my father, who still lives in the rural township where I grew up, and in talking with him, settled on a story that enriched my knowledge about my identity.

Then

Where It All Began: My Father's Story

My father told me the story of how we ended up living in a rural township called New Glenmore, the place where I spent my childhood. I asked my father to tell me about his experiences of rural living, as part of my trying to figure out my own identity. The two of us sat in a rondavel[2] opposite the chicken coop. According to my father, whenever he wanted to clear his mind or if anything was bothering him, he preferred to be close to the livestock, watching them. He believes that looking at the livestock awakens his heart. Since my father was not comfortable with his voice being recorded, we both agreed that I would take notes and ask him if anything was unclear. We talked about his experiences and the pain of being forcibly removed[3] from his home.

When I started the conversation, asking him how we ended up in this particular village, my father became emotional. The question brought back bad memories that he had forgotten and memories that he had never shared with anyone else besides the other people who experienced the forced removals with him. When we started our conversation, my father commented: "Your mother would have been the best person to tell you exactly what happened, as she was at home when the forced removal sergeant brought the news." Among the amaXhosa, my people, the tradition is that mothers are the people who speak to their children, especially daughters. My late mother used to tell us how we were relocated, but not in detail. She passed away a year ago, and so my father had to do the recounting.

In 1979, my family and other residents of Klipfontein, a village in the Alexandria District in Eastern Cape, South Africa, were forcibly removed from their homes by the then apartheid government. These forced removals were not negotiated with the residents nor did they know about them beforehand. Five days before the day of the removals, a police sergeant visited each household and instructed its members to start packing their belongings in time for the relocation. As my father recalled, at first people thought it was a joke. After all, how could about 1,400 people be forced to leave their homes without any explanation? But, according to my father, in the apartheid years anything that oppressed Black African people was possible.

On 2 April 1979, my parents arrived from work to find that their home had been demolished by government workers who had instructed residents to pack their belongings into the waiting trucks that were to take them to their new houses. Human beings, livestock, furniture, and clothes were all loaded into one truck and covered with a tarpaulin. The families left Klipfontein after six in the evening, travelling through the night without being told where they were going. Everybody was afraid of the truck drivers, and no one felt they could even ask where they were going for fear of being beaten. In the early hours of the morning, they arrived somewhere and were told to get their belongings off the truck and to hurry since the drivers needed to go back to Klipfontein to fetch the other families. They were off-loaded and found makeshift houses made of wood with asbestos roofs and mud floors. As Platzky and Walker (1985) have written, people were to discover that the so-called houses to which they were allocated were bitterly cold in winter, scorching hot in summer, and leaked during the rainy season. Forbes (1980, p. 19) observed: "In February 1980, twenty-six of these houses had flooded," given the appalling quality of the structures. Regardless of the apartheid government's claims that the site was temporary, these makeshift structures in Glenmore were to become the displaced people's permanent home.

The actual place where my parents were taken, Glenmore, was a farm located on the eastern side of the Great Fish River, about 40 kilometres by road from Grahamstown in Peddie District, Eastern Cape. It is directly opposite Committees Drift, which was the place originally chosen by the apartheid government in the early seventies to hold displaced people, including my father. Before the incorporation of the homelands[4] into South Africa, Glenmore was situated in the Ciskei. The Ciskei was designated for Black settlement and, as such, served as a destination for forcibly removed Black people. Glenmore is the result of such social engineering, and those who live in this area all have roots elsewhere.

According to my father, things turned bad as soon as they arrived in Glenmore. He recalled that, immediately after their arrival, there was a drought, which killed much of the livestock that had survived the journey. Maclennan (1987) wrote of that time:

> The Glenmore farm was taken from its white owners in 1976. The owner of the farm, Mr. Knott, was at this time rearing cattle and had some land under irrigation. His land, which prior to the enforcement of the National States Constitution Act No 21 of 1971 had allowed for five thousand orange trees and some grapes under intensive irrigation, was bought for R283 000 by the government, and it was proudly announced that an R26 million township would be built at Glenmore over five years. However, the area was so drought prone that the people [were] unable to subsist off the land. (p. 17)

There was also a lack of medical services on the farm turned village, which resulted in the death of many children. The apartheid government had provided only one clinic, which operated from 7:30 a.m. to 4:00 p.m. on weekdays and was closed during weekends. There was no doctor, and serious injuries had to be treated in the Nompumelelo General Hospital in a small town called Peddie, more than 45 kilometres away. The community was angry with the government because they felt that, if they had stayed where they were in their birthplace, their family members would not have died.

Whisson (1981) has written: "About 250 families from Klipfontein [from where my parents were forcibly removed], Coega, Colchester, and other small settlements between the Great Fish River and Port Elizabeth were [also] dumped in this area" (p. 74). People were promised fertile land to feed their livestock and generate income from farming. Men were promised work as labourers and women as domestic workers. On arrival, none of the promises were fulfilled. There were high levels of unemployment and great poverty in the community, with many households depending on the old-age grant of one or two people. There was no electricity and no fences, which made it easy for thieves to steal the livestock. Everyone lost their job, livestock died, children's schooling was disrupted, homes were destroyed, and people got sick and died. In all, they were left with nothing. Men had to go elsewhere to find employment as migrant workers, leaving women and children vulnerable to violence, including rape. These conditions contributed to high levels of violence in the community as the different groups clashed with each other.

In 1979, residents of Glenmore marched against the forced removals and the conditions in their new home. According to the Unemployed People's Movement (2013) press statement, the march was directed at the government to find a solution that would restore the dignity of the people who had been forcibly removed. The march resulted in one of the protesters being arrested for throwing stones through the window of the High Court, the same High Court that had ordered the eviction of these people earlier in 1979. Residents of nearby Grahamstown also marched against the forced removals and in support of the Glenmore residents. In response, the director of the then Eastern Cape Administration Board, Mr. Louis Kock, informed the residents that each home would have running water, a flush toilet, and electricity and that all main roads and bus routes would be tarred. The director further promised that "there would also be job opportunities in a proposed canning industry and in local administration" (Malila, 2000, p. 40). Of course, none of these materialized; there were no jobs, no roads, no running water, and no flush toilets.

According to my father, in 1983, the year I was born, there were rumours that people would have to relocate again to a new place because of Glenmore's proximity to the Great Fish River. During the rainy season, the river tended to overflow its banks, and the flood water damaged the makeshift houses. In addition, there were complaints from the residents that the brackish water was making people ill, so the government once again relocated the community to another place called New Glenmore. The residents gave the settlement this name when they saw two-roomed brick houses in a rural township with an outside bucket toilet for every household. According to my father, no one told them the name of the place to which they were relocating, but they had heard that it was not too far from where they were. New Glenmore would become my home, the place where I was born and where my family still lives.

While I was listening to my father, I cried as I imagined what they had gone through, and many questions came to mind. My father was unable to answer some of my questions, such as why the apartheid government chose this place and why the people were not told where they were going. I thought of *Ubuntu* (I am because you are), an African philosophy of valuing each other, and could not understand why human beings could be so cruel to others. I became angry, but then again I saw my father's resilience in being strong and managing to raise us, with the support of my mother, under those difficult circumstances. Talking to my father and hearing about my past made me realize the importance of knowing my own history. It gave me a chance to hear things that my father never shared with us – the good choices and the poorer ones he made to ensure that I would not repeat his mistakes. My past, as told to me by my father, taught me to love, forgive, and strive for a better future.

Growing Up as a Girl in a Rural Village

Reflecting on my life as a girl growing up in a rural village, I recall that I was able to walk alone to school, play with other children after school, and help my parents cultivate crops in the fields. Life seemed carefree. In a village, everyone knows everyone else, which helps to find a perpetrator when any violence has been committed. Children were taught to respect people, even if they did not know them, which made people respectful of each other and of their lives.

However, looking back on my childhood, I realize that I was never involved in any community activities. In my teenage years, I do remember people marching and protesting on the roads of the village. For example, in 1992, roughly 80,000 protesters from the African National Congress gathered outside Bisho, South Africa, to demand that the Ciskei leader Oupa Gqozo resign and that Ciskei be reintroduced into South Africa (see Gastrow, 1992; South African History Online, 2011). Twenty-nine people were shot by the Ciskei Defence Force in what became known as the Bisho Massacre. This protest was led by African National Congress (ANC) leaders, including Chris Hani, who was then the South African Communist Party secretary. In 1993, the year before the first democratic election in South Africa, Chris Hani was assassinated. The Bisho Massacre, followed so soon after by Hani's death, shook the country because many South African citizens believed that Hani would be the next president after Nelson Mandela.

However, as teenagers, my friends and I would follow a march without knowing anything at all about its mandate. We would progress to the community hall and not listen to what was being discussed. We had boarded a bus so that we could join the protest march to Bisho, and we were just singing at the back, not even knowing the meaning of the songs we were singing. Then we realized that we were far from home and had to find our own way back. On the way, we saw a police van, and we ran and hid in the bushes because of how brutal the police officers were in those days. We arrived at our homes very late, and I was beaten for coming home late, hungry, and dirty. As adolescents, we knew very well that we were not supposed to join any march because we would disturb the event and make a noise, so I could not tell my parents where I had been.

As a child, my passion was reading, looking at photo albums, and singing. I used to read books in my home language, isiXhosa, and create songs from what I had read, holding a teaspoon as if it were a microphone and pretending that I was someone else. I would sing the songs I had composed. As a sociable child, at ten, I was the lead singer and a performer in my school. I participated in every play in primary school until my mother said that I needed to give other children a chance too. I left the stage and started playing netball, but I was not good at it, so I quit. Growing up in a rural township seemed pleasant because I did not know any other life than township life. The only good thing about growing up in New Glenmore was having access to education, unlike other neighbouring farms in the district, where learners had to walk long distances. I remember that some of my schoolmates had to travel 12 kilometres because there were no schools on farms.[5]

Life in the township also had many disadvantages. People are far from everything, such as town, hospitals, and government offices. There were only two *bakkies* (small trucks) that went daily from the area to town. I went to town only once every two or three months; this trip was a treat in those days. It never worried me because I was one of the few lucky ones in my community. Most children went to town only during the December school holidays.

In secondary school, I was one of the top ten learners with a good academic record, and I was motivated by my father to study hard in order to have a better life than his. I grew up reminding myself of those words every day. In those days, there was only one public telephone that worked with a phone card for 540 houses and their inhabitants. When I was in grade 12, I wanted to apply to the university, and my father bought a phone card for R20.00 (the cost then of about 50 loaves of bread). The next morning, I called the university requesting application forms to be posted. The receptionist at the university kept on transferring the call, so my R20.00 ran out before I had accomplished anything. I cried that night because my father was going to town again only in two weeks. I had to wait that long to get another phone card to call the university. I was assisted the next time around.

Right up to grade 12, I did not know how to use a computer, and I was concerned that I would lack the necessary skills when I got to university because I knew that I had to type my assignments. Also, I knew I should be able to speak English, a second language, with which I was not that familiar. When I started university in 2002, I was often embarrassed and scared to return the next day because I did not know how to use a computer mouse. However, with support from our end user lecturer, I managed to learn, gain the skills, and continue with my studies.

Now

Working with Girls to Address Sexual Violence in Rural Communities

I have been employed as a researcher in a project that involves a number of universities in South Africa and Canada, "Networks for Change and Well-Being: Girl-Led 'From the Ground Up' Policy Making to Address Sexual Violence in Canada and South Africa" (hereafter referred to as the Networks4Change project). Mitchell and Moletsane (2018) describe it this way:

> It is a project that is situated at the centre of renewed intensive national and international attention to the impact of sexual violence on girls and young women, especially Indigenous girls and young women in Canada and South Africa. (p. 2)

I also enrolled as a PhD[6] student to conduct fieldwork as part of the Networks4Change project and do research with girls from a rural town. As part of my duties and studies, I conducted focus group discussions (FGDs) with the seven young girl participants in Patterson, a small rural town in Eastern Cape Province who were involved in an arts-based project. The girls, who are currently between the ages of fifteen and sixteen, are participants in the Networks4Change project. They named their group the Young Girls Leading Change (YGLC), after a group of young women university students participating in Networks4Change who named their group Girls Leading Change (GLC).

In these focus groups, I explored the girls' lived experiences of gender-based violence (GBV) in order to establish their existing knowledge and come to understand their agency as young girls. Asking these questions also enabled me to position myself in a rural community different from my own and with a different generation of girls. I posed questions in isiXhosa, our mother tongue, to explore the following questions about the various cellphilms (short videos made with cellphones) the girls made and the action briefs they produced as part of the project.

- How does your production represent issues of GBV?
- What inspired you to create this production?
- If you could create your work all over again, what could you do differently?
- You might have had several different audiences in mind when you were creating your work. Who do you think should see it?
- What would you like the audience to do as a result of your production?

The girls responded confidently. They had been working in the project for three years when I came in. They knew the people leading the project and were comfortable and relaxed in the research space. As Denzin and Lincoln (2013) have suggested, in conducting focus groups, facilitators need to pay attention to participants' responses and encourage all of them to be part of the discussion. I did not need to encourage anyone; the girls willingly offered their responses. I asked them whether I could record the FGD so that I could transcribe their responses at a later stage. I asked them to talk about the main message in the work they are doing. There was no prescribed order of who should start talking, and each girl responded to each question when she was ready to do so. I was surprised to see how confident these girls were, how able they were to speak up about sexual violence, and how they encouraged their peers as well as their parents to seek help when needed. With the opportunities they now have, as I illustrate below, the girls were able to engage in a dialogue with a large community audience in addressing GBV, a critical problem that is hardly discussed in communities (Michau et al., 2015), especially in rural areas. While most parents are often unwilling to discuss sex and gender equality with their children, as Binnie and Klesse (2012) have noted, and children are unwilling or unable to discuss sex with their parents, these girls were pushing the boundaries set by community practices in being very open in addressing GBV and how it affects the young girls and the community at large.

I also asked the girls to create drawings depicting how they saw or experienced GBV in and around their school. The exercise was a bit challenging for them, since they were unsure of how to draw their experiences. I explained what they needed to do, and the girls started discussing this assignment with each other; in doing so, they enhanced collective learning, which enabled them to both enjoy the activity and come up with meaningful drawings. This exercise started an additional discussion for the whole group on how to introduce the topic of GBV using drawings with their peers at school. Following Denzin and Lincoln (2013), I encouraged the participants to talk to one another, discuss, and build upon or challenge each other's opinions. The discussions were rich and revealing.

The Girls' Stories

The members of YGLC are, I realized, engaged in youth activism; they present their work confidently to their peers, teachers, and community members, including elders and peers, and they effect meaningful change. One of the YGLC members is a prefect in her school, where she advises other learners about what to do when they are faced with GBV challenges. For example, one learner was beaten by her boyfriend, and this prefect was called by the principal to speak to her. The prefect said: "This is not acceptable. You need to go to the police and report your boyfriend, otherwise he will continue beating you." In addition, the YGLC members understand that their parents might not have the knowledge they have, and some are patient in coaching them. One of these girls said: "Ma, you need to attend the project meeting so that I can speak freely to you about my boyfriend." Furthermore, these girls gained new skills, including the computer literacy that enabled them to create a PowerPoint presentation, policy posters, and action briefs, as well as learning how to make cellphilms.

In relation to the YGLC members, I remembered that, when I was their age, I would not have been able to lead a march and present work in front of the community. I did not have the confidence to speak out or any knowledge about GBV. I used to hear older women being beaten by their partners, but I had grown up believing that, as a child, their experiences did not concern me since that is what I had been taught. By contrast, the YGLC members took a stand and led a march on 9 August 2018 – Women's Day in South Africa – and raised awareness about GBV in their rural community (Figure 11.1). During the march, the girls proactively sang songs that described how their rights as girls were being violated. At the same time, they called on community members to join

Figure 11.1. YGLC leading the march through their village.
Courtesy of Ntomboxolo Yamile.

the march in support of the fight against GBV. The girls' engagement illustrates the extent of their agency in working towards social change.

The girls' parents and family members, as well as other community members, gathered in front of the police station to join the march devised to raise awareness of GBV. The YGLC members talked about their work in grappling with GBV in their community. They showed their policy posters to make the message visible, along with their action briefs that articulate what they and the community can do to help stop GBV. The march was aimed at contributing to transforming gender norms within the community and to ensure gender equality. After the march, the girls led the marchers to the community hall, where they engaged in identifying the complex nature of GBV in the community and proposing strategies to address it. Several speakers, such as a pastor of a local church, the ward councillor, and the police sergeant, encouraged the girls and women to break the silence and report the violence.

Looking Back, Looking Forward

As an adult woman who moved to the city to study after high school, I realize that I have much more to learn and to do, especially in rural areas. Looking at my own rural village when I visit, I see that people no longer seem united as a community, with each person minding his or her own business. As a result, the level of violence and GBV is high, since no one seems to be looking out for anyone else. I also note that people do know what GBV is, so this behaviour seems to be accepted as the norm. There is no community group working towards addressing GBV or sexual violence. Parents are still nervous to discuss sex with their children because they do not know what to say or are scared to say what they know. For instance, the older women from church always remind me to have a talk about menstruation and sex with their daughters because they do not know what to say to them. The older people are worried about their daughters being infected with HIV and getting pregnant, but they are still not willing to start the discussion.

The YGLC members are in a different space in their rural area because, through the strategies they have learned in the Networks4Change project, they are developing their understanding of GBV along with the confidence to address this issue. The YGLC members are talking to their parents about their work, and by so doing, they disseminate what they know not only at meetings in the school and community but also through informal conversations at home. Compared to me when I was their age, I note the girls' awareness and agency, and their willingness to take a stand against GBV in their community.

Seeing young girls like me from a rural area leading a march was exciting. I was amazed to see them taking a stand as young activists and not looking only to adults to address an issue that is ravaging their community. Seeing young girls being unafraid about how the community would look at them after the march highlighted the many ways in which my own childhood was different. As a teenager, I was constrained by social norms that defined women and girls as submissive to men and boys. An example that comes to mind is how, in the afternoons after school, I worked in the field with my mother, while other girls and boys were taking part in athletics. We would harvest vegetables, bring them home, and sell them in the community to earn money towards paying for school fees or buying school uniforms. As a woman, my mother did not want to depend on my father; she also wanted to provide for her children. However, one day when we came back very late from the fields, my father told my mother that, from that day on, we should stay at home like other women. My mother ignored his instruction and went to harvest again the following day. At the end of the month, she bought some groceries with her money, and my father was not happy at all. This attitude reminds me of the work of Parsons et al. (2015) who, among many other scholars such as Hicks (2018) and Renold (2005), have confirmed that GBV is rooted in gender inequality and social expectations of what it means to be a girl and a woman. In my childhood and adolescence, gender inequality did, of course, play itself out, but I was not aware, even of what it was.

A second example relates to how, as a young girl, I was uninformed about menstruation, family planning, and GBV. The only thing my mother told me was that, if I slept with a boy, I would get pregnant. Similarly, when I first met the YGLC members, they told me they, too, had heard about menstruation, family planning, and sex from older girls at school. In our upbringing, both then and now, there was and is no interaction between different generations about the issues pertaining to sexual health. The similarities between my girlhood and that of the YGLC members surprised me because they were born twenty years later. Parents are still not having open discussions regarding sexual and reproductive health (SRH) issues or gender equality with their children (see Binnie & Klesse, 2012). Equally, schools provide no support for boys and girls to develop skills aimed at ensuring gender equality and coping with SRH issues in their own lives, as Bhana (2012) has reminded us.

Conclusion: Where Am I in This Picture?

This autobiographical reflection has enabled me to consider how being a girl during my mother's generation, my generation, and the current generation of girls has changed and is changing in relation to experiences of, and responses to, gender inequality and GBV. The members of YGLC and other girls and young women are now taking the lead, not waiting for their mothers or their grandmothers to take action against inequality and violence in their rural communities (Moletsane, 2018). I, too, have learned from the work of the YGLC and the Networks4Change project and the value of paying it forward to other girls and young women. My father's prayer left me thinking about where we are as women and girls in relation to GBV. While it is intensifying (Statistics South Africa, 2018), some girls and young women are breaking the silence and demanding respect. Clearly, this demand calls for interventions steered by girls and young women, especially from the rural areas, to enable engagement and dialogue, which, with reference to the work of bell hooks, might work towards "restor[ing] their humanity to where they are valued and seen as equally human" (Adam & De Lange, 2018, p. 143). I am taking the lessons I am learning from the YGLC members and other girl groups in the Networks4Change project to other young girls in the rural village where I grew up, and where I now return every summer holiday, hoping to motivate them to start working together to address GBV and other social ills in the community.

The lived experiences of girls growing up in a rural context – then and now – show how different and how similar we are. These contemporary young girls seem more able with ever increasing sources of support to make informed decisions, take action, and contribute to change in their communities. Young girls, hoping to improve their lives and the lives of other young women and girls, are ready for social change in society. My being in the picture with contemporary girls can be part of changing it with them.

NOTES

1 Young Girls Leading Change is a group of seven schoolgirls in a rural town who have been working together as a girls' group to address gender-based violence in the school and the community. They are part of the Networks4Change project funded by the Social Sciences and Humanities Research Council and the International Development Research Centre (2013–20).

2 A rondavel is usually a round or oval house and is traditionally made with materials that can be found locally in raw form.

3 Before 1994, Black Africans were removed from their homes and forced into segregated neighbourhoods as a result of apartheid legislation.

4 Homelands were lands set aside by the apartheid government for Black people to prevent them from living in the white urban areas of South Africa.

5 While my family lived in a rural village, others lived and continue to live on farms owned by white people.

6 Yamile, N. (2022). *Girl-Led Intervention to Address Gender-Based Violence in a Rural School Community: Using a Digital Dialogue Tool* [Unpublished doctoral dissertation]. Nelson Mandela University.

REFERENCES

Adam, M., & De Lange, N. (2018). Seeing things: Schoolgirls in a rural setting using visual artefacts to initiate dialogue in resisting sexual violence. In C. Mitchell & R. Moletsane (Eds.), *Disrupting shameful legacies: Girls and young women speaking back through the arts to address sexual violence* (pp. 139–54). Brill.

Bhana, D. (2012). "Girls are not free" – In and out of the South African schools. *International Journal of Educational Development, 32*(2), 352–8. https://doi.org/10.1016/j.ijedudev.2011.06.002

Binnie, J., & Klesse, C. (2012). The politics of age, temporality and intergenerationality in transnational lesbian, gay, bisexual, transgender and queer activist networks. *Sociology, 47*(3), 580–95. https://doi.org/10.1177/0038038512453792

Brockmeier, J. (2001). From the end to the beginning: Retrospective teleology in autobiography. In J. Brockmeier & D. Carbaugh (Eds.), *Narrative and identity: Studies in autobiography, self, and culture* (pp. 39–58). John Benjamins.

Denzin, N.K., & Lincoln, Y. (2013). *Collecting and interpreting qualitative materials*. Sage.

Domecka, M., Eichsteller, M., Karakusheva, S., Musella, P., Ojamäe, L., Perone, E., Pickard, D., Schröder-Wildhagen, A., Siilad, K., & Waniek, K. (2012). Method in practice: Autobiographical narrative interviews in search of European phenomena. In R. Miller & G. Day (Eds.), *The evolution of European identities* (pp. 21–44). Palgrave McMillan.

Forbes, D. (1980). *Glenmore: Where people have no future*. Black Sash.

Frost, N.A., Eatough, V., Shaw, R., Weille, K.L., Tzemou, E., & Baraitser, L. (2012). Pleasure, pain, and procrastination: Reflections on the experience of doing memory-work research. *Qualitative Research in Psychology, 9*(3), 231–48. https://doi.org/10.1080/14780887.2010.500355

Gastrow, S. (1992). Oupa Joshua Gqozo. In *Who's who in South African politics*. Ravan Press.

Haug, F. (1999). Memory-work as a method of social science research: A detailed rendering of memory-work method. http://www.friggahaug.inkrit.de/documents/memorywork-researchguidei7.pdf

Hicks, J. (2018, 6–7 March). *Gender-based violence and sexual violence in South Africa: Legal and policy frameworks* [Paper presentation]. Colloquium on the Use of Participatory Visual Methodologies in Addressing Gender-Based Violence in and around Post-Secondary Educational Institutions, Durban, RSA.

Lapadat, J.C. (2009). Writing our way into shared understanding: Collaborative autobiographical writing in the qualitative methods class. *Qualitative Inquiry, 15*(6), 955–79. https://doi.org/10.1177/1077800409334185

Maclennan, B. (1987). *Glenmore: The story of a forced removal*. South African Institute of Race Relations.

Malila, B. (2000). *Rural underdevelopment in the former Ciskei with specific reference to Glenmore village* [Unpublished master's thesis]. Rhodes University.

Michau, L., Horn, J., Bank, A., Dutt, M., & Zimmermann, C. (2015). Prevention of violence against women and girls: Lessons from practice. *The Lancet, 385*(9978), 1672–84. https://doi.org/10.1016/S0140-6736(14)61797-9

Mitchell, C., & Moletsane, R. (Eds.). (2018). *Disrupting shameful legacies: Girls and young women speaking back through the arts to address sexual violence*. Brill.

Mitchell, C., & Pithouse-Morgan, K. (2014). Expanding the memory catalogue: Southern African women's contributions to memory-work writing as a feminist research methodology. *Agenda: Empowering Women for Gender Equity, 28*(1), 92–103. https://doi.org/10.1080/10130950.2014.883704

Moletsane, R. (2018). "Stop the war on women's bodies": Facilitating a girl-led march against sexual violence in a rural community in South Africa. *Studies in Social Justice*, 12(2), 235–50. https://doi.org/10.26522/ssj.v12i2.1655

Parsons, J., Edmeades, J., Kes, A., Petroni, S., Sexton, M., & Wodon, Q. (2015). Economic impacts of child marriage: A review of literature. *Review of Faith & International Affairs*, 13(3), 12–22. https://doi.org/10.1080/15570274.2015 .1075757

Platzky, L., & Walker, C. (1985). *The surplus people: Forced removals in South Africa*. Ravan Press.

Renold, E. (2005). *Girls, boys and junior sexualities: Exploring children's gender and sexualities*. Routledge.

South African History Online. (2011, 17 February). Oupa Joshua Gqozo. *South African history online*. https://www.sahistory.org.za/people/oupa -joshua-gqozo

Statistics South Africa. (2018). *Crime against women in South Africa*. Report No. 03-40-05. Pretoria, RSA.

Unemployed People's Movement. (2013, 14 November). SA: Statement by the Unemployed People's Movement on National Assembly of the Unemployed. *Polity*. https://www.polity.org.za/article/sa-statement-by -the-unemployed-peoples-movement-on-national-assembly-of-the -unemployed-14112013-2013-11-14

Whisson, M. (1981). Glenmore: A case study. In N. Nash & N. Charton (Eds.), *An empty table?* South African Council of Churches.

12 Positionality at the Centre: An Epistemological and Methodological Approach for Conducting Research in the Postcolonial

CATHERINE VANNER

Introduction

As a Western feminist, I have supported gender equality in education in postcolonial contexts in numerous roles: as a researcher and as a bilateral donor supporting international, Canadian, and African non-governmental organizations (NGOs). Always political, positionality and identity are especially so for Western researchers in postcolonial contexts. For this chapter, the term "postcolonial" refers to a previously colonized space that is now technically independent. It can describe a nation-state or an area, a group of people, texts, or ideas within a nation-state that may or may not be postcolonial itself. These spaces are officially decolonized but are usually characterized by a new imperialism (Harvey, 2003; Tikly, 2004), shaped by the economic, political, military, and cultural hegemony of the West within the context of globalization (Tikly & Bond, 2013). Therefore, the Western researcher represents not only a colonial past but also a neocolonial present. In light of postcolonial critiques of Western researchers and international development, I have often wondered: "Am I doing more harm than good?" The privilege that accompanies my social location as a white, upper class Canadian academic woman means that, despite good intentions, my efforts to support education in postcolonial contexts risk being patronizing, insulting, threatening, imperialist, and recolonizing.

This chapter will explore epistemological and methodological approaches to answer the questions: Should Western feminists like me do research in postcolonial contexts? And if so, how? It is widely acknowledged that the research process is infused with power, conceptualized here using a Foucauldian understanding of power as exercised and productive, dispersed through social interactions, operating at the micro-level, and best analysed by examining strategies, tactics, and procedures (Elaber-Idemedia, 2002; Foucault, 1980). Strategies, tactics, and procedures that characterize power dynamics in research include participant selection, privacy, disclosure, interviews, observation, analysis, and the (re)presentation of research participants and their communities. Even with methodologies that seek input from participants and local stakeholders, the researcher is usually the primary decision-maker and thereby the dominant figure in the research process. This dominance is true of most research and acutely so for research with vulnerable populations. Due to the legacy of colonialism, combined with ongoing neocolonial relations that characterize postcolonial locations, most research subjects in postcolonial contexts are considered vulnerable (Shamim & Qureshi, 2013), although to varying degrees. Patriarchal structures combined with colonial/neocolonial systems make postcolonial women a particularly disempowered and therefore vulnerable group (Spivak, 1988). Consequently, feminist research in postcolonial contexts has the potential to challenge and/or reproduce power inequalities; the latter is an especially strong risk for Western researchers, who represent a physical and historical embodiment of colonialism and neocolonialism. Yet, neglecting and ignoring postcolonial contexts because I am not a member of a community that is directly and negatively affected by colonialism and neocolonialism similarly reflects and reproduces my privileged position without drawing attention to or challenging unequal and oppressive structures. As Alcoff (1991–2) writes, the decision not to speak on behalf of others "may result merely in a retreat into a narcissistic yuppie lifestyle in which a privileged person takes no responsibility" (p. 17). In response to this deliberation, I provide a tentative framework designed to address my positionality and inherent power and privilege, while creating an ethical research process for working in the postcolonial. Clarifying this framework prior to data collection, modifying it throughout, and then reflecting upon it afterward proved a useful process for reconciling my social location with my topic of analysis, while crafting my identity as a researcher and academic, and navigating the requirements of a doctoral program. The process of setting out an epistemological and methodological framework that integrates and accounts for the power connected to positionality is recommended for all researchers but particularly for new researchers seeking to establish the principles that will guide their research.

In discussing "cultural differences" in postcolonial contexts, it is overly simplistic to talk of community, language, daily functioning, and understandings of research without also addressing questions of power, privilege, and position. The following outlines a two-pronged approach to navigating cultural differences for Western feminists conducting research in postcolonial contexts. The term "Western" is used as a simplified adjective for products, peoples, knowledge, and systems emerging from Euro-centric high-income countries and cultures that are historically and contemporarily privileged by domination of global and local social and economic knowledge, power, and production systems, often at the exclusion of knowledge and perspectives of Indigenous persons and/or groups originating in the Global South. The first step is to identify the researcher's positionality, the objectives of the research, and the guiding theoretical framework(s) to situate the researcher and her research in relation to the participants and context. I position myself as a *bricoleur* (Kincheloe & McLaren, 2005), layering feminist standpoint theory and postcolonial theory to establish my positionality and research objectives. *Bricolage* is a phenomenon of leaning into the hybridity and cross-disciplinarity of research perspectives, stepping back from conventional understandings of research rules, and drawing from "numerous modes of meaning making and knowledge productions" that are useful for understanding forces of domination and intersecting determinants of social location (Kincheloe et al., 2011, p. 169). In this sense, the research process is developed to respond to the specificity of the local context and the critical theoretical perspectives driving the research. The second step is to identify a methodological design that will minimize the negative effects of power on the research participants and maximize their empowerment. I propose the integration of participatory and collaborative data collection and analysis techniques, with particular attention to ethical and cultural sensitivity, into a social constructivist approach to grounded theory. Privilege and positionality make undertaking research in postcolonial contexts difficult and risky but also, for me, essential to contribute to the empowerment of those disadvantaged by the same systems that have advantaged me.

The framework provided here is supplemented with examples and reflections from my doctoral thesis data collection, which consisted of two qualitative case studies of two public primary schools in central Kenya. My research examined the relationship between gender safety in schools (GSS) and student learning processes in Kenyan public primary schools. Building on the extensive literature demonstrating the high prevalence of gender violence in schools (GVS) in Kenya (Abuya et al., 2012; Ruto, 2009; Wane, 2009), and in sub-Saharan Africa more broadly (Parkes et al., 2013; Saito, 2013), and the recent proliferation of NGO projects seeking to eradicate GVS, my thesis seeks to elaborate on the factors that contribute to GSS and the relationship between GSS, GVS, and students' learning processes and outcomes. A gender safe school is defined by Stein et al. (2002) as a place where girls and boys

> have freedom to learn, explore and develop skills in all academic and extracurricular offerings, to be psychologically, socially and physically safe from threats, harassment or harm in all parts of the school ... [acknowledging and challenging] how conventional beliefs about masculinity and femininity constrain and undermine learning, participation and movement. (pp. 41–2)

Data collection methods included seven months of participant observation, individual semi-structured teacher interviews, and open-ended art-based individual student interviews with students aged eleven to fifteen. Data collection took place in two schools, one in a town with a population of approximately 10,000 and the other in a nearby rural area. Both schools were co-ed public day schools with approximately 500 students, ranging from nursery to standard 8. Necessary government and university approvals were obtained at two stages: Initial approval was granted for participant observation prior to starting data collection. I then submitted another round of applications and received approval from the Kenyan government and my university's research ethics board (REB) for interviews midway through my participant observation stage. Submitting ethics applications and research permits after spending several months conducting observation allowed me to become more familiar with the context and obtain input from school stakeholders before finalizing the methodology for the more high-risk interview stage of the research. Interviews were audio recorded unless the participant preferred they not be recorded, in which case extensive notes were taken; this option was requested by several teacher participants. Teacher interviews were conducted in English, but student interviews used a combination of English, Kiswahili, and Kikuyu with the assistance of a translator. The following includes a description of my methodological framework as well as reflections on the planned elements that ultimately needed to be adapted due to the requirements of either my Canadian university or the local context.

Positionality

There is no neutral or apolitical research (Halse & Honey, 2005; Lather, 1991; Mohanty, 1988). My opinions, values, beliefs, and social background accompany me through the research process, shaping each methodological and analytical decision that I make. I am a Canadian feminist and children's rights advocate; I believe that quality education leads to positive individual and social outcomes. I am particularly interested in education systems in sub-Saharan Africa, but most of my own formal education has taken place in Ontario, Canada. In my previous role as an education specialist at a bilateral donor, I felt mildly uncomfortable with the paternal systems through which we (the donor) dealt with NGO and recipient government partners, but I participated in them, eager to help facilitate what I believed was positive educational programming for children and young people in postcolonial contexts. I now seek to question these assumptions and undertake participatory and emancipatory research to understand, from the perspective of children, parents, and teachers, what their vision of quality education is. Although my social position is a detriment to this research in some ways, I can use my position to leverage less powerful voices to speak back to the powerful about their understanding of what education in the postcolonial is and should be. Said (1985) described a need for greater cross-disciplinary activity, characterized by an awareness of the political, methodological, social, and historical situation in which intellectual work is undertaken, a commitment to dismantling systems of domination, and a heightened sense of the intellectual's role in both defining a given context and changing it. I therefore tentatively deduce that it is possible for me to research and write about the postcolonial if I am aware of my influence, ensure that the representation of my participants aligns with their self-identities and emancipatory objectives, and continuously reflect upon the impact of my positionality and research on the participating communities.

Recognizing that research remains an inherently hierarchical process, the researcher should continuously explore opportunities to work in collaboration with participants to respond to community needs and contribute in a sustainable way to enhancing opportunities for participants and other stakeholders, within and also potentially outside the immediate scope of the research project. For me, it involved exploring opportunities to give back by enhancing the skills of students, teachers, and community members in ways that were deemed valuable by those individuals instead of acting on the preconceived notions I had brought about how I might contribute. My contributions resulted in a makeshift assortment of computer training, child-centred teaching activities, editing scholarship applications, letter exchanges with Canadian students, career days that brought in local professionals to speak to students, and advocating on behalf of the schools to local government bodies. These contributions were made at the request or with enthusiastic interest from community members. They did not inherently shift the power dynamics at play but sought to use the advantages of my positionality to contribute positively to the empowerment and enhancement of opportunities and skills for interested participants and community members.

What Kind of Feminism?

Concern with power and representation is fundamental to almost all kinds of feminism, which is rooted in an exploration of the power relations that characterize social interpretations of gender. As Lather (1991) writes, "to do feminist research is to put the social construction of gender at the center of one's inquiry" (p. 159). Feminist research involves a reframing of traditional approaches to research (Marshall & Young, 2006) in order to be considerate and reflective of the "multifaceted nature of gender" that permeates all research and social systems and practices (Beetham & Demetriades, 2007, p. 199). Feminist standpoint theorists assert that the starting point of knowledge about the structures and practices through which girls and women are oppressed and empowered should be their daily lived experiences, from which feminist researchers can work upward to critique the principles, practices, and influences of dominant institutions (Harding, 2007; Smith, 1990). Feminist research's emancipatory objective seeks to challenge and ultimately change power structures to become more equitable, in part by illuminating the voices and experiences of the less powerful and enabling the expression of "subjugated knowledge" (Collins, 2000). Emancipation and empowerment, in this sense, are not conceived of as the liberation of participants by the researcher and her knowledge but rather as a more subtle shift in opposition to oppressive social structures that arises through a process of individual and collective self-reflection, the deepening of social knowledge, and the development of critical problem-solving skills and resources (Reid, 2004). This process may be initiated by the researcher but is dependent on the active engagement of the participants and on critical exchanges between the researcher and participant as well as between participants. Research participants' understanding of their own context should be enhanced through a combination of individual self-reflection and engagement with the researcher during the process; this, for many feminist researchers, is even more important than generating new knowledge and theory (Lather, 1991; Reid, 2004).

Some research designs extend the participatory process significantly beyond what is described here by engaging participants as researchers, which has been done in many types of research, including with children and other vulnerable groups (Åkerström & Brunnberg, 2012; Nind, 2011; Pahl & Pool, 2011). While a fully participatory process like that described above had initially been my goal, it was considered to be too ambitious and complicated for a doctoral dissertation. While it may well be feasible, the candidate would need to have significant resources as well as a thesis committee and ethics board that were willing to recognize the importance of a highly flexible methodology. As a doctoral student, I was not the only individual controlling the research decisions in relation to my methodology, and I faced time and resource constraints that tenured professors may not have. Therefore, a fully participatory approach (where participants act as researchers and are engaged in every step of the research process, from development of the research question and methodology throughout the analysis and writing) was considered too ambitious for my doctoral dissertation. Thus, the researcher's positionality can be simultaneously highly privileged by social location in relation to knowledge, education, racial, and socio-economic status but still be constrained by a relatively subordinate status in the hierarchy of the university.

Postcolonial Theory

Western feminists are often critiqued for an essentialist concentration on the category of "woman" without analysing how gender intersects with other forms of marginalization, including race, class, nationality, sexuality, and ability. Consequently, white middle/upper class feminist scholars often appear to speak on behalf of all women, obscuring the narratives of women whose lives are radically different and less privileged. When used in reference to postcolonial contexts, a simplifying and patronizing portrayal of victimized "Third World women" emerges in contrast to liberated (white) Western women. Mohanty's (1988) "Under Western Eyes" critiques Western feminists whose research nurtures this dichotomy in which the heterogeneous lives of postcolonial women are produced and singularly represented. The dichotomy is created through practices that portray women's oppression as a global phenomenon; ignore the effects of racism, colonialism, and imperialism; and depict postcolonial women as the subjects of power, dominated by legal, economic, religious, and familial structures without individual agency. Mohanty's powerful critique pushes feminists, particularly Western feminists writing about a postcolonial "other," to carefully examine their research and representation for these colonizing devices. Alcoff (1991–2) similarly encourages academics to reframe their approach to "speaking for" people in less privileged social locations by first attempting to listen and critically examine the impetus to speak on behalf of others; deconstructing the social location from which one is speaking and the effects that the location has on the truth and content of what is said; being accountable and responsible by inviting dialogue, conversation, and critique from the people about whom one is speaking; and finally, analysing the probable or actual effects of one's words.

Feminism is not inherently Western but rather is historically rooted in postcolonial contexts as well as Western ones (Akin-Aina, 2011; Eltahawy, 2015; Mannathoko, 1999). Mohanty (2003, p. 46) points out that global intercultural alliances are possible in an "imagined community of Third World feminism" comprised of women with diverse histories and social locations united by political opposition to systemic forms of domination. Community members recognize that race and gender are relational terms, disadvantaging some and advantaging others. This idea fits with other discursive understandings of gender as "always relative to the constructed relations in which it is determined" (Butler, 1990, p. 139). The challenge for Western feminists is to expand their idea of social construction to include racial, colonial, and neocolonial influences, as well as other forms of marginalization that contribute to different constructions of gender. Postcolonial theory is concerned with ways that power and language address the nature of cultural identity, gender, race, social class, ethnicity, and nationality in postcolonial contexts (Burney, 2012). The theory privileges postcolonial knowledge, both academically and in the research communities studied. Conventional research paradigms in European and North American universities are characterized by a set of values; attitudes; conceptualizations of time, space, subjectivity, knowledge, theory, and language; and structures of power that frame them as superior approaches (Smith, 2012). To counter the historic roots of feminist standpoint theory and constructivist grounded theory (CGT) in Western intellectual traditions (Harding, 2007), postcolonial academic discourse can provide an effective critique that decentres Western knowledge assumptions. The research design should also be sufficiently flexible to adapt as it becomes informed by local forms of knowledge that emerge throughout the research process. Postcolonial theory is thus instrumental for me to analyse data and to critique my own research methodology.

Feminist standpoint theory is applicable in postcolonial contexts, given its emphasis on knowledge as locally situated and socially constructed and on producing knowledge for women instead of politically dominant institutions (Harding, 2012). While standpoint theorists have been criticized as essentialist (Flax, 1990), the attention brought by women of colour and postcolonial theorists to the intersectionality of oppressions has forced standpoint theory to evolve and insist upon the recognition of multiple, often conflicting, experiences of women and feminists (Harding, 2007). The "research context" should therefore include micro-level forces that shape participants' understanding as well as macro-level ones that influence the local community, aligning with Mohanty's (2003) call for an imagined community of feminists who encourage relational and systemic understandings of race, gender, and domination. Standpoint theory is possible in research about a community where the researcher is not a member, but it requires collaboration between the researcher and community members to ensure that the standpoint is properly understood, and the members of the marginalized group should always have the last word about their representation (Collins, 1991; Harding, 1993). To embrace the postcolonial, the researcher must deconstruct the power embedded in traditional approaches; recognize the validity of non-Western forms of knowledge; and integrate non-Western researchers, practices, and forms of knowledge through a process of intercultural collaboration that brings postcolonial perspectives and epistemologies to the forefront (Jankie, 2004; Swadener & Mutua, 2008). As theory establishes the groundwork for methodological choices (Marshall & Young, 2006), I now turn to an examination of the methodological, ethical, and analytical considerations with which I conducted research rooted in feminist standpoint and postcolonial theories. This discussion is accompanied by reflections on my experiences applying the framework in my thesis data collection and the inherent challenges and opportunities presented.

Constructivist Grounded Theory

Grounded theory is an analytical method with which to determine the essential themes and theory that emerge from a research project. Its methods are defined by Charmaz (2005, p. 204) as "a set of flexible analytic guidelines that enable researchers to focus their data collection and to build inductive middle-range theories through successive levels of data analysis and conceptual development." When the theory was originally developed by Glaser and Strauss (1967), its defining components included simultaneous data collection and analysis, analytic codes constructed from the data, constant comparison across data sources, the development of theory at each stage of the research process, memo-writing, and theoretical sampling. CGT maintains most of these components but with a significant epistemological difference: a constructivist perspective rejects the idea that theory "emerges" from the data independently, recognizing instead the role of the researcher in shaping the narrative by drawing on her own experiences and beliefs, and through her interactions with participants and the data (Charmaz, 2006). Constructivism denies the existence of an objective reality, "asserting instead that realities are social constructions of the mind"

(Guba & Lincoln, 1989, p. 43). This notion is relevant for participatory research, as it emphasizes the interrelationship between researcher and participant in the co-construction of meaning (Mills et al., 2006).

Grounded theory is frequently employed in feminist research (Clarke, 2012; Keddy et al., 1996; Kushner & Morrow, 2003), and elements, including an emphasis on direct quotes and the development of a situated theory based on the data, align with feminist principles by emphasizing participants' lived experiences to build a legitimized theory and analysis (Arnot, 2006; Harding, 2012). While the researcher inevitably brings her ideological beliefs and assumptions to the project, the constant comparison between multiple data sources and simultaneous analysis and data collection allows the researcher to identify a theory that is empirically based, rather than imposing theory on the data (Clarke, 2007). The resulting theory is described as inductive or emergent because it is developed through an ongoing process, while the researcher is situated within the data collection process, providing her with the opportunity to conduct regular member checks, discuss the analysis with participants, and pursue relevant sources. The researcher brings her prior theoretical knowledge and perspectives with her (Bruce, 2007), but the immersion of the researcher within the data collection process allows the data sources to become the focal point in light of which external theories are considered, instead of a subsequent analysis that would be more likely to prioritize the theoretical perspective(s) and manipulate data to fit within them. As Charmaz (2006) states, questions from the coding process "arise from [the researcher's] reading of the data, rather than emanating from an earlier frame applied to them" (p. 45). The emphasis on situated knowledge and the interrelationship between local and global systems makes CGT particularly relevant for postcolonial feminist research, described as starting with "sensitizing concepts that address such concepts as power, global reach and difference and end[ing] with inductive analyses that theorize such connections between local worlds and larger structures" (p. 256). Given its accordance with the principles of participatory, postcolonial, and feminist approaches to research, CGT is an ideal analytical method with which to scrutinize data and identify the relevance of feminist and postcolonial theories, while inhibiting the imposition of theoretical perspectives if they do not reflect the participants' lived experiences.

I applied CGT, starting with the continuous and ongoing initial coding of my field notes and interview transcripts and memoing on the trends and themes that appeared to be emerging as I was still conducting research. To validate and explore the authenticity of my interpretation of the emergent themes from the initial coding, I held a series of member check interviews with teachers and students to ask them the extent to which they agreed or disagreed with the initial findings and to explore them further. I chose a non-traditional approach to member check interviews by conducting them mostly with new participants who had not been initially interviewed. The role of these member check interviews was not to validate the accuracy of our interview records or to confirm the direct interpretation of what had been said in a specific interview but rather to verify that the emerging themes and analysis from the interviews reflected the lived experience of students and teachers in the schools. Morse (2015) asserts that the practice of sharing initial findings with other participants and asking how these findings relate to them provides a stronger assurance of reliability than sharing transcripts with initial participants by determining normative patterns of behaviour and understanding. New participants and teachers were also used as a means of expanding the number of participants, as the interest in conducting interviews exceeded my expectations and I wanted to increase the opportunities for more individuals to participate. The validation process also took place through many non-formal conversations as I spent time in the schools on a daily basis. Sharing initial findings with participants and inviting their reflections helped me to correct assumptions and extend and sharpen emergent themes with both formal and non-formal input from participants; it also served as a form of theoretical sampling by strategically and specifically exploring theoretical categories previously identified for greater depth and detail (Charmaz, 2014).

Ethical Protocols

The ethical review process institutionalized in Western universities, and increasingly present in non-Western universities as well, is inadequate, particularly for research in postcolonial contexts (Kiragu & Warrington, 2012; Shamim & Qureshi, 2010). The review process is itself oriented towards a Western cultural framework, and so conventional ethics review processes must be complemented by local ethical clearance (Schnarch, 2004; Shamim & Qureshi, 2013). Several models for establishing this complementarity exist, including Simons and Usher's (2000) call for "situated ethics" that reflects specific local practices. The specific local practices of a given context must be determined through continuous negotiation with research participants and community leaders in each individual research project so that the community has the final say on what is and is not acceptable (Denzin & Lincoln, 2008; Renold et al., 2011). This process is not straightforward, as communities are not homogenous, and there may be conflicts or points of contention within the community. It is therefore important for the researcher to consider the repercussions of her decisions, particularly for the most vulnerable participants or affected parties, ask whose voice is being privileged and why, and always prioritize the safety and requests of community members over the depth of data collection. Ethical points of contention that may arise based on cultural context include privacy, disclosure, written versus oral consent, signed forms, and recording devices, among many others. These challenges vary by context, making a general postcolonial ethics procedure impossible; a situated ethics must be determined based on discussion and negotiation within the local context and is not transferable to another locale. It is complicated, however, by the need to respond to the REB requirements of most Western universities prior to beginning data collection, meaning that the methods and ethical protocol have to be predetermined before approval for the project can be obtained and changes to be more responsive to the local context often result in a lengthy delay. One way to effectively address this challenge is to spend time in the community where data collection will take place beforehand, discussing and formulating the methodology with the participants prior to drafting a proposal or an ethics application. For graduate students, however, cost and time limitations can prohibit this early consultation from taking place. Breaking the ethical approval into two stages was an alternative approach that enabled me to first obtain approval for participant observation and, during that time, gain input from participants about the proposed methods and design for the interviews. I then reapplied for research permits and ethical approval for interviews after adjusting the methodology to respond to the local context.

To meet the REB requirements, some of the more participatory elements of the methodology had to be removed due to the board's concern over my inability to ensure confidentiality when discussing initial findings with groups of participants. Another major concern was the lack of clear protocol for reporting cases of child abuse should they be uncovered during data collection, as the legal obligations to report such abuse are much less clear in Kenya than they are in Canada. I was concerned, however, that an obligation to report could expose participants to more harm. Eventually, it was agreed that, instead of declaring that I would or would not report cases of abuse, each case would be dealt with individually through joint consultation with my local Kenyan supervisor (also one of my thesis committee members), my Canadian thesis supervisor, and other local stakeholders if relevant. This protocol did eventually get applied in numerous cases where children were perceived to be in danger and in one very complicated case in particular.

Near the end of my data collection, a teacher informed me that a standard 6 girl at one of the schools where I was conducting data collection (not an interview participant) was being regularly raped by her stepfather, who was rumoured to be HIV positive. The teacher was unwilling to report the incident to the Children's Services Department responsible for dealing with these issues for fear of dangerous repercussions. I therefore worked with my supervisors and my translator/research assistant to determine a solution whereby we could report the case so that the girl would be removed from the abusive situation without revealing the identity of the teacher. After months of pursuing the case, it was ultimately reported to Children's Services, the stepfather was arrested, and the girl was taken to the hospital for a medical exam. She reported the same story to the police that she had to the teacher, but the next day the doctors proclaimed her to be a virgin with a mental illness that had caused her to make up the story. Both the girl and her stepfather were released and returned home, but there remain questions about the veracity of the medical report and the potential for corrupt influences. At the time of submission, we continue to struggle to determine what is true and to guarantee the girl's safety. This case shows that the obligation to report child abuse should not be taken lightly. The researcher assumes responsibility to protect her participants without necessarily having a clear mechanism for how to do so. I take this opportunity, however, to recognize the incredible support and dedication of my research assistant, Mary, whose conviction, perseverance, and ingenuity in navigating local official and non-official systems to guarantee the girl is safe and protected, has garnered my eternal gratitude and admiration. Mary has been instrumental in helping me better understand the local context and relevance of our data more broadly, but she has been particularly crucial in advancing this case. We are now seeking assistance from a local child protection NGO and remain hopeful that our ongoing efforts will achieve a solution whereby we can rest assured that this child is safe, protected from harm, and receives necessary medical treatment and social support.

Cultural and Linguistic Sensitivity

While there are many variables to consider in determining how to make a research project culturally situated and ethically strong, I focus on three elements commonly identified as central to postcolonial research ethics: language, consent, and giving back to the community.

Language is a clear starting point for making the research process more accessible and comfortable for research participants. As a linguistic expression of culture and the main mode of communication, language is a critical factor through which to demonstrate respect for Indigenous cultures. Ngũgĩ wa Thiong'o (1986) asserts that the cornerstone of cultural preservation and the "decolonization of the mind" in Africa are African languages. Thus, the use of local languages in research demonstrates respect for the local community and culture, and commitment to decolonization, and helps to develop trust between the community, participants, and researcher (Griffiths, 1998). A multilingual research project is inevitably characterized by a struggle for the researcher and research participant to understand each other. By using a local language, combined with translation to enhance accurate understanding and representation, the struggle for self-expression falls on the shoulders of the researcher and not the researched. The researcher should provide numerous options so that the language decision can be made by the participant(s). Teachers adamantly told me they wanted the interviews to be conducted in English, firmly turning down the option to do them in Kiswahili or Kikuyu. For the student interviews, Mary and I together introduced the art-based draw–write–narrate method (Ogina & Nieuwenhuis, 2010) to the class of participating students in each school, explaining the process in English and Kiswahili to ensure accurate understanding. During the individual interviews, students were presented with the option of doing the interview in English, Kiswahili, or Kikuyu. Most selected to use a combination of the three languages, and Mary provided clarification between us where necessary. Mary accompanied me on the interviews and conducted the transcription and translation of audio recordings so that the words were not taken out of context. Critical to the success of the project was a strong working relationship between Mary and myself, so that she fully understood the objectives of the project and had the opportunity to contribute to and critique the process and the emerging analysis formally and nonformally. This working relationship was essential for guaranteeing that both the translation and my interpretation of the data captured the nuances of the participants' voices. That said, translation always holds the possibility of miscommunication and loss of nuance (Mackenzie et al., 2007), and my lack of Kikuyu and Kiswahili language abilities remains a limitation of the research.

Guaranteeing the full consent of research participants, minimizing the possible risks to participants, and ensuring that participants fully understand existing risks is possibly the most important ethical consideration. Most projects solicit consent from participants at the outset, usually through a written consent form or a recorded oral statement. Shamim and Qureshi (2013) claim that this method is inadequate and that continuous negotiation and reaffirmation of participants' comfort and commitment throughout the research process is more appropriate. Kiragu and Warrington's (2012) study in Kenya provides some positive practices and points of consideration. To ensure that their child participants fully understood the consent forms, the authors started individual interviews by briefing their participant on the project and providing written ethical guidelines in the language of her choice (Swahili or English). They then asked the participant to explain in her own words what she had read and to ask some questions to ensure that she understood the significance of the consent form. The authors also stressed the voluntary nature of the project and that she would not get into trouble if she declined to participate. But the authors ran into an ethical dilemma when, during the interviews, they learned of potentially harmful situations some girls were facing. Feeling bound to the confidentiality they had entered into, they did not disclose the situation to others in the school or the community but, in retrospect, decided that, in future, they would renegotiate consent and ask the participant for permission to share her information with a person in authority. Conceptualizing consent as continuously negotiated might have avoided this dilemma, as they would have been prompted to discuss consent with the interviewees during and after the interviews, at which point they could address the situation with the participants.

An unexpected challenge I faced in negotiating consent was the cultural premium in Kenya given to welcoming and accommodating guests, which was particularly pronounced in relation to me as a white person from a Western country who had the support of the local and national Kenyan government. When I first introduced the concept of consent to a group of teachers prior to commencing participant observation, explaining to them that they could tell me they did not want me to observe their class at any point, the room full of teachers burst out laughing. One teacher then assured me in front of all the staff: "You are here to help. I think we will not say no to you." While this welcoming attitude was appreciated, it made it difficult to determine when an individual was actually consenting to participate and not just conforming to the expectation that they will do what I ask them because I am a high status guest. I adapted my protocol to make an individual request to observe a specific class each time and would back away at any sign of hesitation. Through this process, teachers did tell me that they were uncomfortable at various points, for example, because they were planning a review session and wanted me to watch the more structured lesson planned for later in the week. I also learned that few people would tell me outright that they did not want me to observe a class or conduct an interview with them but that many would resist scheduling a time. In these instances, I would try to reschedule once or twice; if scheduling proved unsuccessful, I took it as a cue that the unavailability of the participant represented her discomfort with the interview or observation, and I made the decision to exclude that individual from the study. For both students and teachers, we asked them to self-identify whether they wanted to do an interview by writing yes or no on a blank paper with their name and their or a parent's contact information. With students, Mary then contacted the parents and orally explained the interview process and the risks and opportunities to obtain their consent. We only interviewed students who both had indicated their consent to participate and whose parents had also provided consent, but we then paid close attention to their comfort level during the interview. After stressing at the outset that they could stop at any time and asking some questions to ensure their understanding, we asked students who appeared uncomfortable whether they wanted to stop during the interview, assuring them that stopping would not be a problem. A few took us up on this option, while others stated they preferred to continue.

Feminist scholars assert that projects must give back to the research communities so that the community and participants benefit from the research project. There are multiple interpretations of how to do so: gifts, volunteer work, or other support; raising awareness within the community about the research topic; building the capacity of the research participants; bringing critical attention to the research topic within the community; and, ultimately, influencing structural and policy changes related to the struggles of the community. I believe that all these elements are important and can be explored, based on the needs of the community, but that one of the most significant is the development of the capacity building and critical reflection of the participants. A condition of marginalization is often unequal access to certain forms of knowledge (Wylie, 2004); thus, while the local population may be experts in understanding local power relations, they are often unaware of how the oppression they face originated and is maintained (Narayan, 1988). The capacity building and critical reflection of participants is therefore essential so that participants can effectively engage with the researcher, contribute to the analysis, and become critically aware and able to advocate at the local level if they choose to, following the project's completion, ideally in collaboration with the researcher. "Catalytic validity" is the extent to which research "moves those it studies to understand the world and the way it is shaped in order for them to transform it" (Lather, 1991, p. 159).

Attempts to integrate opportunities for participants' critical reflection into the methodology were again challenged by the need to respond to my university REB's concerns regarding potential risks to the participants from collectively discussing the sensitive topic of gender safety and violence in school. The project had initially intended to host focus groups and participatory discussions with school community members throughout data collection to collectively discuss the emerging themes and their relevance to the schools and participants. This concept had to be eliminated, however, as it was felt by the REB that it posed too great a risk to the participants to be discussing even broad findings about issues of safety and child protection without being able to control confidentiality. Thus, for the protection of the participants, the focus group discussions were eliminated in favour of individual student and teacher interviews. Results were instead presented separately to different stakeholders; I met separately with teachers, students, and government administrators to share findings and collect feedback. In doing so, all mention of teacher malpractice was removed for the protection of the students and staff. For the students, we held a reflective activity where the findings about what the students liked and did not like about their school, based on the interview data from both schools, was presented in child-friendly language, and students worked in small groups to come up with strategies about how to make their schools safer. The students' strategies were then presented to the class, and we discussed their strengths and opportunities. The teachers were not forthcoming with feedback in a large group setting, but critical reflection occurred more informally on an individual basis, with certain teachers discussing the findings with me before and after the interviews on an informal basis throughout my time in the school and following the presentation of initial findings. The catalytic validity was therefore not present in the open and obvious way that had initially been planned but rather in a subtler and simmering process that some teachers selected to engage in, while others did not choose to share their reflections with me. This alternative conception of catalytic validity resulted from a necessary flexibility and adaptability required to meet the principles and objectives of the methodology while respecting and prioritizing the safety of the participants.

Participatory Research

My interpretation of participatory research focused on providing space for participants to influence the research process, including the design, data collection, analysis, and writing stages. The researcher must use a flexible design, open to adaptation and redefinition of methodology and even the research questions, as feedback from participants shapes the researcher's understanding of the culture and relevance of the research design (Henstrand, 2006; LeCompte & Goetz, 1984). This interpretation reflects Smith's (1992) power-sharing model for research undertaken by non-Indigenous researchers about Indigenous peoples, whereby the researcher seeks the community's assistance to meaningfully support the development of a research project. The model can be facilitated either by establishing a research committee, made up of a selection of participants and community members (such as students, teachers, parents, the head teacher, and community leaders) who are consulted at each stage of the project, or through the more informal but continuous negotiation of the research process with participants and community members. Participatory processes are sometimes criticized for compromising the analysis so that the results can be easily understood by participants (Morse, 1988), but they ultimately prioritize analysis that, at its essence and in its most basic terms, can be understood by the research community. This process echoes the principles of feminist and postcolonial research described above, as well as Lather's (1991) measure of "construct validity," which is determined when constructs are actually occurring rather than existing solely in the researcher's perspective. Member checks that share initial analysis with participants to solicit their feedback have been called "the most crucial technique for establishing credibility" (Lincoln & Guba, 1985, p. 314). Participatory research is undeniably complicated and challenging, but the choice to use participatory approaches is one concerned with both the empowerment of participants and the reliability of results. If the researcher seeks to empower the communities she works with, she "cannot sloganize the people, but must enter into dialogue with them, so that the people's empirical knowledge of reality, nourished by the [researcher's] critical knowledge, gradually becomes transformed into knowledge of the causes of reality" (Freire, 1970/2012, p. 210). With CGT, the researcher(s) are continuously analysing data for emerging theories and identifying new sources that may support or contradict an emerging theory. A participatory approach would have the researcher discussing her thoughts on emerging theories with her participants or committee, gaining feedback, conducting member checks throughout, and asking participants for help identifying new data sources that could otherwise go unrecognized. This process could be taken further by involving research participants directly in analysis so that the narrative is co-constructed and the participants become more involved and invested in the process and outcomes of the analysis (Coad & Evans, 2008; Koelsch, 2013; McIntyre, 2008).

My experience attempting participatory research demonstrated to me that the concept of participatory research can itself be a Western researcher–driven initiative that is irresponsive to the participants' interests. It is a concept based on the premise that participants or local stakeholders want to be involved and contribute to the research process. What if the participants do not want to be researchers? Just as a non-participatory process can be imposed on participants who desire to be involved, so too can a participatory process be imposed on participants who do not want to be involved. This realization became abundantly clear to me during an early consultation with a group of teachers to gain their input on the proposed interview methods in order to adapt them to become more suitable to the school priorities and context. In response to my explanation and questions, only one teacher offered a suggestion. Most looked bored and frustrated to be kept in a meeting during one of the few breaks in their busy day. One teacher put her head down on her desk and slept through the consultation. I met similar issues trying to meet and consult with the administration alone. The schools were highly welcoming towards me and open to my research; many teachers and students were visibly eager and enthusiastic to participate in the interviews and observation. Yet, the teachers and administrators had little interest in contributing to the research design, which they perceived to be my job and responsibility. Ultimately, I informally discussed the methods with teachers and administrators on an individual basis. On several occasions, a participant would then demonstrate significant engagement, input, and even follow-up to adapt the methods to enhance their relevance. But this participation was always on an individual basis when there was visible interest and enthusiasm. The reluctance to contribute to the research design may have been due in part to the fact that the research topic arose out of demand from donors and NGOs and a perceived knowledge gap, as opposed to demand from the local community. Had the process been participatory from the beginning in the formulation of the research topic and question, participants may have been more interested in contributing to the research process.

Conclusion

To do research in postcolonial contexts, feminists from all social locations, but particularly Western feminists who carry a legacy of privilege, must maintain vigilance in analysing the power dynamics of their research process to avoid misrepresenting, exploiting, and endangering their participants. The research should be responsive to the local community and driven by an emancipatory objective that is rooted in dialogue with participants and other community members. A perspective that embraces a combination of feminist standpoint theory and postcolonial theory provides a useful framework with which to conduct postcolonial feminist research, but it must be accompanied by the adaptation of research methods to be culturally sensitive using situated ethics. CGT and participatory research principles can guide the research design, data collection, and analysis processes to ensure that research is rooted in the local context, considers data from multiple perspectives, and puts participants at the forefront. This discussion intentionally avoids specifying whether traditional qualitative methods such as interviews, focus groups, and observation or more innovative methods such as art-based or participant-led enquiry should be utilized, as the ideal methodology will be different for each project. Similarly, the ethical and cultural considerations must be locally situated and cannot be automatically transferred. Issues of inequality, violence, poverty, and oppression are among the most important challenges our inherently global society faces today. For Western researchers, with unearned privilege and authority, to ignore these challenges is to reproduce and strengthen unequal structures. Mohanty's (2003) call for an alliance of Third World feminists from all social locations to collaboratively confront political structures of inequality reverberates internationally. All feminists who are willing to critically examine themselves and their privilege should respond to the call with humility, openness, and eagerness to work together and learn from each other. Research is infinitely complicated; the more researchers of all social locations learn to lean into discomfort, invite criticism, and genuinely reflect upon it, and the more we establish cross-cultural partnerships and understandings, the greater the potential contribution of our work for the participants, our partners, and ourselves. The reflexive processes described here are a fundamental undertaking for all researchers but are especially informative for new researchers establishing and modifying practices that will set the stage for a lifetime of ethical research.

Acknowledgment

This chapter has been reprinted by permission of Sage Publications, Inc., from the following source: Vanner, C. Positionality at the Center: Constructing an Epistemological and Methodological Approach for a Western Feminist Doctoral Candidate Conducting Research in the Postcolonial. *International Journal of Qualitative Methods* 14(4), pp. 1–12. Copyright © 2015 by the Author.

REFERENCES

Abuya, B.A., Onsomu, E.O., Moore, D., & Sagwe, J. (2012). A phenomenological study of sexual harassment and violence among girls attending high schools in urban slums, Nairobi, Kenya. *Journal of School Violence, 11*(4), 323–44. https://doi.org/10.1080/15388220.2012.706874

Åkerström, J., & Brunnberg, E. (2012). Young people as partners in research: Experiences from an interactive research circle with adolescent girls. *Qualitative Research, 13*(5), 528–45. https://doi.org/10.1177/1468794112451035

Akin-Aina, S. (2011). Beyond an epistemology of bread, butter, culture and power: Mapping the African feminist movement. *Nokoko, 2,* 65–84. https://ojs.library.carleton.ca/index.php/nokoko/article/view/1828

Alcoff, L. (1991–2). The problem of speaking for others. *Cultural Critique, 20* (Winter 1991–2), 5–32. https://doi.org/10.2307/1354221

Arnot, M. (2006). Gender voices in the classroom. In C. Skelton, B. Francis, & L. Smulyan (Eds.), *The SAGE handbook of gender and education* (pp. 407–21). Sage.

Beetham, G., & Demetriades, J. (2007). Feminist research methodologies and development: Overview and practical application. *Gender & Development, 15*(2), 199–216. https://doi.org/10.1080/13552070701391086

Bruce, C. (2007). Questions arising about emergence, data collection and its interaction with analysis in a grounded theory study. *International Journal of Qualitative Methods, 6*(1), 51–68. https://doi.org/10.1177/160940690700600105

Burney, S. (2012). *Pedagogy of the other: Edward Said, postcolonial theory and strategies for critique.* Peter Lang.

Butler, J. (1990). *Gender trouble: Feminism and the subversion of identity.* Routledge.

Charmaz, K. (2005). Grounded theory in the 21st century: Applications for advancing social justice studies. In N. Denzin & Y. Lincoln (Eds.), *The SAGE handbook of qualitative research* (3rd ed., pp. 507–35). Sage.

Charmaz, K. (2006). *Constructing grounded theory.* Sage.

Charmaz, K. (2014). *Constructing grounded theory* (2nd ed.). Sage.

Clarke, A.E. (2007). Feminisms, grounded theory, and situational analysis. In S.N. Hesse-Biber (Ed.), *The handbook of feminist research: Theory and praxis* (pp. 345–70). Sage.

Clarke, A.E. (2012). Feminism, grounded theory and situational analysis revisited. In S. Hesse-Biber (Ed.), *The handbook of feminist research: Theory and praxis* (2nd ed., pp. 388–412). Sage.

Coad, J., & Evans, R. (2008). Reflections on practical approaches to involving children and young people in the data analysis process. *Children & Society, 22*(1), 41–52. https://doi.org/10.1111/j.1099-0860.2006.00062.x

Collins, P.H. (1991). *Black feminist thought: Knowledge, consciousness, and the politics of empowerment.* Routledge.

Collins, P.H. (2000). *Black feminist thought: Knowledge, consciousness, and the politics of empowerment* (2nd ed.). Routledge.

Denzin, N., & Lincoln, Y.S. (2008). Introduction: Critical methodologies and Indigenous inquiry. In N.K. Denzin, Y.S. Lincoln, & L.T. Smith (Eds.), *Handbook of critical and Indigenous methodologies* (pp. 1–20). Sage.

Elaber-Idemedia, P. (2002). Participatory research: A tool in the production of knowledge in development discourse. In K. Saunders (Ed.), *Feminist post-development thought* (pp. 227–42). Zed Books.

Eltahawy, M. (2015). *Headscarves and hymens: Why the Middle East needs a sexual revolution*. Harper Collins.

Flax, J. (1990). Postmodernism and gender relations in feminist theory. In L. Nicholson (Ed.), *Feminism/postmodernism* (pp. 39–62). Routledge.

Foucault, M. (1980). *Power/knowledge* (C. Gordon, Ed.; C. Gordon, L. Marshall, J. Mephan, & K. Soper, Trans.). Vintage Books.

Freire, P. (2012). *Pedagogy of the oppressed*. Continuum International. (Original work published 1970)

Glaser, B., & Strauss, A.L. (1967). *The discovery of grounded theory*. Aldine.

Griffiths, M. (1998). *Educational research for social justice*. Open University Press.

Guba, E., & Lincoln, Y. (1989). *Fourth generation evaluation*. Sage.

Halse, C., & Honey, A. (2005). Unraveling ethics: Illuminating the moral dilemmas of research ethics. *Signs: Journal of Women in Culture and Society, 30*(4), 2141–65. https://doi.org/10.1086/428419

Harding, S. (1993). Rethinking standpoint epistemology: What is "strong objectivity"? In L. Alcoff & E. Potter (Eds.), *Feminist epistemologies* (pp. 49–82). Routledge.

Harding, S. (2007). Feminist standpoints. In S.N. Hesse-Biber (Ed.), *Handbook of feminist research: Theory and praxis* (pp. 45–69). Sage.

Harding, S. (2012). Feminist standpoints. In S.N. Hesse-Biber (Ed.), *Handbook of feminist research: Theory and praxis* (2nd ed., pp. 46–64). Sage.

Harvey, D. (2003). *The new imperialism*. Open University Press.

Henstrand, J.L. (2006). Seeking an understanding of school culture: Using theory as a framework for observation and analysis. In V.A. Anfara, Jr., & N.A. Mertz (Eds.), *Theoretical frameworks in qualitative research* (pp. 1–22). Sage.

Jankie, D. (2004). "Tell me who you are": Problematizing the construction and positionalities of "Insider"/"Outsider" of a "Native" ethnographer in a postcolonial context. In K. Mutua & B. Swadener (Eds.), *Decolonizing research in cross-cultural contexts: Critical personal narratives* (pp. 87–105). SUNY.

Keddy, B., Sims, S.L., & Stern, P.N. (1996). Grounded theory as feminist research methodology. *Journal of Advanced Nursing, 23*(3), 448–53. https://doi.org/10.1111/j.1365-2648.1996.tb00005.x

Kincheloe, J.L., & McLaren, P. (2005). Rethinking critical theory and qualitative research. In N. Denzin & Y. Lincoln (Eds.), *The Sage handbook of qualitative research* (3rd ed., pp. 303–42). Sage.

Kincheloe, J.L., McLaren, P., & Steinberg, S.R. (2011). Critical pedagogy and qualitative research: Moving to the bricolage. In N.K. Denzin & Y.S. Lincoln (Eds.), *The Sage handbook of qualitative research* (4th ed., pp. 163–78). Sage.

Kiragu, S., & Warrington, M. (2012). How we used moral imagination to address ethical and methodological complexities while conducting research with girls in school against the odds in Kenya. *Qualitative Research, 13*(2), 173–89. https://doi.org/10.1177/1468794112451011

Koelsch, L.E. (2013). Reconceptualizing the member check interview. *International Journal of Qualitative Methods, 12*(1), 168–79. https://doi.org/10.1177/160940691301200105

Kushner, K.E., & Morrow, R. (2003). Grounded theory: Feminist theory, critical theory: Toward theoretical triangulation. *Advances in Nursing Science, 26*(1), 30–43. https://doi.org/10.1097/00012272-200301000-00006

Lather, P. (1991). *Getting smart: Feminist research and pedagogy with/in the postmodern.* Routledge.

LeCompte, M., & Goetz, J. (1984). *Ethnography and qualitative design in educational research.* Academic Press.

Lincoln, Y.S., & Guba, E. (1985). *Naturalistic energy.* Sage.

Mackenzie, C., McDowell, C., & Pittaway, E. (2007). Beyond "do no harm": The challenge of constructing ethical relationships in refugee research. *Journal of Refugee Studies, 20*(2), 299–319. https://doi.org/10.1093/jrs/fem008

Mannathoko, C. (1999). Theoretical perspectives on gender in education: The case of Eastern and Southern Africa. *International Review of Education, 45,* 445–60. https://doi.org/10.1023/A:1003866707061

Marshall, C., & Young, M.D. (2006). Gender and methodology. In C. Skelton, B. Francis, & L. Smulyan (Eds.), *The Sage handbook of gender and education* (pp. 63–78). Sage.

McIntyre, A. (2008). *Participatory action research.* Sage.

Mills, J., Bonner, A., & Francis, K. (2006). The development of constructivist grounded theory. *International Journal of Qualitative Methods, 5*(1), 25–35. https://doi.org/10.1177/160940690600500103

Mohanty, C.T. (1988). Under Western eyes: Feminist scholarship and colonial discourses. *Feminist Review, 30*(1), 61–88. https://doi.org/10.1057/fr.1988.42

Mohanty, C.T. (2003). *Feminism without borders: Decolonizing theory, practicing solidarity.* Duke University Press.

Morse, J.M. (1988). Validity by committee. *Qualitative Health Research, 8*(4), 443–5. https://doi.org/10.1177/104973239800800401

Morse, J.M. (2015). Critical analysis of strategies for determining rigor in qualitative inquiry. *Qualitative Health Research, 25*(9), 1212–22. https://doi.org/10.1177/1049732315588501

Narayan, U. (1988). Working together across difference: Some considerations on emotions and political practice. *Hypatia, 3*(2), 31–47. https://doi.org/10.1111/j.1527-2001.1988.tb00067.x

Nind, M. (2011). Participatory data analysis: A step too far? *Qualitative Research, 11*(4), 349–63. https://doi.org/10.1177/1468794111404310

Ogina, T.A., & Nieuwenhuis, J. (2010). Gaining access to the experiences of orphaned children: A draw-write-narrate approach. *Qualitative Research Journal, 10*(2), 51–64. https://doi.org/10.3316/QRJ1002051

Pahl, K., & Pool, S. (2011). "Living your life because it's the only life you've got": Participatory research as a site for discovery in a creative project in a primary school. *Qualitative Research Journal, 11*(2), 17–37. https://doi.org/10.3316/QRJ1102017

Parkes, J., Heslop, J., Oando, S., Sabaa, S., Januario, F., & Figue, A. (2013). Conceptualising gender and violence in research: Insights from studies in schools and communities in Kenya, Ghana and Mozambique. *International Journal of Educational Development, 33*(6), 546–56. https://doi.org/10.1016/j.ijedudev.2013.01.001

Reid, C. (2004). Advancing women's social justice agendas: A feminist action research framework. *International Journal of Qualitative Methods, 3*(3), 1–15. https://doi.org/10.1177/160940690400300301

Renold, E., Holland, S., Ross, N.J., & Hillman, A. (2011). Becoming participant: Problematizing "informed consent" in participatory research with young people in care. In P. Atkinson & S. Delamont (Eds.), *Sage qualitative research methods* (Vol. 4, pp. 55–74). Sage.

Ruto, S. (2009). Sexual abuse of school age children: Evidence from Kenya. *Journal of International Cooperation in Education, 12*(1), 177–92. https://cice.hiroshima-u.ac.jp/wp-content/uploads/2014/03/12-1-12.pdf

Said, E. (1985). Orientalism reconsidered. *Cultural Critique, 1*(Autumn), 89–107. https://doi.org/10.2307/1354282

Saito, M. (2013). Violence in primary schools in Southern and Eastern Africa: Some evidence from SACMEQ. *SACMEQ Gender Series, 1*, 1–13. https://healtheducationresources.unesco.org/library/documents/violence-primary-schools-southern-and-eastern-africa-some-evidence-sacmeq

Schnarch, B. (2004). Ownership, control, access, possession (OCAP) or self-determination applied to research: A critical analysis of contemporary First Nations research and some options for First Nations communities. *Journal of Aboriginal Health, 1*(1), 80–95. https://jps.library.utoronto.ca/index.php/ijih/article/view/28934

Shamim, F., & Qureshi, R. (2010). *Perils, pitfalls and reflexivity in qualitative research in education.* Oxford University Press.

Shamim, F., & Qureshi, R. (2013). Informed consent in educational research in the South: Tensions and accommodations. *Compare: A Journal of Comparative and International Education, 43*(4), 464–82. https://doi.org/10.1080/03057925.2013.797729

Simons, H., & Usher, R. (2000). *Situated ethics in educational research.* Routledge.

Smith, D. (1990). *The conceptual practices of power: A feminist sociology of knowledge*. Northeastern University Press.

Smith, G.H. (1992). Research issues related to Māori education. In *The issue of research and Māori*. Research Unit for Māori Education, University of Auckland.

Smith, L.T. (2012). *Decolonizing methodologies: Research and Indigenous peoples* (2nd ed.). ZED Books.

Spivak, G.C. (1988). Can the subaltern speak? In C. Nelson & L. Grossberg (Eds.), *Marxism and the interpretation of culture* (pp. 271–313). University of Illinois Press.

Stein, N., Tolman, D.L., Porche, M.V., & Spencer, R. (2002). Gender safety: A new concept for safer and more equitable schools. *Journal of School Violence, 1*(2), 35–49. https://doi.org/10.1300/J202v01n02_03

Swadener, B.B., & Mutua, K. (2008). Decolonizing performances: Deconstructing the global postcolonial. In N.K. Denzin, Y.S. Lincoln, & L.T. Smith (Eds.), *Handbook of critical and Indigenous methodologies* (pp. 31–43). Sage.

Tikly, L. (2004). Education and the new imperialism. *Comparative Education, 40*(2), 173–98. https://doi.org/10.1080/0305006042000231347

Tikly, L., & Bond, T. (2013). Towards a postcolonial research ethics in comparative and international education. *Compare: A Journal of Comparative and International Education, 43*(4), 422–42. https://doi.org/10.1080/03057925.2013.797721

Wane, N. (2009). Sexual violence and HIV/AIDS risks in Kenyan and Ugandan schools: Social implications for educational policy development. *Journal of Contemporary Issues in Education, 4*(1), 71–91. https://doi.org/10.20355/C5C88H

wa Thiong'o, Ngũgĩ. (1986). *Decolonizing the mind: The politics of language in African literature*. Heinemann.

Wylie, A. (2004). Why standpoint matters. In S. Harding (Ed.), *The feminist standpoint theory reader: Intellectual and political controversies* (pp. 339–51). Routledge.

13 Going the Distance: Theorizing Forward in the Time of a "Rural Turn"

CLAUDIA MITCHELL, KATARINA GIRITLI-NYGREN, AND RELEBOHILE MOLETSANE

Introduction

It is perhaps ironic that, at the very moment we are finishing this book, the notion of distance – one of the fundamentals of rurality, as Balfour et al. (2008) have observed – has become a central feature of all lives, rural and urban, now that we are immersed in the COVID-19 pandemic. When Canada first introduced physical distancing early in March 2020, Claudia's cousin and his wife talked about moving from a small city in Manitoba to their cottage on a lake at the edge of a small prairie town. He pointed out: "Everyone lives at a distance here; there is only distance." Perhaps more than at any other time in recent history, we are all participants in a social experiment that includes space and distance, two key features of rurality. But it is also ironic that rurality, long thought to belong to the outskirts, so to speak, of the mainstream, is quickly becoming the centre. A quick scroll through various newspapers and social media posts from late March 2020 to April 2021 reveals such headlines as "The Rural Escape: How COVID-19 Is Prompting Canadians to Renounce City Living and Move to the Country" (CHIP, 2023); "The Coronavirus Pandemic Is Pushing Canadians Out of Cities and into the Countryside" (Ashleigh Weeden, 2020); "Younger Canadians Moving Away from Big Cities at Record Levels" (Hertzberg, 2021); "COVID-19 Is Pushing Americans Out of Cities and into the Country" (Roper, 2021); "The Pandemic Is Making People Reconsider City Living, Trading Traffic for Chickens" (Kelly & Lerman, 2020); "More People Quitting Cities for Country Life in Italy as Result of Lockdown Restrictions" (Euronews, 2020). At the same time, there is something paradoxical in that, as so many people from the Global North retreat to rural areas to get away from COVID-19, other research from the Global South highlights the new dangers of leaving the city for rural areas, where there are limited health resources. The example of India is particularly dramatic and troubling, as can be seen in headlines such as the following: "Coronavirus: Poor Indian Workers Flee to Villages amid Strict COVID-19 Measures" (Jamkhandikar & Waydande, 2020) and "India's Migrants Flee to Their Villages as COVID-19 Prompts New Lockdown" (Agarwal & Bellman, 2021). How then, to both wrap up the chapters that were all written pre-COVID-19 and reflect forward in the context of what might be described as the rural turn?

As co-editors, we realized that we had landed ourselves into some new thinking about the idea of "Where am I in the picture?" and that it would be useful for each of us to draw on the new thinking about this new rural turn in the form of three reflexive pieces as a way to reposition some of the initial questions of the book, as outlined in chapter 1 and developed across its various sections. Indeed, where are we are in the picture? And what is the picture? In keeping with the idea of working with images as a key feature of this "Where am I in the picture?" book, we start with Claudia's piece on reframing rurality, which highlights how perspectives can shift, even in relation to the same piece of land. Then, Katarina's piece on reading from the periphery challenges us anew to work in solidarity and transnationally. Finally, Relebohile's piece on "Where are *they* in the picture(s)?" is a compelling call to reassess in the time of COVID-19 with whom, why, how, and with what consequences those of us in the academy (typically urban) engage with girls and young women in rural contexts.

Reframing Rurality: Perspective-Taking while Taking Pictures – Claudia (Canada)

I cannot help but be drawn back to the visual of this book. One of my favourite book covers is the image on Lucy R. Lippard's (1997) *The Lure of the Local: Senses of Place in a Multicentered Society*. The caption on the back of the book, related to a photograph taken by Peter Woodruff, notes: "This houseboat, moored in the Kennebec River, was the summer home of a nomadic local woman." I am not that nomadic local woman, but there is something about the image that somehow encapsulates the sense of our book's title, *Where Am I in the Picture?*, and hints at why, as co-editors, we want to fuel the flames of this question, which takes us back to visual sociology. As a generous reviewer of an earlier version of our book's manuscript observed, we've had "long roads, Scandinavian forests, the snow, the dust, South African rural schools, the imagery concerning the leaving of rural home places," and, of course, the book is full of photographs, maps, images of installations, and drawings.

For eight months during COVID-19, my partner and I lived on the East Coast of Canada on Prince Edward Island (PEI), one time zone and 1,000 kilometres away from urban Montreal where we reside. PEI is Canada's smallest province, has a population of 145,000 people, and is situated on a small island land mass. The Island, as it is fondly referred to, is decidedly rural and coastal: potatoes and tourism are its two main industries. The first two months of being there were somewhat normal for us. It was July and August, and we have had a summer cottage there for several decades. Aside from having to quarantine when we first arrived, and aside from being masked and cautious, our summer life by a lovely bay leading into the Gulf of Saint Lawrence was its usual idyll of bay breezes and beautiful sunsets. Given that all classes and meetings back in Montreal at McGill were on Zoom, it was possible to even extend our summer away by a couple of weeks into September. While at first we occasionally joked about staying on into the fall, it was never meant very seriously, especially since our cottage is not winterized. At most, it was a question of how long we could stay before freeze up. Then two things happened. Montreal went into a more drastic Red Zone lockdown that made us rethink going back, especially given some health conditions of my partner. And then, a neighbour who lives just one field over (with the same view of the bay) indicated that her house would be available to rent for the fall and winter. It was a dream come true, although we still never expected to stay for the whole winter. We stayed in our cottage until the end of October. Then there was November. December came. Obviously, we wanted to be back in Montreal for Christmas. Maybe we would go and then return to PEI? But we did not go back for Christmas. Montreal was in such intense lockdown that it would have been madness. And then it was January. And then it was February. And then came March. What I want to convey here is that, without leaving the almost exact physical space of our summer cottage, a place overlooking a bay and the dunes across the water and leading out to open sea, we moved to living in what we can only call a rural area.

During those eight months, I took hundreds of pictures on my phone. Some (many?) were of our cats, but the bulk of the pictures were taken on my many walks. At first, I just took pictures of whatever was preoccupying me on the walk, although I kept thinking that I should focus on something – maybe taking only pictures of birds, or the position of the sun, or the types of clouds – and that, at the end of this time (which seemed to have no real ending), I would have this wondrous thematic array of photos of something profound or surprising. I had not started a journal to document these repeatedly called "unprecedented times," nor had I done anything else.

But the pictures, as I look over them chronologically, seemed to just go in phases rather than in themes. Not surprisingly, as we moved into fall, we became more aware of the houses and farms along the main road and lost our preoccupation with wanting to be in our cottage. In the novelty of the early days of staying and not leaving, I suddenly felt inspired to document something of the rural. I have dozens of pictures of barns, especially barns engulfed in the fog, capturing something of a romantic rural notion. The barn photography lasted for a little while and also included rustic-looking wagon wheels and falling-down fence posts. Then I have farmers' fields. I wanted to capture those spaces, so specifically and mathematically demarcated by trees, bushes, and the shoreline, as they, too, changed over time from abundant greenery to the brown grasses in the sun or touched by frost. Once the snow came, I was enchanted by the tracks of foxes and birds – such a recognition of post-humanism and the riparian nature of our existence. Sometimes the bay itself, especially when it was frozen over, was the subject.

But, as time went on, I also started to recognize some preoccupation with construction and changes on the main road and less with nature. Down the road, I watched and photographed a "For Sale – 20 lots" sign become "Sold" and, days later, saw a bulldozer clearing a road among the trees. I became obsessed with photographing a two-story house being erected in one of those farmer's fields further down the road and returned to it almost every day to see what was happening. Our very long driveway seems to have also preoccupied me: How far was the main road from us? Or was it a question of how far were we from the main road? Then it was the view of the bay from the road, and then, sometimes, I was just trying to capture pictures of the snowdrifts across the laneway or the ruts and the mud. Could we manage the mud ruts in our small car so that we could go to town?

Thematically, I think one could say that, in one sense, nothing really came to me, and I did not have a photo project. I do not have a thousand pictures of the life of one little pebble or of the daily flight patterns of the eagle that swooped by almost every morning. Perhaps, if I had just accepted that we were going to be living rural for an indefinite period of time and developed a go-with-the-flow attitude on uncertainty, I might have been able to assign myself a daily photo shoot. But I did not think our rural existence was going to span several seasons, and the very uncertainty of it all seems to be something that is key here. Now, newly recovered from having been in the middle of living rural and back in urban Montreal, I recognize how much my photos reveal, for me at least, that the physicality of the rural is also a state of mind. Ulrich (1983), in his article "Aesthetic and Affective Response to Natural

Environment," noted a "consistent tendency for North American and European groups to prefer even unspectacular natural scenes over the vast majority of urban views" (p. 110). He wrote that, beyond the aesthetic preference and emotions of interest, this response "is probably also expressed in neurophysiological activity" (p. 120). Further, Woods (2010) observed that "the practice of rural geography is closely tied to the performance of rurality, and rural geographers are revealed not only as observers and recorders of the rural but also as active agents in producing, reproducing and performing rurality" (p. 844). To read back over the various chapters in this book, we can appreciate anew the notion of "active agents," something we can see in examples such as Sheppard's (chapter 3) "correction line" discussions, Nyhlén's "entangled selves" (chapter 8), and the "outsider" reflections by MacEntee (chapter 10) and by Wiebesiek and Treffry-Goatley (chapter 9).

Finally, reflecting on my visual practices during this time is something of an awakening in relation to the intimacy of the visual in participatory fieldwork, especially in rural areas. As a member of a research team working with girls and young women in rural contexts, I do not think I had ever really appreciated the state of mind of taking pictures, producing visual images, creating digital stories, and so on. I recall that, when Relebohile Moletsane, Naydene de Lange, and I began our fieldwork in rural areas of South Africa in 2003, we decided that it was absolutely critical that, in any PowerPoint we produced for a conference, we include photographs that showed the rural, even if the images (of a classroom, for example) produced by the participants themselves were not explicitly rural. Such images were meant to act as establishing shots pointing out that this is where we are. This is rural. Somewhat absurdly in retrospect, I even recall a debate on a panel at a conference in South Africa about whose rural setting being discussed was "the real rural." Now, of course, after my eight months of what I might call my state of mind rurality, I am wondering if this whole issue of what is the real rural and how do you picture rural was a type of spectacle-building, aimed at trying to capture, as Susan Sontag (1977) observed, that which cannot be captured. But, pertinent to the themes of this book and the idea of the rural turn, it is more of a reminder of both the limits of, and challenges to, the broader project of rural girlhoods.

Troubling Urban Ontologies or Reading from the Periphery – Katarina (Sweden)

As the headlines above highlight, there are many signs that COVID-19 has made people leave urban areas and settle down in rural places.

Perhaps in the beginning, it was with the intention of doing so temporarily; but as time has passed, and they, like us, are still living with the pandemic, what was thought of as temporary might not be so temporary any longer. Whether rural living will become more desirable post-pandemic is a question being raised, and there are many media reports about people who have made such choices, at least in Sweden. In parallel with writing this final chapter and following the development of a rural turn in social media, I was also finalizing an edited collection about commitment, resistance, and care in rural villages of northern Sweden, so I had many images of the rural cross my mind. Although I somehow felt pleased that the pandemic made the shortcomings of urbanization visible and that images of rural life as a good life were being extolled on different media sites, I could not help being disturbed by how these stories were being told. The kind of rural that was displayed in these different reports is somehow so disconnected from the community life and struggles that I was reading about in the collected volumes on which I was working. I asked myself: "Why this interest in telling the story of rural life as a story of leaving the urban?" Such communication of rural life tends to reproduce the normative power that maintains the hegemonic structures of society in that the periphery is seen from the point of view of the centre. The right to represent is, in other words, linked closely to power.

In this book, the contributors have explored their relation to the rural sites to which they have come as researchers. Much of the reflection has focused on the way in which the researcher's own position influences the kinds of stories told during interviews and the ways in which they are read. It is challenging as a researcher, if even possible, to position oneself outside of the power dynamics inherent in representations of the rural. Scientific knowledge production in itself is part of colonial modernity and has promoted images of urbanity and urban life as desired, desirable, and normative figurations, as well as grounds for progress and development. Universities and university hierarchies are embedded in such normative figurations of urbanity, particularly visible through what is regarded as top universities; most often located in cosmopolitical centres, these institutions are considered to be producers of universal knowledge (see Connell, 2007). Questions on how to trouble the urban ontologies inherent in scientific knowledge production and on the ways in which we learn to see when we are trained to be researchers are topics with which many of the authors in this book engage as they try to find solutions to the problems these issues raise. If, as Sheppard (chapter 3) suggests, "the very language ... with which to comprehend land is rooted in a colonial ontology," what can we then do?

One way, as Sheppard suggests, is to try to find ways to make colonial ontology, such as data sets and mapping, visible in familiar languages, texts, and part of various approaches as a means of holding the settler body to account. To be honest, I have not previously reflected that much on the concept of the settler and settler colonialism. However, while working on this book, I have come to do so, and many of the reasons why I have not encountered this concept before applies in the Swedish context. Of course, first and foremost, it was a function of my own ignorance. Having done research in the Swedish north where I grew up, for many years criticizing the peripheralization of rural sites in both political and economic processes as well seeing the large-scale urban as the norm (see also Larsson, chapter 7; Nyhlén, chapter 8), I have not once considered how I and these processes are implicated in the ongoing settler colonialism of Sami land, as if we, in Sweden, do not need to be held accountable.

So, disturbed by the media reports about urban dwellers leaving urban life for a more secure, slower, environmentally friendly, and socially distancing life while trying to write the final chapter of this book, I found myself also writing a research proposal together with Emelie Larsson and another colleague, Angelika Sjöstedt. The proposal draws on insights from this book; we pick up on conceptual contributions on how to adopt a decolonial researcher position in order to try to disrupt settler colonial and/or apartheid scripts from the Canadian and South African contexts, respectively. More specifically, we attempt to explore how the concept of settler colonialism, a concept less often used in the Swedish context, can illuminate our own position at Mid Sweden University. In relation to some Swedish academies, Mid Sweden University is often deemed peripheral in terms of geographical location. From the South Sami perspective, our university is centrally located and the only university on South Sami land on the Swedish side of Saepmie.

In this book, authors with rural backgrounds – both settlers and the colonialized – are also reflecting on how urban ontologies and epistemologies are embedded in the ways in which we are trained to become researchers. For example, Samukelisiwe Khumalo (chapter 6) writes about the challenges with which South African rural-origin students might be confronted in a cosmopolitan university (see also Yamile, chapter 11). Sara Nyhlén (chapter 8) reflects on her rural past; she feels that she occupies two very different positions – that of rural girl and urban-based researcher. Starting with a feeling of being the one who got away, she ends up asking if it is at all possible to leave the rural. From the Canadian perspective, Lisa Starr and Claudia Mitchell (chapter 2) elaborate on how their rural past and settler bodies inform the way in which they participate today in colonial spaces. They believe that their "prairie-ness" has given them a particular lens through which they view the world. This idea is interesting, because, in most of the chapters, the rural background of the authors, although they are today implicated in the norms and standards of city-centred scientific knowledge production, are considered as giving them access to ontologies beyond the urban ones. The authors who have grown up urban reflect on their lack of access to such ways of seeing. For example, Emelie Larsson (chapter 7) and Lisa Wiebesiek and Astrid Treffry-Goatley (chapter 9) bring up the position of being outsiders with urban backgrounds. In their chapter, Wiebesiek and Treffry-Goatley also reflect on their position as white, English-speaking outsiders from privileged, urban backgrounds in a South African context and ask whether they should engage in this work or leave it to other researchers with different pasts and presents, and different subject positions.

So, does it then matter whether we view the world from the high streets of academia or from the prairies? Feminist philosophers of science (see, for example, Collins, 1990; Haraway, 1985; Harding, 1991; Hartsock, 1998) have criticized traditional research for its claims to objectivity and general vision or what Haraway (1985) refers to as "playing the God trick." She has redefined scientific methodology and its analytic categories. By moving the Enlightenment's epistemological assumptions into the sphere of politics and ethics, arguing that science itself is political, these feminist writers have contributed significantly to the discussion.

Following these insights, inspired by feminist theorizations of reading from the margin (hooks, 1984) and standpoint theory (Harding, 1991), the research proposal I am writing with these colleagues in parallel with working on this concluding chapter brings reading from the periphery to the forefront as a methodology for our study. Reading from the periphery refers to using embodied experiences of spatial marginalization as a source for understanding and theorizing social relations in order to restructure relations and ground our academic practice in the local setting of our university. Learning across transnational explorations of what it means to do rural research and to reflect on where I am in the picture has been to me a process of becoming aware of where it is that I reflect on my position. Although I did reflect, I had not really figured out where I actually stood. April Mandrona (chapter 4) suggests a building of solidarities across rural sites: in the proposal we are writing, this solidarity is expanded. At least in the Swedish context, we have also seen the importance of not getting stuck in the duality of urban/rural divides when we talk about how solidarity is constructed between what are usually deemed to be peripheries. There are many similarities between peripheralization processes in different geographic contexts, such as rural areas and suburbs. We believe that solidarity across "often conflictual locations and histories ... [derives from] ... the political links we choose to make among and between struggles" (Mohanty, 1991, p. 5). While rewalking the road from the margin to the centre, we might first continue the walk started with this book – to create solidarities across peripherialized places from the Global North to the Global South, from the woods to the hoods, from the prairie to the reserve, and from the village to the township.

Where Are *They* in the Picture(s)? Transnational Feminist Research and Activism in the Age of COVID-19 – Relebohile (South Africa)

The year 2020 was to be the final year of the "Networks for Change and Well-being" project, a transnational partnership project that involves mainly Canadian and South African researchers and communities. But the year also became one of reckoning with COVID-19 and the restrictions it brought to field-based research internationally. Central to the project has been its emphasis on working *with* rather than *on* or *about* girls and young women in rural and Indigenous communities in researching the issues that have an impact on their lives and developing and/or identifying ameliorative strategies for change. Over the years, using participatory visual methods and local stories *with* and *by* girls and young women, we have built transnational networks of rural and Indigenous activism and cultural production (Córdova & Salazar, 2008; Moletsane et al., 2021). However, the work of these networks and our research was abruptly halted by the implementation of the COVID-19 restrictions, which occurred at a time when we desperately needed to hear the voices of the girls and young women in our network. We were anxious on many counts: What challenges are they encountering, including the much-reported increases in domestic violence from the early days of lockdown and stay-at-home regulations? What coping resources or strategies are they able to draw on, if any, as they are forced into lockdown, in many cases with their abusers? How do these experiences differ from one community to another or from one national context to the next? What and how are the various groups hearing from their counterparts in other rural communities across their countries or in different countries? Importantly, are we able to get the pictures (through participatory visual research) that address these questions, and if so, where are we as a transnational team of researchers in these pictures?

The chapters in this collection address these questions as they relate to transnational research and girls' activism before COVID-19. Our international partnership in Networks for Change and Well-being allowed for the sharing of experiences, exchanging of ideas, and co-creating solutions within and across borders (see Ashutosh, 2008; Blunt, 2007). Our aim was to "[break] down traditional boundaries in research to embark on a transgressive process of scholarly dialogue and inquiry that positions girls and young women at the center of a transnational girlhood movement" (Moletsane et al., 2021, p. 40). We wanted to "prioritize the voices of traditionally marginalized [girls and] women from [rural and Indigenous communities in] a critical counter-hegemonic call for global systemic change" (Vanner, 2019, p. 117). Yet, it seems that COVID-19 has reversed the gains we had begun to make towards achieving these goals. In reflecting on the chapters in this book, and on COVID-19 and its impact on research, particularly in the rural and Indigenous communities we have been working in for the past six years, my own privilege as a middle-class urban dweller and my audacity to conduct research in poorly resourced rural communities, and with members of the most oppressed groups in those communities (girls and young women), came face to face. As I continued to maintain safe physical distance and to work remotely with access to resources that allow me to continue communication and collaboration with my colleagues in the country and around the globe, the equation has suddenly changed. While our transnational partnership had enabled our participants to be at the centre of the images and stories they produced, COVID-19 restrictions have removed them from the picture(s). Instead, the internet and the digital platforms it enables (Zoom, Skype, and so on) have placed adult researchers at the centre of transnational conversations *about* the lives of girls and young women in rural, Indigenous, and other marginalized communities. What right do we have to continue doing research on or about girls and young women from the comfort of our homes in the cities? Who benefits? As transnational researchers, as we reorganize research in the second year of COVID-19, it is imperative that we conduct what Jackie Kirk, Claudia Mitchell, and Jaqueline Reid-Walsh referred to as identifying and analysing potential points of "convergence among those studying girlhood ... to discover what we can learn/lose by crossing disciplinary [and national] borders" (Kirk et al., 2010, p. 15) about the impacts of the pandemic on the lives of girls and young women in rural and Indigenous communities. Such transnational feminist mapping, according to these scholars, would allow us to put girls and young women back into the picture. In turn, it would allow us "to better understand girls and girlhood in national, transnational, and international contexts and learn more about the social issues affecting girls and young women in differing contexts" (Moletsane et al., 2021, p. 41) and how to address them. As the chapters in this book have collectively illustrated, analysing the experiences of girls and young women across cultural, community, and national borders provides opportunities for transnational communication and the transfer of cultural production and understanding about how we might rethink research and facilitate girls' activism in poorly resourced rural and Indigenous communities, particularly in the context of COVID-19 (Moletsane et al., 2021).

Conclusion

Exploring how we position ourselves in relation to what sorts of concepts of rurality we use might also encourage us to ask how they could possibly be developed in order to go beyond this problematic performativity. However, to theorize forward is not only about how we view, and participate with, people in colonial spaces; it is also about space itself, how we see physical space in nature, and how we understand and use the colonial language of mapping space. We must reject the ways in which industrial patriarchy has told us to be indifferent and not to feel with the wind, trees, land, and melting ice.

REFERENCES

Agarwal, V., & Bellman, E. (2021, 14 April). India's migrants flee to their villages as COVID-19 prompts new lockdown. *The Wall Street Journal.* https://www.wsj.com/articles/indias-migrants-flee-to-their-villages-as -COVID-19-prompts-new-lockdown-11618392602
Ashleigh Weeden, S. (2020, 2 September). The coronavirus pandemic is pushing Canadians out of cities and into the countryside. *The Conversation.* https:// theconversation.com/the-coronavirus-pandemic-is-pushing-canadians -out-of-cities-and-into-the-countryside-144479
Ashutosh, I. (2008). (Re-)creating the community: South Asian transnationalism on Chicago's Devon Avenue. *Urban Geography, 29*(3), 224–45. https://doi.org/10.2747/0272-3638.29.3.224
Balfour, R.J., Mitchell, C., & Moletsane, R. (2008). Troubling contexts: Toward a generative theory of rurality as education research. *Journal of Rural and Community Development, 3*(3), 100–11. https://journals.brandonu.ca/jrcd /article/view/139

Blunt, A. (2007). Cultural geographies of migration: Mobility, transnationality and diaspora. *Progress in Human Geography, 31*(5), 684–94. https://doi.org/10.1177/0309132507078945

CHIP. (2023, 13 March). The rural escape: How COVID-19 is prompting Canadians to renounce city living and move to the country. *CHIP.* https://www.chip.ca/reverse-mortgage-sresources/lifestyle/are-canadians-migrating-to-rural-areas/

Collins, P.H. (1990). *Black feminist thought: Knowledge, consciousness and the politics of empowerment.* Unwin Hyman.

Connell, R. (2007). *Southern theory: The global dynamics of knowledge in social science.* Polity

Córdova, A., & Salazar, J.F. (2008). Imperfect media and the poetics of Indigenous video in Latin America. In P. Wilson & M. Stewart (Eds.), *Global Indigenous media: Cultures, poetics, and politics* (pp. 39–57). Duke University Press.

Euronews. (2020, 2 December). More people quitting cities for country life in Italy as result of lockdown restrictions. *Euronews.* https://www.euronews.com/2020/12/02/more-people-quitting-cities-for-country-life-in-italy-as-result-of-lockdown-restrictions

Haraway, D. (1985). A manifesto for cyborgs: Science, technology and socialist feminism in the 1980s. *Socialist Review,* no. 80, 65–108. https://monoskop.org/images/4/4c/Haraway_Donna_1985_A_Manifesto_for_Cyborgs_Science_Technology_and_Socialist_Feminism_in_the_1980s.pdf

Harding, S. (1991). *Whose science? Whose knowledge?* Cornell University Press.

Hartsock, N. (1998). Standpoint theories for the next century. *Women & Politics, 18*(3), 93–101. https://doi.org/10.1300/J014v18n03_06

Hertzberg, E. (2021, 14 January). Younger Canadians moving away from big cities at record levels. *BNN Bloomberg.* https://www.bnnbloomberg.ca/younger-canadians-moving-away-from-big-cities-at-record-levels-1.1548707

hooks, b. (1984). *Feminist theory: From margin to center.* South End Press.

Jamkhandikar, S., & Waydande, P. (2020, 21 March). Coronavirus: Poor Indian workers flee to villages amid strict COVID-19 measures. *Global News.* https://globalnews.ca/news/6712256/coronavirus-india-migrant-workers-COVID/

Kelly, H., & Lerman, R. (2020, 1 June). The pandemic is making people reconsider city living, trading traffic for chickens. *Washington Post.* https://www.washingtonpost.com/technology/2020/06/01/city-relocate-pandemic/

Kirk, J., Mitchell, C., & Reid-Walsh, J. (2010). Toward political agency for girls: Mapping the discourses of girlhood globally. In J. Helgren & C. Vasconcellos (Eds.), *Girlhood: A global history* (pp. 14–30). Rutgers University Press.

Lippard, L.R. (1997). *The lure of the local: Senses of place in a multicentered society.* The New Press.

Mohanty, C.T. (1991). *Third world women and the politics of feminism*. Indiana University Press.

Moletsane, R., Wiebesiek, L., Treffry-Goatley, A., & Mandrona, A. (Eds.). (2021). *Ethical practice in participatory visual research with girls*. Berghahn Books.

Roper, W. (2021, 19 January). COVID-19 is pushing Americans out of cities and into the country. *World Economic Forum*. https://www.weforum.org/agenda/2021/01/rural-life-cities-countryside-covid-coronavirus-united-states-us-usa-america

Sontag, S. (1977). *On photography*. Penguin Books.

Ulrich, R.S. (1983). Aesthetic and affective response to natural environment. In I. Altman & J.F. Wohlwill (Eds.), *Human behavior and environment: Vol. 6. Behavior and Natural Environment* (pp. 85–125). Plenum.

Vanner, C. (2019). Toward a definition of transnational girlhood. *Girlhood Studies*, 12(2), 115–32. https://doi.org/10.3167/ghs.2019.120209

Woods, M. (2010). Performing rurality and practising rural geography. *Progress in Human Geography*, 34(6), 835–46. https://doi.org/10.1177/0309132509357356

Editors and Contributors

Editors

Claudia Mitchell is a Distinguished James McGill Professor in the Faculty of Education, McGill University, where she is the director of the Institute for Human Development and Well-being and the founder and director of the Participatory Cultures Lab. She has an honorary doctorate from the Mid Sweden University and is an honorary professor at the University of KwaZulu-Natal, South Africa. Her research focuses on participatory visual and arts-based approaches to working with young people and communities in relation to addressing critical social issues such as gender equality and gender-based violence. Much of this work is in rural contexts. She is the co-founder and editor-in-chief of the award-winning journal *Girlhood Studies: An Interdisciplinary Journal.*

Katarina Giritli-Nygren is a professor of sociology at Mid Sweden University. She is interested in the sociology of gender and in intersectional analysis. Her research addresses different forms of governance relationships, with a general focus on inequalities and a particular focus on the spatial and temporal aspects of intersectional disparities in the context of centre and periphery in industrialized economies as well as between the Global North and Global South. She grew up on an island in the northern part of Sweden and has struggled with her relationship to urban norms with both desire and resistance during her professional and personal life.

Relebohile Moletsane is professor and the JL Dube Chair in Rural Education in the School of Education at the University of KwaZulu-Natal. She works with South African rural schools and communities, focusing on teacher development, poverty alleviation, HIV and AIDS, gender inequality, gender-based violence as barriers to education, and the development of girls' education. Currently, she is working with girls and young women to address sexual violence in rural communities. She was co-principal investigator with Claudia Mitchell on an International Partnerships for Sustainable Societies (IPaSS) grant: "Networks for Change and Well-being: Girl-Led 'from the Ground Up' Approaches to Addressing Sexual Violence in Canada and South Africa." She co-edited, with Lisa Wiebesiek, Astrid Treffry-Goatley, and April Mandrona, *Ethical Practice in Participatory Visual Research with Girls and Young Women in Rural Communities* (2021).

Contributors

Naydene de Lange, born in a small rural town in the Eastern Cape province of South Africa, is Professor Emerita in the Faculty of Education at Nelson Mandela University, Port Elizabeth, South Africa. Her research focuses on using participatory visual methodologies in addressing gender and issues related to HIV and AIDS in rural communities. Her background in educational psychology and her interest in inclusive education provide a framework that sees research as social change, within which she locates the work she does to include the marginalized. Her book *Participatory Visual Methodologies: Social Change, Community and Policy*, co-authored with Claudia Mitchell and Relebohile Moletsane, came out in 2017.

Katja Gillander Gådin is a professor in public health science in the Department of Health Sciences at Mid Sweden University and a member of the managing team at the Forum for Gender Studies. Her research focuses on gendered violence and health among youth, with most studies being conducted in sparsely populated areas in the north of Sweden. She is currently involved in projects that focus on sexual harassment and other forms of violence, such as harassment through social media and sexual harassment and racism in the hospitality business. She is also involved in a participatory visual method project on gendered violence against girls and young women in rural areas.

Samukelisiwe Khumalo is a senior lecturer in curriculum studies discipline at the University of KwaZulu-Natal and Academic Leader for Teaching and Learning in the School of Education. She completed her undergraduate degree at the University of Zululand and earned her PhD at the University of KwaZulu-Natal. Her research interests lie in rurality and in success, throughput, and academic support in higher education, along with multigrade teaching. She attended both primary and secondary school in a rural area where she grew up. She has been a teacher in South African schools and has taught physical science, chemistry, and biology, as well as AS-level biology at Albany Secondary School and across the United Kingdom.

Emelie Larsson has a PhD in sociology from Mid Sweden University. Her research interests include gender, risk, eco-social criticism, and the implications of the construction of urban areas as the centre and rural areas as the periphery. She grew up in a suburb of Stockholm, but now lives in a village in the countryside outside of Sundsvall. Her interest in rural studies has developed along with her PhD dissertation project on a maternity unit closure in Sweden's northern inland, and rurality continues to be central in her research.

Katie MacEntee is the postdoctoral fellow in the Dalla Lana School of Public Health at the University of Toronto. Her research focuses on the use of participatory visual methodologies in rural and urban settings to address HIV and AIDS, transactional sex, gender-based violence, LGBTQ2S youth and homelessness, and sexual and reproductive health.

April Mandrona is an associate professor at the Nova Scotia College of Art and Design (NSCAD) University where she developed and directed the new Master of Arts in Art Education program. She earned her PhD in art education from Concordia University and was a Social Sciences and Humanities Research Council (SSHRC) postdoctoral fellow at McGill University. Her current SSHRC-funded community art education research with historically excluded groups focuses on the social roles of artistic production and innovative approaches to understanding narrative, belonging, well-being, and participation. She has published on rurality, young people, art education, ethics, and participatory research. Co-edited volumes include *Visual Encounters in the Study of Rural Childhoods* (2018), *Our Rural Selves: Memory, Place, and the Visual in Canadian Rural Childhoods* (2019), and *Ethical Practice in Participatory Visual Research with Girls: Transnational Approaches* (2021).

Sara Nyhlén is an associate professor in political science in the Department of Humanities and Social Sciences and the head of the Forum for Gender Studies at Mid Sweden University. She grew up in a rural area in Sweden, and even though she moved away, this experience is rooted in her as well as in her research, which focuses on critical policy analysis in different empirical areas with a particular interest in intersectionality, power, and policy, as well as in methodological development in the field of political science. She is currently involved in projects focusing on social inequality in housing and planning, digitalization politics, cultural heritage, and gendered violence against girls and young women in rural areas.

Lou Sheppard is a Canadian artist working in interdisciplinary audio, performance, and installation-based practice. His work focuses on climate crisis, colonial histories, and queer resistance, responding to the material and discursive histories of sites, bodies, and environments. Lou's research is evidenced through graphic notations, scripts, and scores, which are often performed in collaboration with other artists and in community gatherings. Lou graduated from the Nova Scotia College of Art and Design in 2006 and then studied English and education at Mount Saint Vincent University. In 2018–19, he was artist-in-residence in the Faculty of Education at McGill University. Lou is a settler on the traditional and unceded territory of the Mi'kmaq in Mi'kma'ki / Nova Scotia.

Lisa Starr is a professor and dean for the Faculty of Education at the University of Lethbridge. She is the past president of the Canadian Association for the Study of Women and Education (CASWE). She earned her doctoral degree in the Department of Curriculum and Instruction at the University of Victoria in the area of educational leadership. Her earlier career as an international teacher in Pakistan, Kuwait, and Mongolia informed her current research and commitment to international development. She is the principal investigator for the project "Designing and Implementing Pedagogical Strategies for Addressing Sexual and Gender-Based Violence in Teacher Training Colleges" in Mozambique.

Astrid Treffry-Goatley is a South African researcher with a background in ethnomusicology and ethnographic research, based at Stellenbosch University. Her areas of interest include gender and health, girlhood studies, film studies, and ethnomusicology, while her current research interests lie in understanding the social and ethical aspects of conducting collaborative health research with young women in low-income settings with specific focus on gendered vulnerability, health-care systems, community engagement, and policymaking. She has extensive experience with using participatory methods to understand and address key health challenges, including HIV-drug adherence and gender-based violence.

Catherine Vanner is an assistant professor of educational foundations at the University of Windsor. Her research uses qualitative and participatory methods to examine the relationship between education and gender-based violence in diverse country contexts. Previously, she worked as a postdoctoral fellow at McGill University and as an education advisor at Plan International Canada and the Canadian International Development Agency (now Global Affairs Canada). She earned a master's degree in international affairs from Carleton University and her PhD in education from the University of Ottawa.

Lisa Wiebesiek is the research manager of the Centre for Visual Methodologies for Social Change at the University of KwaZulu-Natal, South Africa, where she earned a PhD in education. She has previously worked in the fields of HIV prevention and rural education development. Her current work focuses on working with girls and young women to better understand and address gender-based violence in rural communities. Her research interests include adolescent sexual and reproductive health and rights, gender and sexuality education, rurality, girlhood studies, and participatory visual methodologies.

Ntomboxolo Yamile has a PhD in education from Nelson Mandela University in Port Elizabeth, South Africa. She is working with Young Girls Leading Change, a group of girls from a rural township in Eastern Cape, South Africa, as part of the "Networks for Change and Well-being: Girl-Led 'from the Ground Up' Approaches to Addressing Sexual Violence in Canada and South Africa" project, focusing on addressing sexual violence in their community. Her research interests include gender and education, with an emphasis on rurality and girls and women. She currently works as a workplace-based learning coordinator for Technical and Vocational Education and Training in the Department of Education, Nelson Mandela University.

Index